RETURN TO ANIMALIA

Yea, though I walk through the valley of the shadow of death
I will fear no evil for thou art with me
thyne rod and thyne staff they comfort me
.... and I will dwell in
the house of the LORD forever

Psalm 23
A Psalm of David
(tehillim xxiii)

To the Memory
of
Elizabeth Law

war is inevitable
whom are the winners and whom the losers is irrelevant
for war is a condition of humankind!

ISBN   9780994315700

Longership Publishing Australia
Victoria 3896 Australia
ABN 73446736413

email: longership@email.com
First published in Australia 2015
Copyright © Tom Law   2015
Cover design Tom Law

The right of Tom Law to be identified as the Author of the Work has been asserted in accordance with the Copyright, Designs and Patents Act 1988.

Law, Tom
Return to Animalia
ISBN 9780994315700
pp ~ 264

Return

to

Animalia

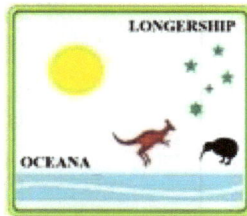

LONGERSHIP

in association with

British Manhood Motor Cycle Club Australia

BRITISH MANHOOD

MCC

AUSTRALIA

DEFEND THE RIGHT

BMMCC

Australia

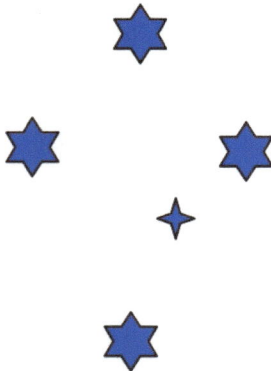

Contents

Introduction…. Right is Right is Right!

Introduction....   Right is Right is Right!

It was a hot Saturday afternoon, around 41^0 C and we were going to the river for a swim to be followed by a barbeque. As we arrived in our local small hamlet I noticed some fifty plus motorcycles parked close to the pub... 'The Albion', Ingland's olden name! Walking into the local shop to purchase some drinks I noticed three or four members standing inside the shop. They were oldish men wearing their club jackets with full Nazi regalia and the name "Fourth Reich" emblazoned on the back of their jackets. "Hey mate, what's with all the Nazi regalia? Where are you from?" I inquired to a portly and grey bearded man. "Are you guys Jermans, is this some sort of joke?"

"From Wollongong. It's no joke mate, it's not a joke, just our club" he replied. I bought my drinks and left leaving him to mumble to his friend about my questions. Afterwards I felt I should have asked him about the 27000 Animalian service men and women killed in WWII fighting these bastards (a further 23000 injured) and that I perceived his dress and manner to be un-Animalian. But there was one of me and dozens of them. Later with some difficulty I searched for the Fourth Reich on the internet. I noticed they were related to the extreme right wing group in Amerika, Stormfront, (http://stormfront.org) with all its hatred propaganda about coloured races and the Jews. Same old stuff pedalled by Hitler and his thugs!

So why are we tolerating such a group here in Animalia? Are our memories short? Is it an Animalian's born right to dress up in Nazi Regalia and parade about the countryside free of harm? Is this part of our democratic values? Had I a Kalashnikov (AK47) at hand, I would have felt not a qualm in sending them off into their wooden boxes; but then 'the other law' would have descended upon me!

Notable bike gangs outlawed from nightclubs at Kings Cross, Sydney, include the Bandidos, Black Uhlans, Coffin Cheaters, the Comancheros, Finks, Fourth

Reich, Gladiators, Gypsy Jokers, Highway 61, Life & Death, Lone Wolf, Mobshitters, Nomads, Odins Warriors, Outcasts, Outlaws, Phoenix and the Rebels.

One reporter quoted the Fourth Reich as being community minded and good blokes… I refer to Shakespeare who said "a rose is a rose is a rose and by any other name would smell as sweet" … consequently a turd is a turd is a turd! (My Irish friend did tell me he thought the Fourth Reich was born out of the earlier club, Der Turd Reich!)

But then there is a myriad of extreme right organisations in Animalia including the notorious "League of Rights" which still totes some rather nasty publications on its website bookshop aimed at the Jews and Holocaust Denial! (… most of them, i.e the Jews, ran away to Rusha and Cheena.)

As a nation of immigrants (predominantly boat-people) it is hard to fathom the minds of these extremists. But then again if anyone is honest enough to face a 'self-examination' of views, mores and values, I can see that we all carry some baggage and possess conflicting ideas. We tend to label and compartmentalise … it is not our fault, but just the mechanisms of our brains trying to continuously make references in order to make some sense of the world. Consensus is clearly a good approach for settling differences of opinion but consensus does not necessarily reflect either truth or the best path. Its value lies in the alternative to aggression and sometimes bloodshed. Having made these noble gestures, I personally (as perhaps we all) find it difficult to accept the new world order as it unfolds each day with the chip chipping away at traditional value systems that bind a society. It seems to me that many things in contemporary society have a downside, the significance of which is either neglected or deliberately ignored in the ostrich head-in-sand fashion and filed away in the "never-to-be-opened" circular cabinet! It's a slippery slope with normality forever sliding to the right (or down the plug hole) as perceived by the majority on their U-tubes, Facebooks and current social media Apps. I see society as becoming a herd of Antarctic penguins seeking the best light and warmth. A signal goes out and we all run to this spot. A new signal goes out and we all run to a new spot… and so the game goes on. Eventually we look more like headless chooks than penguins! Fashion, fashion, fashion; money, money, money; things, things, things; labels, labels, labels! What the duck's wrong with us????

I had been in Cheena for six years as a Chemistry teacher teaching the South Animalian Matriculation in a Cheenese 'qango' International School in the very wealthy and modern city of Changzhou (pr: chang-joh). But more on that later. On returning home I went to my local hospital as my vision in my right eye was failing. I spoke to the receptionist who asked my name, address etc. to which she then responded "I'm sorry Mr Law, but you don't seem to be on our database!"

"But I have been here many times over the past thirty years- it's not possible that I am not there!" I replied indignantly.

"Well we updated our system just a year ago, when did you last come in?"

"About two years ago for an x-ray"

"I'm sorry, I will have to enter your details again" … and so I tediously went through all the questions as she entered my personal info. I was then asked to wait and after a brief interval was shown to a small room with some equipment and a chair. I sat. Firstly a youngish Indyan lady in tight blue jeans, wearing her stethoscope in necklace style (too many Amerikan hospital soapies?) came into the room to which I had been ushered. "I am Dr Rimbavi, what seems to be the trouble?"

"I seem to be losing my sight in my right eye."

"OK let me have a look at it". She closely examined my eye then suggested I sit behind a piece of equipment for closer examination. She tried to adjust the instrument but without success. After a few minutes she was joined by a middle aged doctor also from Indya dressed in neat grey trousers, a dapper shirt and flamboyant tie. "I am Dr Patel, has my intern given any diagnosis yet?"

"No, she was trying to adjust the equipment".

"Ah, let me have a look then" … after several minutes of fiddling he said "the machine doesn't seem to be calibrated, I cannot focus on your eye to see the problem. I will have to call the equipment supervisor to get it working!" At this point another receptionist came in and called the doctor away, requesting I return to the waiting room. After twenty minutes I asked at reception whether the doctor was returning to continue with the consultation. Just my luck, there were several critical patients arriving from a road accident. "I'm afraid the doctor will not be available for some time, could I record a new appointment time for you?"

My next stop was to my local branch of Westpac. Fortunately there are still people there to actually see and talk with face-to-face, but I cannot see that situation remaining after another few years! I spoke with the girl at the front desk "Good morning, I wonder if I might speak with someone regarding a short-term loan please"

"Certainly sir, take a seat and someone will be with you in just a minute"

Eventually I was in the partitioned office with a middle aged thin wiry lady with grey hair. "How can we help you today Mr Law?" she said in a most polite manner.

"Well you see I have this problem with all my stuff from Cheena. It has arrived at the Port of Melbourne but the fees are considerably more than anticipated from the logistics company and I will need to borrow $1000 on a short term in order to be able to pick the items up. After next week I will commence to incur warehouse fees charged on a daily basis."

"And what is your current employment situation Mr Law? How much is your fortnightly income?"

"Well actually I am retired and am awaiting my pension from Centrelink" (the org with all link but actually no centre... but I didn't say this!)

"I see, please wait a minute whilst I talk with the manager" After several minutes the dear lady came back. "I'm so sorry Mr Law, we cannot assist you at present; may I suggest that you go back to Centrelink and make a request for an emergency advanced payment?"

I was thinking how many years I had been with this bank and this was my first request for a loan... a measly $1000, but excessive for the scrupulous and over-careful employees of my branch at the end of 2013!

I was again on the telephone to the shipping brokers to get my stuff cleared. "I am living in far East Gippsland, can I get all the paperwork done online and send a cheque in the mail?"

"Certainly Mr Law, I will forward the forms to you by email and you can return them as soon as you have completed all the details. From the actual date of unloading you must have all the details to us, including payment, within seven days after which you will start to incur storage fees on a daily basis"

"OK, not a worry, I look forward to receiving the documents"

Unfortunately it was Christmas in just another three days. We were to travel via the Snowy River to my brother's house in Canberra for the festive season... but I did not concern as he has an excellent computer and good internet connection. The night by the banks of the Snowy was serene, beautiful and soul enriching. I had been in Cheena daily soup for too long and had forgotten the pleasure of the smells and sounds of the bush with the gentle murmur of the river flowing by.

After returning the pdf file to the broker via email with all the detail with the exception of my signature (the stupid form would not permit a paste of a signature, only typed text was permissible) I sat back to enjoy my Christmas. Three days later a returned email said "the customs people will not accept your forms due to the lack of a signature". On returning home I was back at the Shire Office to email again... "but you guaranteed that I could do all this online". Then after a phone call "I am so sorry Mr Law but you need to sign the forms and return them asap. I must warn you that your time is almost out and you will soon be receiving added storage charges of $200 per day."

Now I was receiving urgent emails from the Cheenese shipping company in Shanghai asking why I had not yet picked up my goods.

I won't bore my reader with the rest other than to say by the time I picked up all my stuff we had paid the true value of the goods two times over in shipping fees, customs duties and the dreaded broker fees (what the hell do they do? .. just sit in plush offices on their fat bottoms raking it in!!)

Despite all these hurdles I was so happy to be back in Animalia amongst familiar faces with air one could breathe, starry nights and the aromas of the forests of eastern Victoria. I was so glad to be home!

Went to the local Doctor for a referral for my seven year old daughter to see a paediatrician… she was born with a heart murmur and we thought we would get it checked. Got the referral and a telephone number. "Sorry Mr Law, there was a paediatrician but he resigned, you will have to try a Melbourne hospital."

Went to the local Doctor for a referral for grandad's knees to see an orthopaedic surgeon for knee surgery. Got the referral and a telephone number. "DO YOU HAVE PRIVATE INSURANCE MR LAW?"

"…err, no I don't, neither has grandad. Could I make an appointment at our nearest big town please?"

"Sorry Mr Law but it will be more than twelve months. Mr De Vries only comes there once a month and currently is all booked out 'til June of next year; but you could make an appointment for here in Trag."

"OK then, but it's a long way!"

"Ah, I have a spot for you on the 25th November at 1.30 pm."

"but that's seven months away, does he have a friend in Singapore or Beijing?"

"I don't think so! I can fit you in if we have a cancellation… please fax the referral."

Cancellation I thought; what- due to sudden death from boredom? Am I living in Victoria or some remote Abo community in the backblocks of Western Animalia?

I was hoping to build a house of concrete and rock on a lightly forested block 10 k out of the village. I had done all the paperwork from Cheena and had had the site and access track cleared some two years earlier. I had my planning and building permit but had jumped the gun somewhat having stayed in Cheena for a little longer than expected. My 'four years' were almost up so I applied for an extension. "We are so sorry Mr Law, but you did not complete your house within the four years of your permit. Also, the fire regulations have altered". I tried to tell them I was an aging 'owner builder' and that the house was to be built of cement blocks with a stone façade. No joy! I also pointed out that the Council were still issuing planning permits for houses made entirely of timber in the High Country. No joy! I also pointed out that Liverpool Cathedral was started circa 1906 and not completed til 1974. No joy! (obviously one could not build anything of substance or so grand in this shire!)

"What we suggest Mr Law is that you resubmit your plans and reapply for your permits". The money grubbing bastards wanted me to start over!

I notice that both this shire and the Alpine shire in eastern Victoria will no longer give building permits for small acreages (under 25 hectare in fact). Reasons given are mainly:

- We wish to give farmers "the right to farm"
- We don't like or want "lifestyle choice persons" spoiling the view
- Providing services is a financial burden on council

I get the impression that perhaps the "Bonegilla Blackshirts" have finally taken over the Alpine Area with a view to making it like a Piedmont-cum-Bavaria utopia for a select clientele! (more on this group later). Building permits have been handed over to private companies and even the distribution of water from rivers to farmers for irrigation has also been given over to private companies.

The telly told me that in the first 17 weeks of this year (2015), 34 women in Animalia as a whole were killed by acts of domestic violence. That equates to *two* per week! Other murders are around *five* per week and deaths due to road accidents around *twenty two* per week. Murders by Animalian Islamic Terrorists … *zero!* Drugs and suicide… tens of thousands per year!

A local lad in his early twenties got extremely angry one evening and smashed the grocery shop window and beat up the garage mechanic on account that he was refused a purchase of some alcohol. Evidently, I was told later, he was taking a drug called 'ice' freely available in this small remote community. I had watched the Amerikan drama "Breaking Bad" whilst in Cheena. I had no inkling that the drug was now available almost everywhere in Animalia including small remote rural communities. I had been away more or less for fourteen years. It only took me a couple of months to realise that Animalia was *in a state of war…* and I am not referring to participation in conflicts in Afganiston or the Middle East. There was an insidious creeping war on our own turf and no one seemed to recognise its existence.

A war tearing at the heart and fabric of Animalian society with thousands of casualties each year with the dark enemy unidentified and suffering hardly a single casualty.

I looked around aghast at our sterility, immobility and stupidity on a grand scale! I have decided that we are now at the point of Kessen (決戦), which literally means "decisive battle".

16

1.   Sodomy

t is a topic that clearly the media continue to avoid and to a great extent the public also wish to avoid in every day conversation. However, characters in Amerikan TV soapies such as the ladies in 'Sex and the City', openly mention the perverse desires of 'one-night-stands' regarding anal sex. In the movie 'Bridgette Jones Diary' there was the brief 'morning after' scene where Bridgette refers to the anal intercourse she was subjected to by her boss... but she obviously didn't say 'no' at the critical moment of entry! There are many internet sites with graphic video of normal sex and, unfortunately, anal sex. Examples include: bravoteens.com, tubewolf.com, 21sextury.com and *hundreds* of others. (Which reminds me of the Primary grade student that the teacher asked to make use of the internet to write a story about her favourite pet. The innocent child typed into the search engine "Black Pussy". You may titter at this, but it is not so funny for parents to see their children subjected to these sites.) Our courts and especially our reporters when following such cases as wayward Priests tend to use safe and more sensitive expressions such as 'sexually abused' when the truth is *"the bastard sodomised the nine year old boy!"* Let us not cower away from truth and reality! Currently we see a priest that abused more than one hundred children over his long career since the 1960s bringing pell-mell to the Catholic Church in Animalia. At least for the Inglish speaking countries of the world, is it not time that Catholic priests be allowed to marry, bringing some normality and renewed trust!?

It may not be a shared opinion, some may violently disagree; however, I put it to you: "a society that is tolerant of *sodomy* between consenting adults whether of the same sex or no, is a *decaying society* soon doomed for the scrap heap!"

Scoff as you will but the history of human societies of the past have clearly demonstrated this. King Solomon decreed "no sodomite shall live in close proximity to the Temple". In the West there seems to be a creeping adage that "we can do just about anything we wish to without reprisal". Sounds a bit strong? Well drug abuse, murder and general criminal activity are on the rise. Belief systems such as religion and the rule of law are on the wane. TV and film have a lot to answer for in shaping the values of modern society over the last fifty years or so and now the internet also has its 'down-side' regarding its infiltration and attack on social values.

Tolerance of sodomy between humans is a criterion in the dividing line between civilisation and animalism. I am a scientist. But I am humble. For all the grandeur of our collective knowledge and state of the art technology, we will always be just scratching the surface. To reason that "there is nothing new to be discovered" is absolute nonsense. However clever, we still are here for our three score and ten and not much more. We are at a point in time where the lessons of history are being ignored. We are both sentient and spiritual in nature. Without those qualities we are nothing much above other animals. If you wish to regard this epistle as being anti-homosexual, that is for you to judge. If you wish to label me homophobic I challenge that on two counts: Firstly homophobic means 'a fear of homosexuals' which I have not. I suffer no fear! Secondly, and here is the nub, I am focussed on the act of *sodomy* whether it be between males or between a male and a female (and I'm not going to be diverted here into hermaphrodites or other oddities and acute minorities). It is my firm belief that the act of sodomy should remain on the statutes as being unlawful and that it is a punishable offence. Any man or woman sodomised should report it to the police and an investigation followed. Otherwise the next phase will be consenting marriage between farmer Brown and his prized sheep or cow. "I couldn't help it me Lard, I jest loves Buttercup so much!" Baaah!

The Irish Republic voted on the equality of same sex marriage into law and their constitution but to what extent of equality were they voting for? (Amerika has recently done the same, but imposed by law, NOT by referendum). For instance, should two men in a gay marriage be permitted to raise children in an odd family? My value is a resounding 'NO'. The very definition of a family is man, woman and children. But Ireland has already been subject to severe economic depression necessitating a 'hand out' from the EU. Why it wishes to slide further I cannot fathom? Recognition of same sex marriage on a legal basis has many other associated connotations and complications such as the raising of children. Tom is a 'vote NO' person on this issue.

We are certainly on the downhill with so many issues and it seems to me that now is the time to act. If not, the 'Sounds of Silence' will permeate society and we will soon be irreparably broken as a nation. The goodness, the greatness, the value of being human, the virtue and righteousness of a developed society will sink into the abyss of conceit, greed, disrespect, cruelty and all the outpourings of a hedonistic tribe rushing in no particular direction like the confusion of 'Looking Glass Land'! *We cannot do anything we like!* A society can only exist based on some rules. For millennia, the stronger societies are those with respect for the normality of family life and the rearing of children in a unit where the guardians are man and wife. I understand that the single mum or dad is unavoidable but I am strongly against homosexual couples being permitted to raise children (in modern parlance I mean here both gay and lesbian.) Why you ask? Simple answer: "It is my value". And I will *not* yield from these values expressed here. This value is generally held by all the major religions of the world. Yet the West is now not only committing societal suicide but condemns those sensible nations that are trying to hold on to their norms and values. What arrogance! An Afrikan nation with the highest occurrence of Aids in the world being dictated to on its stance against sodomy and homosexuality? What's wrong with the West? If certain nations wish to

19

bring in new laws to guarantee their own destruction so be it. But keep your smelly noses out of other nation's politics and social mores that are (i) not fully understood and more importantly (ii) have served these nations for hundreds if not thousands of years. Permitting sodomy is not a criterion of a civilised society. It is the mark of the beast!

A pre-sodomy sexual act is to lick and suck the anus… also called rimming. Again, I would file this under 'base animal behaviour' to be associated with that of cats and dogs.

I confess that I do not have persuasive statistics regarding feminine views on sodomy. However the few that have openly expressed their view retain the value that they are against the practice. The majority of those women that have experienced being sodomised by their partner, husband, boyfriend etc. state that *it is unpleasant, painful, lacking in sexual fulfilment and leaving them with a feeling of low worth.* Most stated that they did not like it and would prefer their partner not to inflict it upon them. So why do we allow the internet to promulgate the act on many disgusting explicit sites? Why do we allow the internet to be used as a tool of hatred for terrorists, perverts, murderers and a whole gamut of con artists? Is this justified under freedom of expression and democratic values? Is there no line to be drawn in the sand for common decency and the survival of human society?

Perhaps the licensing laws for personal computer ownership and those of web sites are not tight enough on a global basis. Also, countries that invade us with viruses, cons and hideous exploitation should be temporarily disconnected until they get their house in order.

A person 'convicted of sodomy' should be excluded from holding a position in local, state or federal government; the armed forces; the police force; the professions of primary and secondary teaching; the scout and guide movements; youth clubs and societies; health care organisations and anything to do with food handling.

Sodomy must be held for what it is.. an act of animals, not humans! Keep it illegal! Again I repeat: these are *my* values and shared by *all* the major religions.

Punishment for Sodomy?

1st offence: $3000 fine + 3 month imprisonment
2nd offence: $5000 fine + 1 year imprisonment with hard labour
3rd offence: $10000 fine + 3 year imprisonment with hard labour
Further:

Persons *convicted of sodomy* and the *reduction of their work choices*: "any person convicted of having participated in the vilest *act of sodomy* shall not be permitted to enter the following occupations:

Armed Forces

Police Force (State or Federal)

Prison Officer

Primary or Secondary Teaching, Early Childhood Institutions

Other organisations pertinent to youth e.g Scouting Movement, Girl Guides

Health industry: Clinic, Hospital, Pharmacy, Dentistry

Restaurant or served food establishments

Clergy of the Anglican Church or the Church of Ingland

Prime Minister, Premier (i.e Head of a State or Territory)

Ministerial Position for Health or Education (Federal or State)

Ministerial Position for Defence

Representative in local Council, State Government or Federal Government"

It may at first seem a bit unfair but it still leaves a broad variety of permissible jobs, occupations or professional posts! Again, I do not need to justify my advice and opinion. As an Anglican (albeit not the best example and as a sinner) I am appalled by the current stance of the Church of Ingland ... again taking the suicidal road! No, all I have to tell you is that this is my personal value and it is shared by the majority of decent people in the Inglish speaking countries of the world.

Deuteronomy 23:17 There shall be no whore of the daughters of Israil, nor a sodomite of the sons of Israil. (King James Bible)

War on the Net: there seem to be hundreds of pornographic sites that anyone can go to and see couples engaging in sodomy. Once a child knows how to navigate it is easy to reach any one of these sites. And they are mostly "free". Personally I would like to see sites displaying 'normal sex' charging a membership fee so that even these cannot be viewed for free or by minors! Again some international body needs to police unsavoury web sites such as those displaying sodomy, sex, child pornography, bestiality, acts of terrorism, sadistic torture, sadistic mutilation, graphic murder and anything deemed below the standard of human decency. Consequence: minimum fine of $US500 000 and immediate deregistration and shut down [imprisonment for three years if unable to pay the fine!] Not just the site owner, but the owner of the server should also receive a hefty fine for each individual occurrence of an unsavoury site with deregistration and shut down after three such offences, again with the possibility of a prison sentence. Excessive flouting of these laws by any nation may also bring about total internet closure to that nation for a period of time. I suggest that an international body attached to the UN might be the overseer and judge. (see later: Data and Media)

2.   Crime and Punishment

Do we really want or need a memorial to two aborigines executed in Melbourne in 1842 for the murder of two whalers during the period of early settlement? Some guy Dr. Tosser by name (close enough) reckons that such a memorial should rival Captain Cook's cottage as a place we can be proud of to take visitors and overseas tourists. Probably the same tosser is an avid supporter of Ned Kelly, Jack the Ripper and Adolf! He was even brazen enough to compare the struggle of squeezing the tax-payers pocket to the tune of close to half a million bucks with the struggle in Amerika for a Vetnam War Memorial! Clearly the confused doctor feels that the aboriginal struggle is a war... a war with the whites in this country and most of all a war against those of us with Bretish heredity. It has nothing to do with conservatism or denying the past. They were hanged for murder. But Dr Tosser wishes to make them "war heroes" as part of a continuing war. Activists now continuously desecrate Cook's cottage in leafy Melbourne. These 'anti-Bretish' and 'anti- early settlers' rubbish are on a war footing. As a Bretish Animalian of Bretish descent I can only say that "I welcome it! Bring it on!" ... but maybe that's just me!

The Melbourne City Council would be better to channel money into a dignified development of the cemetery under the car park adjacent to the Victoria Market where so many early Animalians (including aborigines) lie forgotten. Some were whalers, sailors, prostitutes. Also labourers that helped build Melbourne in the early 19th century, whilst others were prisoners, vagrants or just poor working class people.

Again we see the attempted projection of the black, red and gold foisted upon us. The clear majority don't want it Mr. Mayor! (see later: Flags and Symbols)

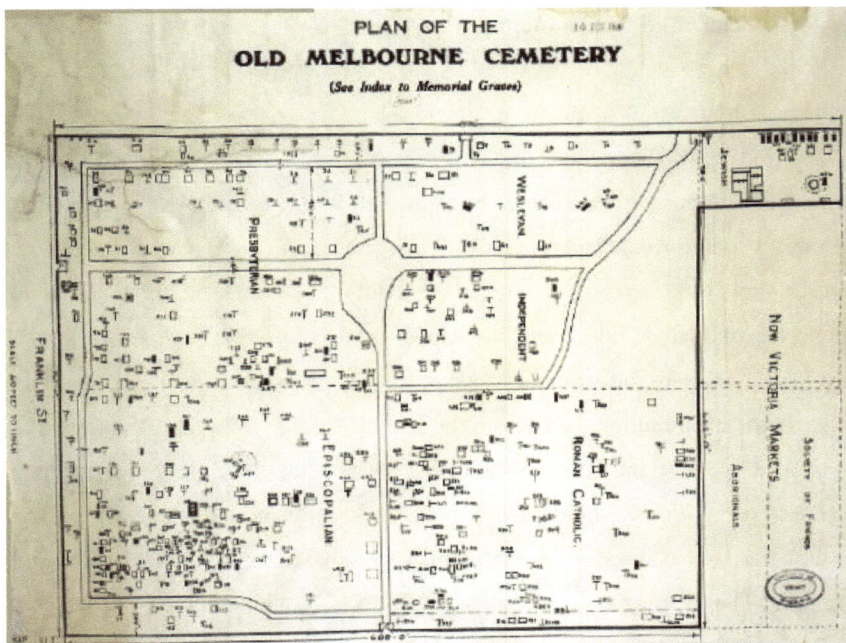

PLAN OF THE
OLD MELBOURNE CEMETERY
(See Index to Memorial Graves)

Now let me look to events, real or possible, at the present time as I write, June 2015:

The system placed a man in prison for murder. After twelve years or so the system decided to release the man on parole. Late one night within weeks of his release, the man dragged a woman off the street into a darkened alleyway, raped her then strangled her to death.

A paedophile lured a thirteen year old boy into his car, took him to a remote bush location, sodomised him and then murdered him by strangulation.

Two men and a woman placed several bombs in a busy shopping precinct and killed a dozen people (including women and children) and seriously injured sixty others, many with severed limbs and extensive burns. The explanation tendered was that 'Animalian servicemen were fighting overseas killing members of their religion and this was retribution.'

A group of four young men in their late teens and early twenties burst into a synagogue with shot guns and murder a dozen men, women and children for reason none other than their Jewish faith.

A young man in his early twenties having taken the drug 'ice' breaks into a house. There is a baby in a cot which is starting to cry. For fear of arousing the family sleeping in another room, the young man bludgeons the baby to death.

A gangland criminal is cornered and decides to use his illegal handgun to fight his way out. In the process he fatally shoots a member of the police force.

A drunk presents himself at a hospital after receiving a serious injury. He is verbally abusive to a nursing sister and with an iron bar bludgeons her to death right there in the outpatient reception area.

Two men attack an Animalian serviceman on the street and hack him to death with knives and machetes for a misguided perception of religious persecution in a foreign land.

Of course there are many other incidences of murder such as crimes of passion, self-defence and even on a humanitarian premise. But each of the examples given above I would categorise as heinous, outrageous, inhumane and a crime against humanity. I remain unapologetic when I state that the only punishment deserved (and for justice served) is for each of the perpetrators above to suffer the *death penalty*. We are not discussing here the lesser types of murder mentioned. We are not discussing punishment for the stealing of a loaf of bread. Since the abolishment of the death penalty society has had to submit to an increasing attack by people that think they can get away with horrendous crime. Our society has become weakened by a value that is just *not sustainable*. If our judicial system cannot adequately deal with the excesses of murder we run the risk of seeing normal individuals taking the law into their own hands. These will then suffer the legal consequences of their actions. Since the abolishment, again we see displays of superiority and finger pointing at other nations where the death penalty still exists. The question to be put is "has our nation benefitted by abolishing the death penalty? Are we living now in a more civilised and safer society than that of the 1920s or the 1950s?"

[It might be of interest to know that surveys questioning the public whether the death penalty should be reinstated in Animalia have *always* resulted in more than 50% in favour!]

Let not the reader be confused here! I find abhorrent the concept of the State taking the life of a human being. I find it sickening to the stomach the idea that someone must perform the actual execution. None the less, these feelings are nullified by the gory details of some killings and I see no alternative. Incarceration with the occasional prospect of release does not seem adequate with regard to certain crimes. And it is not a tooth for a tooth or an eye for an eye mentality I am expressing. How can a single individual be punished for multiple murders? It is expediency, just and brings closure to the case. It brings comfort to society at large that a cancer has been permanently removed. These *special provisions* should be under Federal Law and overriding of State Law.

Offences Tom sees as warranting the death penalty under Federal Law:

Murder of a police officer
Murder of a prison officer
Murder of a member of the armed forces
Murder of a medical practitioner
Murder of a school teacher, primary or secondary
Murder of a member of the judiciary
Murder of a nursing sister
Murder of an ambulance officer

Mass murder or serial murder
Mass murder in a terrorist act
Possession of drugs*
Importation of drugs*
Murder of a minor associated with a sexual attack
Repetitive murder
Murder of a child without compassion
Murder of a member of the clergy

*See relevant table

Notorious killers like the NSW "backpack killer" and similar... well I would provide a retrial. There are most likely up to a dozen more victims not yet found. There is a nice piece of fresh manila waiting for him and others like him!

The mode of execution itself is without doubt problematical. A judge and jury have to take responsibility. A person delivering the final blow has to live with her/his conscience. If the killing is to be humane, perhaps an extremely potent sleeping drug should be administered first, rendering the murderer unconscious; this may then be followed by a deoxygenised atmosphere in a closed room that brings about certain death without pain (despite the wishes of some for the contrary!) The process needs to be witnessed and documented.

Uncivilised you shout? It is a logical consequence of the scales of justice balancing an appropriate punishment to suite the crime committed. Society does not need monsters let loose to recommit their vileness. That is totally unacceptable. But you might execute an innocent you protest? This will always be a possibility but I would argue that for the *specialised* group of murders described taken together with modern forensic evidence, the occurrence of a misjudgement is unlikely. Evidence needs to be weighty and conclusive.

EXECUTIONS IN ANIMALIA SINCE 1822

	LAST EXECUTION	YEAR ABOLISHED
NSW	1940	1955
VIC	*1967	1975
QLD	1913	1922
WA	1964	1984
SA	1964	1976
TAS	1946	1968
NT	1952	1973
ACT	-	1973

*Last hanging Ronald Ryan aged 41 on 2nd March 1967 at Pentridge
Source: Australian Institute of Criminology

Each of us generally cannot bring our conscious mind to ponder on these horrible thoughts. History has demonstrated the most cruel and undignified modes of execution. Our very life blood and awareness dictates that death is an awesome thing that we must avoid contemplating (even though we must all eventually face it!) This however does not remove the problem. As academic as you would wish, the fact remains that some individuals deserve nothing less than termination. For each of the cases described above, I cannot fathom that those particular murderers will somehow "get better" and become useful members of society once again. *They have already forfeited their chance of rehabilitation.*

Morgan Poll 5814: with a representative cross-section of 1307 Animalians on Sept. 19 2014, they were asked: "If a person is convicted of a terrorist act in Animalia which kills someone should the penalty be death?"

52.5% responded YES   47.5% responded NO

Morgan Poll 6044 conducted with a representative cross-section of 2123 Animalians over Jan 23-27 2015. They were asked: "In your opinion, if an Animalian is convicted of drug trafficking in another country and sentenced to death, should the penalty be carried out?"

52% responded YES   48% responded NO

62% said the Animalian Government should **not** do more to stop the executions of Sukurmaran and Chan by Indenosia.

I noticed recently that the Frunch government was trying to reintroduce laws making prostitution illegal. I am uncertain as to the degree of success of the Bill but it certainly has some merit. The biggest joke of all time in our own country was the argument proffered back in the 1960s that legalisation of brothels under licensing laws would (i) take girls off the street and (ii) give the impression of control over the 'oldest profession in the world'. The fact remains that it did neither of these. There are still girls on the street hawking their wares with thuggy pimps not too far away. There are still many unlicensed and therefore illegal brothels in the urban areas. There exist even enslaved girls shipped in from overseas and forced to work in hideous and unbearable conditions with little chance of escape. But what I find the most obnoxious is the fact that some brothels are listed on the stock exchange as registered businesses which of course must pay dividends and tax. By definition, the share-holders as well as the tax department are clearly guilty of pimping!

It was a most extraordinary move by state governments across the nation to encourage the building of casinos. There seems to be either ignorance in high quarters or a total contempt for the fact that there has always been clearly a strong relationship between gambling, prostitution and illicit drugs! I ask again, "what sort of society do we wish to abide in and what sort of society do we wish for our children?" Hard decisions need to be made. But I say that our present three tiered hierarchy of government simply does not have the will to change things. Revenue collection seems to outweigh common sense!

My Irish friend, his wife and children were devastated by the wasteful death of their twenty two year old son viciously kicked and beaten outside a pub in the city of Melbourne at 2 am. in the morning. Another demonstration of the mix of youth, drugs, alcohol and the freedom of the footpath at such a late hour.

Curfews you want? Different strata of society have varying opinions on this. Younger people argue that they are bored and want places to go all through the night. Parents of teenagers are not so sure. I myself feel that 6 pm closing maybe a bit too strong (which we suffered in the 1960s) but why serve alcohol after 11.45 pm? Why are nightclubs open till 4 am? Again, our governments are weak on this issue and I find 'bravehearts' few and far between. It appears that revenue earned from these places is also more important than lives of young people. Some argue that a 'city that never sleeps' is somehow civilised and a mark of modernity. However the cost to young lives seems, to my logic, more powerful than these arguments. The stress placed on the police, ambulance officers and hospital staff is also considerable. The heartache and sorrow of any family losing a son or daughter that has been attacked and killed outside such venues in the wee small hours can be reduced considerably. Midnight to ten am. does not seem unreasonable a space in which alcohol is not permitted to be served or sold. I am not a wowser, nor do I see that total prohibition is the answer. I enjoy an occasional beer or glass of wine. Just the introduction of a modicum of common sense is what is needed. Is that so hard for the power brokers of our land?

The drugs marihuana, methyl amphetamine, heroin, cocaine and others less known but equally dangerous should remain forever prohibited. The damage they are doing to our society is beyond measure. I do not smoke tobacco (I confess I did as a teenager... it was peer pressure ha ha!) But the self righteous that focus on cigarettes and tobacco but with hardly a whisper on hard drugs I find infuriating. There is always a 'push' from some to accept the growing of hemp for clothing and other purposes. However one should regard these lobby groups with suspicion. Political extremists right and left have a common goal... destroy society and replace it with something ugly! Robbery, violence, sexual attacks and murder are all associated with the distorted view of the world possessed by the possessed (i.e those under the influence of drugs). The fact that tobacco and alcohol in excess do extreme harm to one's body and hence to society, is not really a strong argument to permit the introduction of other drugs to be abused (I am excluding essential prescribed medications here). I am again unapologetic when I say that I agree with the actions of those countries having a desperate struggle with the wide use of illicit drugs and the damage caused. Our neighbours all have the death penalty for excessive possession of certain drugs and I agree with it! None of this bullshit of "we are so much nobler and more civilised" attitude. *For we are neither!* [We don't mind joining wars and dropping bombs on people!] We must exercise the death penalty for major importers, manufacturers, distributors and traffickers of these drugs.

If we don't do it soon, we are truly lost. It must by now be accepted that this is the modern form of *warfare* against a country and its peoples. We have been over and over this discussion since the late nineteen sixties and early nineteen seventies into the twenty first century. The number of Animalian lives terminated or severely impaired by serious drug abuse is incalculable. The collateral damage to young children, other family members and friends is also inestimable! Plane, train and motor vehicle accidents are often the direct result of ingestion of harmful drugs alongside serious assault and murder. It cannot go on unchecked or at least with current wishy washy laws. We need to have resolve and stronger action if we truly want a clean up! Again, I think that these laws need to be *Federal Laws* and dealt with as such. The following is an arbitrary table and I am sure it can be tailored somewhat. But it is what Tom thinks we need:

Table: minimum amount of a drug to realise the death penalty

Drug and grade	Amount grams	Action
Ice (methyl amphetamine)		
1^0	> 255 g	Mandatory death penalty
2^0	> 280 g	Mandatory death penalty
3^0	> 335 g	Mandatory death penalty
Heroin		
1^0	> 185 g	Mandatory death penalty
2^0	> 205 g	Mandatory death penalty
3^0	> 330 g	Mandatory death penalty
Hashish		
1^0	> 205 g	Mandatory death penalty
2^0	> 225 g	Mandatory death penalty
3^0	> 255 g	Mandatory death penalty
Marihuana plant (stem and leaf)		
1^0	> 2505 g	Mandatory death penalty
2^0	> 2805 g	Mandatory death penalty
3^0	> 3005 g	Mandatory death penalty
Marihuana (dried)		
1^0	> 2005 g	Mandatory death penalty
2^0	> 2305 g	Mandatory death penalty
3^0	> 2505 g	Mandatory death penalty
Cocaine		
1^0	>195 g	Mandatory death penalty
2^0	>255 g	Mandatory death penalty
3^0	>295 g	Mandatory death penalty

The list is not comprehensive as there are other debilitating drugs out there destroying lives that can be included in the table. But marihuana is legal in some states of some countries you protest? Yes, those countries that have already taken their first step to 'social-suicide'. Those countries whose governments have yielded to the enemy. Those countries whose laws are weak. Why is it that third world countries have stiffer penalties than us? Because they are backward and behind the times? I don't think that is the reason. Some of these nations are closer to the 'golden triangle' where heroin filters down through their land on its way to us. They have a desperate struggle to combat the criminal moguls controlling the trade. They have no other recourse than to execute couriers and manufacturers when caught.

The golden triangle itself has been producing heroin for thousands of years. Opium (the derivative of the opium poppy) is a fine medicine for the operating table and for controlling extreme pain and was used widely during the First World War for army hospitals in the field of battle. But it has a destructive element. (It is unfortunate that there was a black period in Bretish history where opium was permitted to be sold in Cheena as a means of pacifying the people and the fact that the Cheenese have long memories.) A possible solution to end this area of production for the world market is by the use of weaponry to completely destroy the area (thousands of square kilometres in a mountainous terrain). Sounds dramatic but the world can do without the biggest manufacturer! I won't shed a tear. But who will do it?

We have seen the government and others of the "bleedin' hearts club" shed tears of woe over the execution of two Animalians in Indenosia in May 2015. [I do not agree with the *mode* of execution i.e by shooting!] A lot of pressure was brought to bear on Indenosia to abandon these executions. It was on the news every day for months. The two main 'Chess Pieces' on the Canberra parliamentary chess board did not refrain from making several threats about repercussions. When mentioning the Aceh tsunami rescue and the cost, Indenosians laughed at us for our pathetic impudence and started to publicly collect coins to pay us back! Personally I think that was merely an extension of 'White' arrogance on our behalf! [Our government and secret service have a habit of 'kicking' Indenosia on many fronts.] Regarding the above incident I have only praise for the AFP in their joint effort with the Indenosian police to catch heroin smugglers and there is no need to agonise over what eventually happened. It is essential that this close cooperation continue to frustrate would be extremists and drug pedlars. Of course I feel for their families but who was responsible for their grief? Had they not been caught, would they have continued their business? Of course YES. And how much additional grief and despair would they have brought to many young Animalians? In the final analysis I can only say "WELL DONE INDENOSIA!"

Many young Animalians behave in a most outrageous and embarrassing fashion whilst holidaying in Bali or Lombok… behaviour not tolerated at home. A joint effort by Animalian police and Indenosian police might help quell this.

Further, I was sickened by the 'Animalian Catholic University' in their proposal to offer scholarships in the names of the executed criminals. Maybe they could introduce more for Ned Kelly, Jack the Ripper, IRA bombers and perhaps other notorious criminals. It is a ploy to paint and perfume themselves like a rose in the current century whilst ignoring their cruel past! Does the 'sanctity of human life' count for those that have committed horrendous crime?

[As a final note I admit I was disappointed with the earlier President Yudhoyono that should have had the executions take place nine years earlier... I think it was a cowardly act to spare the Animalians but continue to execute other nationalities for the same offence. However some Us states have been known to hold criminals on death row for years before their execution.]

Half a tonne of drugs ('ice' and cocaine) arrived in Sydney from Bogota, Colombia early 2015. Six were arrested including a Colombian national. I repeat... half a tonne! Our police say that they have been cooperating with the police in Colombia. What can I say? If the scale of importation from that country is so large, it almost warrants a military action after a stern warning! After all are they not making war upon us?

The 26 year old Kiwi caught in Guangzhou, Cheena trying to bring 28 Kg of ice to Animalia ... well by now you know my feeling. I just hope the Chenese authorities round up the Triad gangsters as well and give them what they deserve!

Then there are the 'Balkan Drug Gangsters' from Sydney that run international drug cartels along with their Italiano 'Mafia' and 'Coda Nostra' competitors said to be responsible for literary tonnes of ice, cocaine, heroin and weapons importations to Animalia. These scumbags' roots can be traced back to those weak liberal immigration ministers and their mismanagement in the immediate post-war decades (see later). Our state and federal police forces are overwhelmed and need support... special, high priority and immediate! But the chess board pieces are diverted to side issues hardly effecting mainstream Animalian society... why is this the case?

Some Animalians Executed Overseas:

South Afrika		
'Breaker' Morant	War Crimes	1902
Peter Handcock	War Crimes	1902
Vetnam		
Phum Trong Dung	Drug Trafficking	2014
Malaysia		
Barlow	Drug Trafficking	1986

Chambers	Drug Trafficking	1986
McAuliffe	Drug Trafficking	1993
Singapore		
Van Tuong Nguyen	Drug Trafficking	2005
Indenosia		
Chan	Drug Trafficking	2015
SYOUKamaran	Drug Trafficking	2015
Cheena		
Henry Chhin	Drug Trafficking	2005 fate unknown

Interesting that in WWI, many allied soldiers were executed for cowardice or desertion; however none of the 129 Animalians charged with similar offences were executed by order of High Command. Many Animalians along with other allied soldiers were executed in enemy hands however.

It is likely that many other Animalians were executed overseas over the last 100 years or so, but we have no record of these. Currently as I write there are seventeen Animalians on death row around the world, mainly for drug crime and mostly with the intention of bringing drugs here to Animalia. So you see, the problem is really *here* in our society! Regarding the current scourge of 'ice' I feel that every city, suburb, town, village and hamlet around the whole nation need to take action to prevent the drug permeating into their local environ. Governments and the police have a mammoth task and battle that they are losing. This must be recognised and we have no time to be weak, intransigent, complacent and inactive! People and communities need to be vigilant! By what means? That is not for me to infer or to say outright!

As with all of us, our hearts went out to Animalian Woman of the Year 2014 and her crusade on the deep trend of family violence in Animalia. Statistics are horrific with on average two women being murdered each week by their male partner. Many women live and put up with violent husbands and one can only hope that, in such a situation, they seek advice and assistance. Drug abuse is definitely an aggravating factor to violence against women and children. Regarding children, one difficulty is to differentiate between what is seen to be violence and what may be deemed reasonable preventative measures in discipline. Naturally there is a whole gradation of physical punishment from a smack to the leg to serious infliction causing some permanent damage e.g broken bones, excessive bruising, cruel incarceration etc. My culture sees no harm in milder forms of punishment like a smack to the leg or time out from viewing TV and consequences involving similar removal of privileges for a short period. But then the European Union and New Zeeland have placed in law that a child cannot be smacked on the leg, and a parent may be prosecuted for such. As an anglophile I do not agree with that extreme either, nor does my spouse. The lesson of a short sharp smack to the leg indicates to the child an immediate recognition of wrong doing or that they are doing something that might endanger themselves e.g about to run onto the road. With these milder punishments, they are not gender based. A mother that loves and cares for her sibling may equally use a smack on occasions.

The more serious event such as brutality whilst in a fit of rage is however a gender issue. Most males have built in survival instincts that can raise their adrenaline and produce a fit of anger and even rage. We are living in the 21st Century but our genetic makeup has changed little in one million years. So what can trigger rage which often leads to an act of violence and sometimes in the extreme? Sadly and more often than not, the man brings home the pressures of his day. His frustrations with work, his boss or relationships with fellow workers add to the stress and strain which he brings to his own home. I am not trying to make any excuse for extreme behaviour. Many men need some assistance with this problem by education, mentoring and even psychological help from a professional. The most important thing is for a man to recognise he has a problem with how he deals with his stress in life and seek help. Too often it is a question of control... the man wishes to take complete control in his home environment. If he cannot get it, he loses control of himself! Again, he must recognise this problem and realise that sharing responsibility with his partner is the better way. Unfortunately the majority of men fail to heed such advice. But it is a first step to modifying their behaviour. A man with a family loved his partner dearly in the early days of the marriage. The advent of children enriches the lives of both parents and brings great joy.

External pressures can be damaging as can dissatisfaction with the material assets of the family. Too much pressure is brought to bear by the constant bombardment of advertising for material things that we are told we must have. As parents we worry about whether we are providing well enough for our kids. The Smiths down the road have just bought a new four wheel drive car, next door have just obtained a 60 inch plasma TV and so it goes on.

Dissatisfaction with our personal appearance, our sex lives and the thought "does she still love me?" all chip away at what was once a strong marriage. An extramarital affair is often the most damaging, but a sensible couple may work through this without the destruction of their precious family. A lot comes down to personal values which were inculcated during the childhood and adolescence period of our development. Poor values continue in cycles and are difficult to suddenly rectify to attain better values in adulthood where they are absent. Families do not necessarily have to demonstrate strong religious values alone; common sense and decency with mutual respect and caring are sufficient to develop good values in a child. Those men with a problem with violence need to realise that a spouse and children require a sustained safe environment in which to live. A woman that truly loves her husband should not care too much about material things. A marriage is about survival of the family unit and doing one's best in defiance of hard or difficult circumstances.

Rampant capitalism and the media are guilty of damaging the family unit. But then there exists a political agenda of the extremes of right and left to weaken and destroy our society also. Drugs, chemicals, psychological ploys and various diabolical inventions at a sophisticated technological level may be applied to an unwary victim. There are menaces also among us that are not our friends but indeed our enemies and see the family unit as a target for societal destruction. The complexity of modern times is also the bringer of confusion, frustration and a sense of futility to the lives of many. A return to basic values is the path to salvation and restoration and it need be only common sense. Some will find solace and direction in religion and there is nothing wrong with that... it should never be scoffed at for, we as humans, are sentient beings and seek connectivity with each other. That connectivity many conveniently be found by a sincere belief in God and a Creator of all things with purpose and meaning. The advantage of this belief is that it brings calmness, sense of direction, understanding and positive attitudes to an otherwise meaningless life. Those that create are the happiest of all!

It is not for me to point to the enemies of the family unit and our society itself. But it is for each of us to be vigilant and to be constantly aware that the enemy is at hand and takes on many forms and guises! Cherish your family and friends and always assist the stranger in need of your help. Whosoever knows who that stranger may be and the value of that gift of your compassion in a brief moment of need?

Where a man has severely injured his partner, or worse, killed her in some fit of rage, I call for *a blood test of the perpetrator* immediately if possible to look for any anomalies or traces of unusual substances. If men are experiencing abnormal bouts of anger and rage that are out of character, I recommend they too seek a blood test and critical analysis for same. The health system must meet this demand and the instruments of analysis be made available at all hospitals regardless of the cost. As well as basic psychological help, we must make use of sophisticated technology to research the inherent problem. It may be that there *are* causes unrelated to gender in many cases! Know what I'm saying?

Finally, for the woman that has made a sincere and concerted effort to change the behaviour of a violent husband that once was both loving and kind towards her, the best option is to leave the marriage. It might be for a trial period with provisos or a permanent separation where there is no hope of repair or reconciliation.

The chess pieces in Canberra wish to cancel Animalian citizenship for returning citizens of dual citizenship accused of serving in a terrorist organisation or having served with an army fighting against Animalian armed forces. Some wish to include purely Animalian citizens. These powers are to be given to a politician. Whilst Tom does not condone the action of terrorists and those that take up arms against our own armed forces, the implications of such legislation run deep and are fraught with legal difficulties. I remember decades ago that an Animalian attacked Michael Angelo's Pieta sculpture in Italia with a hammer. The media immediately condemned him not as Animalian, but by his former nationality. Typical! The main problem of stripping citizenship is "proof of the charge laid" which to my mind can only be ascertained in a court of law. The chess pieces seem currently to have a secret channel direct to the enemy with absolute certainty as to the identity of participants originating from our shores. Magic!

I see that the intention is NOT to make the new law retrospective. That lets off the Nazis and their quisling supporters (which a liberal/country party government allowed into Animalia in the 1940s, 50s and 60s), the IRA (including thousands of local fund raisers), national service men and women of Israil, Lebanoon and other countries, volunteer soldiers during the last Lebanese civil conflict and a host of other conflicts around the globe where war crimes may have taken place!

Are Animalia's joining in conflicts far from our shores *all* to be deemed legal and ethical without question? Tom sees the war in Siria and Irak as a '*phoney war'* with unprecedented heaps of propaganda to cover up its true nature and purpose. But more on that later!

Stripping citizenship is a 'Pontius Pilate' act of washing ourselves clean without taking responsibility. If Animalians break the law, however heinous, justice must be determined in an Animalian court of law. It is the natural right of all citizens in this nation and must not be removed or eroded by politicians. *That road leads to totalitarianism* as we have seen elsewhere in place and history. We have laws for traitors and murderers already; let them be applied. Let posturing politicians write their memoirs to frighten small children at bedtime and let the legal system do its job.

3.   Manufacturing, Cars and Ships

Surprise surprise, the big guys from overseas wanna run away to Cheena and get their cars made there for a mere fraction of what it costs in Animalia (Toyota, Ford and GM). But even Animalian companies have been going "offshore" for decades now…   Philipeens, Indenosia, Vetnam, Hong King, Bangladash… reducing the manufacturing prowess at home. Heaven help if we are suddenly thrown into a "real" war! We would have to start new factories from the ground up to produce armaments, ships and planes etc. Fortunately we do have a dearth of natural resources to produce all these things; but would we have time to get it all organised, up and running? I doubt it. So with all this running offshore are we placing the nation in jeopardy from some such future war scenario? I suppose we could always surrender! Or alternatively threaten our invading enemy with the prospect of us biting their balls and tits off with our bare teeth!

To decline into solely a producer of agricultural products and exporter of raw materials will lead us into great peril. Now I know that governments with stout hearts have tried to tax the greedy international conglomerates that own a sizeable amount of our mining industries without success. If the bastards won't pay their taxes fairly (due to high salaried accountants and lawyers plus malleable conservative politicians whom shall be nameless here), how about getting them to re-invest a fraction of their trillions into a true blue Aussie car?

Indenosia, Indya, Jepon and Cheena all like our exports and want more. Why not start up an Animalian car manufacturing enterprise before the incumbents pull the plug. We are rich in engineers, scientists, computer heads and resources. How about some arm twisting? How about extending lucrative benefits to some of these close-by clients if they genuinely assist us in this venture? We would not have to reproduce a myriad of models and options; just a few basic cars with some serious industrial research into electric vehicles.

A basic V-6 alloy engine might go into a sports model, family model sedan, family model wagon, 4X all purpose wagon and 4X farm utility. A 1400 cc small engine for a small economic run-about. An electric car would be essential to design and manufacture. The big problem is there seems to be no 'will' to accomplish these things. The Mr. Big is looking out for his shareholders who want the highest return for their investment. Profit can sometimes get in the way of parsimonious action and forward thinking. Consequences logically always follow actions. Often, consequences are not realised until it is too late. A nation and its people are more important than the serving of the few at the expense of the many. Drugs, TV, sporting heroes and public castration of tall poppies are not enough! Excellent schools, hospitals, services and utilities and a feeling of well being and safety are paramount indicators of a high society. A work ethic and available jobs is all people ask. Take these away and decay and decadence set in. A national malaise is enduring if it is allowed to spawn.

Qantas has a proud and noble history and it will damage and hurt the country greatly if it is permitted to go under ('scuse the pun!). Well yes, we suffer the double wammer of both the tyranny of distance in a large country and the weight of a small population of fewer than 25 million. Mathematically this places enormous strains on our economics and the ability to withstand external competition with the quality and quantity of products and technology generally. But we are a resilient people and have achieved bloody miracles in the 200 years plus we have been on this soil. Let no one doubt this or try to take the ideal away for it is a basic truth about this country. And how you might ask? By the sheer will of its people to soldier on and get the job done. It is easier to conjure up seemingly insurmountable excuses why something should *not* be attempted or done than to be stubborn and self reliant and struggle on 'til the goal is achieved. There will always be the poo-pooers heckling at the sidelines. But a people of substance will endure with inner fortitude and achieve. That was the strength of the early settlers, the soldiers of two world wars and can still be seen in most of us today. Resolve is our medicine and mainstay! So what am I trying to say here? Well basically it is about a national value. Money, profit and immediate reward are not necessarily virtuous. Our actions today will logically shape what happens in the future. I think we are making some errors of judgement which will have debilitating effects in the long term. No matter the cost, it is my view that some national icons must be preserved and our national carrier is definitely one of them. A car industry is another. (I know you will tell me here that Holden is owned by GM but the research, design and development was due to many clever engineers and creative locals!)

The Us is well known for its trend of protectionism of its own. We cannot be dictated to by other airlines for a level playing field in everything. We need to look after our own first and maintain our own work forces in fields of expertise that are essential for a sustainable future in a technological sense.

Very overweight politicians with thumbs in coal mining might also be persuaded to consider investing in an *Animalian Car Industry*.

Our ship building industry (including subs) is something we should not permit to slide overseas either. A submarine made in Nippon might have a self-destruct mechanism if that nation ever became aggressive again. What would we defend ourselves with then? The ugly red faces of politicians? (though it might scare some away!) It is sad that the wisdom in Canberra is always looking for someone else to do our manufacturing for us.

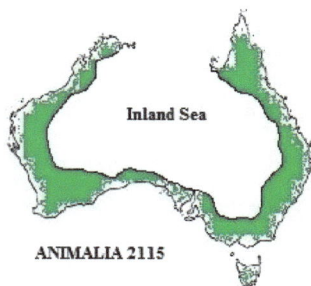

Inland Sea

ANIMALIA 2115

"What happened to Animalia?"

"Awe... it was all dug up and shipped to Cheena and Indya last century!"

"At least it has expanded our fishing industry!"

It might be nice to currently export so much iron ore, uranium, gas and coal to the hungry giants up north but are we keeping a careful eye on our resources? The current thinking is that we have sufficient for hundreds of years to come. How true is that statement? There is not much oil and gas left in Bass Strait. We are sending huge amounts of gas from the North West Shelf overseas. If our population grows to 80 millions in another century will people look back proudly or with resentment?

The sunniest country in the world is still toying with the idea of nuclear energy for domestic use despite all the warnings on the potential effect on our environment. Why are we not making our own solar power cells? Why are we not placing wind generators in the same paddock with solar cells? We don't seem to have quite got it together yet or solved the equations! I propose that a minimum of one tenth of overseas revenue on exporting of uranium and carbon fuels should be poured into these cleaner technologies (including electric auto manufacture).

Those again in Canberra that keep describing nuclear energy as clean 'n green and cheap energy should take a hard look at the figures and the potential for an unhealthy environment!

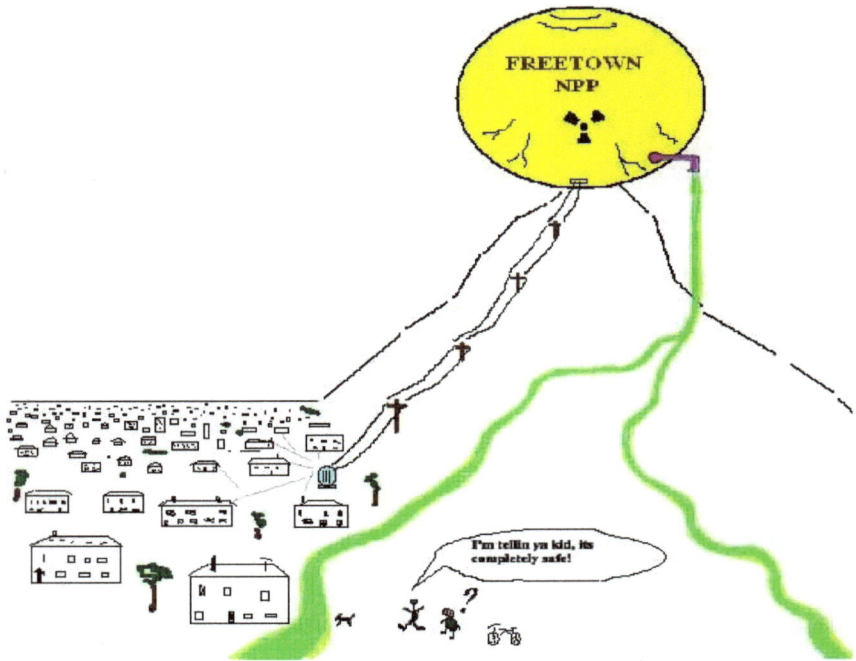

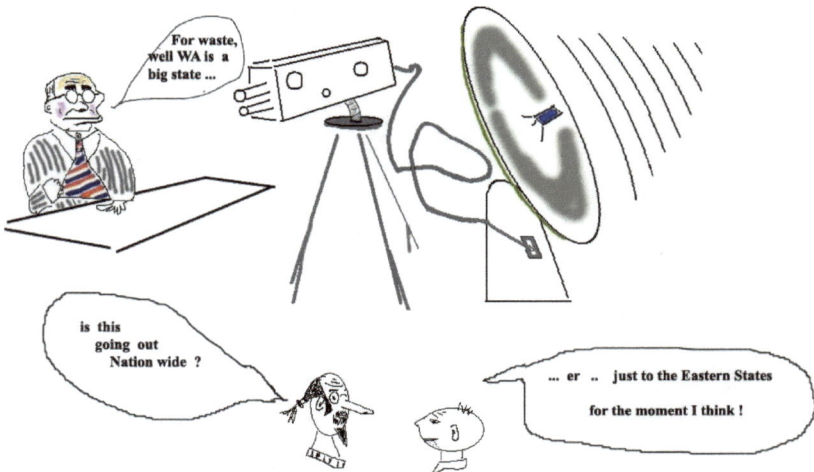

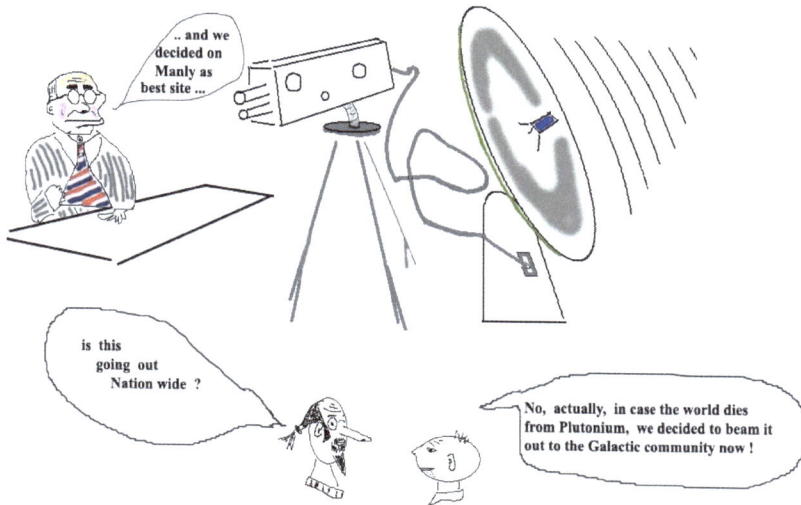

Closing down aluminium smelters, copper and zinc production and many other essential industries with the prospect of making nothing and importing everything will reap dire consequences for our society in the future. We need to turn around this backward thinking and get our trades and manufacturing industries back to full steam ahead. There is something smelly and morally wrong to rely on those countries to our north with big populations and desperately poor people to make everything for us. If we are not smart, we are destined to become a nation of onlookers and beach bums holding out tin cans for the meagre offerings from rich overseas tourists, mesmerised in a drug induced stupor still holding to the belief that we are God's chosen whilst sand is kicked into our grubby faces. The reality is that we will become intellectually and materialistically impoverished, marginalised by a high tech world at our doorstep that will show no pity on us. An extreme point of view you laugh… well maybe!

Well, well, well… submarines surfacing again … but made where? Perhaps Jepon, perhaps Cheena, perhaps Jermany. There's a very cheap Scottesh version the Government might be interested in:

It must be such a difficult decision but Tom advises against overseas production for the sake of our own workers. Animalian jobs must come first! As mentioned elsewhere, our international companies might foot the bill with fair taxation (although it's a basic premise of all banks and tax departments to screw the poor… its easier!)

As an iron ore producing country we should utilise some of that resource in our own manufacturing and maintain our technological expertise. Sure it may not be as cheap as producing a submarine in Cheena but it would be ours and everything on board would also be ours. No good having something that a future potential enemy knows the detail and blueprint!

price:	most expensive	expensive	moderately priced	very cheap		expensive	very expensive
delivery:	10 years	6 years	2 years	next week		4 years (maybe)	2 years
quality:	very good	quite good	excellent	good		quite good	excellent

The turnaround time is slow but does that really matter? … securing jobs is the determining factor. By the way, the above figures and comments are Tom's and are not based on any scientific or economic study ha ha!

On the Board

4.   Boat People and the Gulags

At the age of 16 years I myself was a boat person, arriving at Port Melbourne on the SS Orion in September 1961. My parents were described as 'ten pound poms' due to the migration scheme at the time where citizens from the Old Kingdom were enticed to a long sea voyage to Animalia for ten pounds sterling apiece. It was an excellent scheme and one that my family had no regrets about embracing. Life on a migrant hostel at Fishermans Bend, nestled among factories, was a little hard on my parents but my brothers and I had a whale of a time. In the immediate years following our withdrawal from Vetnam (1975-), many boat people came from that country and were welcomed.

People have been coming to Animalia in leaky boats for thousands of years (although it is thought that people were able to walk from New Guinea during the last ice age some 14000 ya and likely in the two earlier ice ages). White people from Europe started to explore and eventually settle the continent from the end of the eighteenth century. This was a tragic moment for the indigenous peoples of the continent then living a Stone Age culture. There was conflict and diseases new to the aborigines that both reduced their numbers and forced them off their traditional lands.

Why, one might ask, are we now so hard on desperate people that have risked their lives and left their loved ones behind to reach our shores? It is a question that I cannot find a rational answer to. The Government and many conservatives call them 'queue jumpers' and the boat operators 'people smugglers' (We have labels for others also such as terrorists for Freedom Fighters). Whilst there may be a few undesirables, many have escaped war torn countries or persecution in their own country for religious or political reasons. I understand that we cannot take in a flood of people in their hundreds of thousands. Having said this, there is an expectation by us of those countries bordering a country at war to take in up to a million people in a very short period of time placing enormous stress on them (Jardon, Lebanoon and Turkee at present). I see a huge disparity in logic and reason here if not just damn hypocrisy. We are the first to put our hand up to join wars but are we doing enough for those afflicted? I think not. The Animalian encampments in other island countries close to our shores where we have dumped the brave boat people can only be described as gulags. A cruel ending for those weary travellers already wearied by war and deprivation. And the cost of these camps

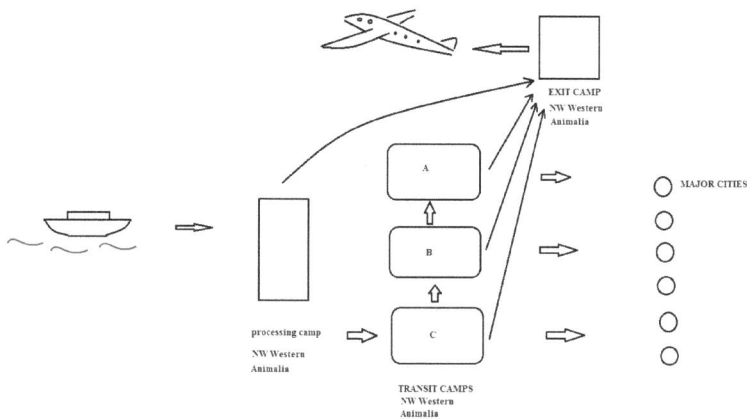

run by private companies is astronomical and a burden to the tax payer. The misery of the inmates unfathomable! The chess board leaders' latest tactic is to mix asylum seekers with violent Animalian criminals at Xmas Island ... certainly an added deterrent having efficacy but lacking in morality! Sadly we are being constantly criticised by both our neighbours and the United Nations; an indictment that our King chess piece must take responsibility for!

"Some of the lower ranks of people undergo more hardships in a single day than those of a more exulted station suffer during their whole lives!" (sic: Oliver Goldsmith)

If these souls were brought to one or two major camps in the north west of Western Animalia (or to the proposed Centrapolis... see later) and processed there, many useful migrants might enter our country and make good citizens.

Those of dubious character might be sent back to their original country after an uncomfortable stay in a transit camp for up to 90 days (but no longer), ensuring they won't return. Instead of languishing whilst in these camps, inmates might be given opportunities to work in a range of factories and support facilities depending on skills, where useful products are made. Those that prove themselves to be hard working and diligent can be accepted as migrants. Aspects of the current system seem both cruel beyond belief as well as expensive. The 'turn back boats' program has just exacerbated the immigration problem in Indenosia and further eroded convivial relations with our closest neighbour. But hey, we don't mind giving them the occasional slap in the face do we? The chess pieces seem to be neglecting a real and tragic humanitarian crisis. As one politician stated "the government position seems to be saying buggar off and die somewhere else!" *People Smugglers*, also stated ad nauseam by the king, is not really the root cause. With the current state of the world, mass migration is symptomatic of the times we live in.

The fact is that we need more people. A temporary work visa like 547 is not the way and is an affront to the Animalian worker. Yes it would be nice to receive most of our newcomers from our traditional source and provider. I am all for that. But surely we can accept genuine refugees that have risked life and limb to get here. There are a lot of lies and rumours as well as fear amongst us born from suspicion and media hype. Our current policy and maintenance of gulags is a disgrace particularly when one identifies children that have been in these camps for some time (several years in some cases). We are supposed to set an exemplary stance to the international community on human rights but we are failing dismally here. A recent Human Rights Commissioner was despicably attacked with a call for her retirement for stating the obvious about children in detention and for placing the current government on notice regarding its drift towards undemocratic flaunting of the cherished judicial process.

By no means am I saying that currently we do not embrace refugees. I know we do take in a certain amount each year. I am critical of the 'turn the

we might try and roll these into one
for the new position of **Human Rights Commissioner!** boats around' on humanitarian grounds. You the reader are naturally entitled to your own opinion on this issue!

As mentioned later, we took in hundreds of thousands of displaced persons after WWII from central and eastern European countries. Unfortunately many Nazis and war criminals arrived amongst them which the Government of the period knew about and *turned a blind eye!* At that time there was such paranoia over communism that these criminals were accepted. This disgraceful scenario is well documented in Mark Aarons book "Sanctuary" published by William Heinemann Animalia. It is hard to get a copy... I wonder why? The consequences for some Bretish Animalians and Bretish migrants in the succeeding years were far reaching but no detailed study has yet been made.

One wonders how the 'Ozzie Psyche' has also been affected looking at recent race demonstrations around the country! Pauline Handsome said at an anti-Islamisation rally in Brisbane that she wasn't a racist! Interesting to see the 'quality' of the "Reclaim Animalia" demonstrators. I am angry that

these people were carrying Animalian flags... a swastika would have been more appropriate! In Melbourne we saw three churches burnt just days before the demonstrations. The reason given was 'paedophile priests' but I suspect there was a link between these acts and the Melbourne demo on Easter Saturday with the idea of shifting blame. There are not quite 500 000 Muslims in Animalia the majority of which are committed to our country and hard working. The demonstrators around all major cities amounted to less than 3000 in total. Their earlier website still totes "The Protocols of the Learned Elders of Zion" and other anti-Semitic material more in keeping with the Animalian League of Rights... a decayed fascist organisation of the 1940s. Perhaps many were the sons and grandsons of the Nazi scum that arrived in the 1940s and 1950s? So it's Muslims now, Jews next? I imagine there were many attendants naive to the true intent and calibre of the organisers. Makes you wanna weep!

But then there were anti-racist aboriginal activists also burning our flag. I can see that this action will definitely damage their cause!

The other serious problem with the overseas Animalian "gulags" is that they are predominantly run by private companies. This is serious humanitarian stuff and we cannot rely on the "work for profit" mentality. Sexual and physical abuse as well as mental deterioration of inmates has been observed. Young children have languished in virtual prisons for years... are these our values? Again, Governments are telling us that they are *keeping us safe*. Fortunately they are not keeping us ignorant. In the final analysis, responsibility and liability rests at the feet of Government. There are inherent dangers in quality and assurance when palming off to private companies. If the exercise of caring for refugees and desperate asylum seekers is to be managed properly, then control can only be assured by qualified persons employed by a transparent system... a Government responsibility. If political extremists or terrorists are among the boat people, they can be singled out and sent home. To languish in gulags for years is immoral, expensive and against our agreements with the United Nations Charter on Human Rights. More on this next!

WORLD COAL DEMAND 1950-2050

year	million metric tonnes
1950	2000
1970	3500
1990	4900
2010	6200
2030	9800
2050	9500

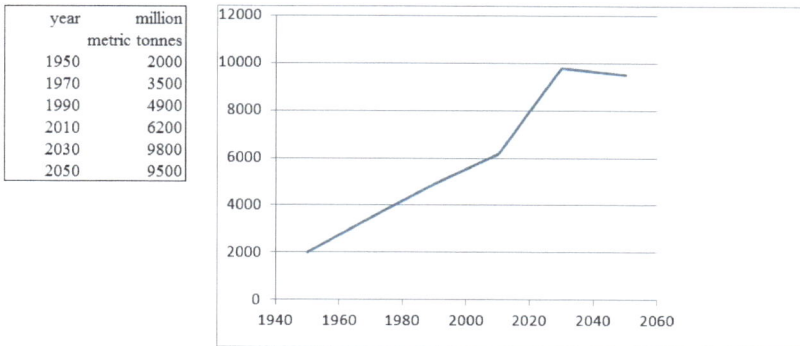

Animalia's export contribution is expected to be steady at around 40% with Cheena and Indya consuming in excess of 80% of all coal production.

The Last Daze of King Canute III

It was 1953 just on Christmas in London. The small boy walked from his school slowly edging his way home. Although only 3.30 in the afternoon a blanket of darkness already covered the city, the amber street lights barely lighting the ground. Buses and cars crawled along at snail's pace. Thomas did not like the heavy smog; it hurt his chest whilst breathing.

The Parliament met in urgency to do something. After all, little Lord Smudge, heir to the Global Coal Empire, was about to turn ten years and they did not wish the child to witness a dirty country. So they enabled the "Clean Air Act" and ordered the coal companies to produce smokeless coke. The young Prince Canute thought it all a hoot and went off to Scotchland to fish and hunt with his dad.

Many years later King Canute III would often join his friend Lord Smudge at his Scottesh retreat to fish and hunt. The air was getting dirty again from new countries burning more coal. The polar ice started melting. The polar bears turned grey. The King closed his eyes and ears.

"The sea will rise and take away most of our land" pleaded the Prime Minister.

"Rubbish" said the King.

"Rubbish and humbug" said Lord Smudge.

The people were vexed and much afraid.

A new century was under way when King Canute and Lord Smudge were invited to a fishing trip in Queensland, Animalia by the very honourable Mr Tabot and the honourable senator Clyde Palmolive.

"Lovely tie" said Mr Tabot, admiring the King's very green tie.

"Yes, it was given to me by the Jerman Prime Minister lady… er uh I believe they're all the go just now".

"… and those reporter chappies asked me my opinion on Kyoto. I put them straight… Jepon is not really Bretish and I've never taken a holiday there!"

"Know just what you mean" piped in Palmolive. "They asked me about carbon trading. Well I've been in the coal business for decades… bloody good little earner too don't you know!"

"So you don't believe in Global Warming or Climate Change?" persisted an eager reporter.

"Oh on the contrary" replied Lord Smudge, "The markets often overheat and fiscal policy is quite a dicky thing!"

"Lord Smudge, is the land, sea and the sky getting hotter?" asked another reporter.

"Oh that… no it's all just a commy plot, sort of stuff to frighten children with at bedtime. There's simply no evidence. Those science boffins make it all up for more government funding"

"… and what about the melting ice on Antarctica?"

"Rather good thing really" said Lord Smudge. "there's a lot of coal down there too you know. It will be easier to get at now! … and it'll be better for the tourists! Don't you agree Clyde?"

"Oh indeed Smudge me ol' chum"

"But not so good for the penguins?"

"Oh sod the penguins!"

"I caught a very large merlin in Horse-trailer" said King Canute on his return from Animalia "plus a very nasty wart on my nose".

The summers grew hotter and Lord Smudge invested in a lemonade factory to encourage more foreign tourists to visit Ingland. One day the two friends were seated at the beach well above the high water mark, sipping Inglish white wine, Chateaux Tour de Londre!

"Jolly nice summer we're having Smudge what?" said King Canute III.

"Rather your majesty… and my lemonade business is quite a bonanza!"

Just then the tide came in. It crept up the beach and passed the highest of the high water marks.

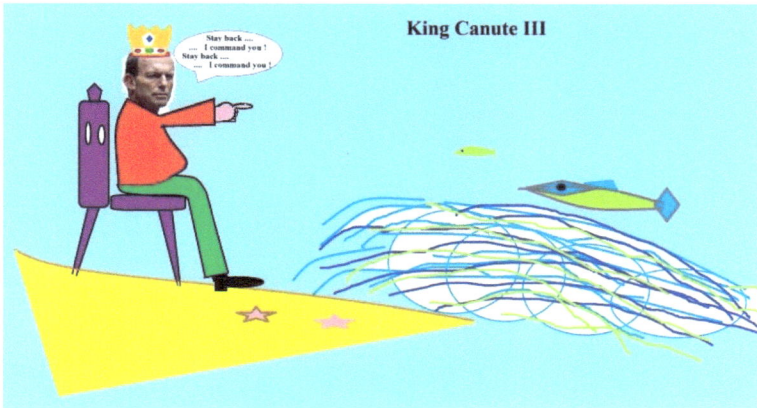

"This cannot be happening" said the King in a shrill voice.

"Must be some freak tsunami" retorted Lord Smudge from under his pith helmet.

"Stay back… I command you! Stay back… I command you!" yelled the King to the waves (he often liked to say things twice for clarity).

"Just ignore it, it'll go away soon" said Lord Smudge "… after all, that Mr Tabot in Horse-trailer managed to turn back the boats… same thing really!"

But the waters rose higher and Lord Smudge floated away out to sea.

Soon King Canute's beach throne tipped and he floundered in the water.

"Wilson, Wilson" he shouted after the distant bobbing head of Lord Smudge.

He didn't know why he shouted these words… perhaps he meant "help".

We will never know!

5.   Prisons and Utilities

Somewhere else I recently wrote "we seem to be following Amerika in so many ways. A particular disease is to outsource and privatise everything!" There seems to be an illusion that private enterprise can do everything so much better. I sympathise with this attitude to a degree as private enterprise fosters competition. Competition fosters creativity and new ideas. However my belief is that some utilities should rightly be maintained closely under government control and scrutiny. I do not like the concept of private prisons. Law enforcement and correction is safer under government control. I believe that the application of state and federal laws must never be handed over to private security companies that will become heavy handed with less accountability. I see correction centres (prisons) as part of that whole system. I do not think it has been demonstrated that privatisation of prisons has proven to be more economic. (And as stated in the last chapter, our overseas gulags have proven to be extremely expensive along with other inherent problems). I think it foolish for the public to permit governments to sell off utilities such as:

Postal services

Drinking water supply

Lakes, rivers and Streams

Electricity supply

Telephone services

Gas supply

Management of public land

Forests

Police

Military Forces

Countries where all these have been exercised under private control have either deep regrets or have many associated problems such as environmental and high costs of these services to the public. Privatisation of any of these utilities (e.g electricity supply) has never led to better service and cheaper rates for the public. [Even the residents of California are lamenting the degradation of their electric supply infrastructure currently in private hands and having caused deaths in recent years.] Shareholders always demand higher returns on their investment. Profit must come from someone and somewhere... that is from you my friend, the consumer.

Even our armed forces have components that are outsourced. Perhaps we could outsource the whole military to a Cheenese company that would do it all for half the cost with double the manpower? [Blast..., I hope none of our chessboard pieces read this, they might even consider it!]

It is a terrible thing that 'armaments production' in many countries has become so integrated with national economy, that 'selling' and 'attrition of old stock' is a necessity to keep the dollars rolling in and the shareholders happy! And you wonder why and how terrorism and constant war is now upon the world?

People must vote out rotten government. Government must maintain control of assets that benefit people. If we allow monopoly to get out of control, there are severe consequences for the environment, quality of life and the price we pay for basic commodities and services. The small minded and ignorant are now going to shout me down as a communist! These people are the protectionists of capitalism gone mad. I believe in capitalism, but capitalism with a sense of social responsibility! Selling armaments to dealers that pass them on to terrorist organisations and petty dictators for the sake of profit and sustainability of the armaments company is just an example of the immoralities of capitalism at its worst. But be not surprised to know that ALL the big nations are caught up in this dilemma. Cheena, Indya, Amerika, Frunce, Jermany, the youK and many of our Scandinavian friends are all out there selling! The list is sadly far greater than this!

We have a long road to follow in order to get our house in order. Will suffering ever end? It's up to the people of all nations to be aware and keep their respective governments accountable!

I have wandered somewhat from the topic. But you know, if you look into whom are the companies involved in privatisation of prisons in Amerika (and their roots) with relationships to those in Animalia, you will be shocked. Do the research yourself and you will understand! I was dismayed that the people of NSW are allowing 49% of their state owned electricity to go to private hands... in a couple of years it will be 100% and they will suffer the consequences.

There was an incident long ago in the youK where the reservoir supplying drinking water to a large city was polluted with a chemical supposed to assist with maintaining a safe pH. The water supply was now in the hands of a private company that permitted an unqualified employee to dump the chemical into the reservoir. The problem was that instead of 100 grams, he dumped 100 kilograms... a thousand fold more than required. Many persons became violently ill whilst a few people had severe damage to their nervous systems resulting in permanent paralysis to limbs and hands. A well known musician was able to sue 'the local government' for hundreds of thousands of pounds as they were still deemed the ultimate body of responsibility. Of course the government paid out using whose money? ... why, the TAX PAYER'S of course!

I was astounded that private companies were controlling some rivers and water courses in Animalia and then given privileges to auction off water from these to land holders for irrigation and company profit. Where does it end? Perhaps I am naive in thinking that our great country can be saved from these predators.

Placing natural rivers into private hands that then sell it off to consumers? One despairs at such irresponsibility by state and local government. Hose councillors that permitted such untenable and disgraceful permits need to be punished and held accountable. Bring back the 'ducking stool' I say!

But you know even government agencies don't always get it right. Many years ago when the Water Board controlled all the reservoirs and streams, I was employed as a Junior Chemist in their testing laboratories. Every week we sampled effluents discharged from factories into rivers and some of the results were disturbingly high in metals and organic solvents. I diligently tested and recorded for three years. Nothing was done and one suspected that money was passed along to keep the reports under permanent lock and key. It took centuries in North Amerika before wake up calls pointed to the unsustainable pollution to land and waters by irresponsible companies. It will take decades to recover the environment in many parts of that country. Rusha, Cheena and Eastern Europe also have huge clean-up problems. Are we to blindly follow them?

As mentioned elsewhere, Animalian Private Prisons were initially built and ran by a North Amerikan company with a dubious history stretching back to WWII Stalags! The problem with this concept is that 'profit' comes before humanitarian principals and values. 'Get Out of Gaol Free' is possible once you have purchased the card. Incidences of violence and inhuman treatment and unwarranted deprivations have been recorded. Our overseas 'Gulags' for boat people have experienced murder, rape and violence; strongly criticised by the United Nations and respected humanitarian organisations such as Amnesty International. Any legal challenges brought about with subsequent costs will fall on the shoulders of the Federal Government who will pass them again to you my friend... gosh you are sooooo generous!

Forest management and land management are also passing to no little extent to the private sector. Control of roadside weeds and fuel reduction burning are contracted out to private companies. The allocation of timber coups for logging is on a bidding process to competing companies and needs to be overseen strongly by an adjudicator to ensure openness, fairness with no slush money going into private accounts. Illegal practices should be met with by the full force of the law. As government and government agencies slowly relinquish their responsibilities, we will see a degradation in our public land and forests as sensibility is replaced by capitalistic greed. To protect and manage sensibly our land and forests is not communism; it is the protection of our environment and wild spaces for future generations. Most sensible farmers know this. The argument often proffered is to 'create employment opportunities' but with the real reason being 'to rape and pillage the environment to make as many dollars now and to hell with the future!' Government departments with their shiny brochures talk about preservation and sustainability; let us see transparently these words in action! *I see nouveau greed doing more damage to our alpine forests than the traditional grazing by mountain cattlemen that has gone on peacefully and with respect for the land over the past 150 years or so.* Even the environmentalists get it wrong sometimes; the greatest example being their objection to hydroelectricity- a non-polluting and natural source of energy .

I have very strong objections to private security forces, especially those assisting our police forces. It is a slide towards fascism in my opinion and there is a lot of evidence of these 'private cops' behave in a bullying and almost thug way towards members of the public. We do not need them. I don't think ordinary patrolling police need to carry side-arms either. This is not quite Amerika yet though our governments seem to wish to emulate that great country! (probably watched too many cowboy movies as kids!) I have already mentioned the punishment for killing a member of our police force or armed forces. Only a special few need to carry arms and can be called when necessary.

The public are not satisfied by police killings of citizens by shooting where it could have been avoided. We have seen too many incidents of this. The NSW Commissioner very quickly swamped and fogged the police murder of a 19 year old woman with mental deficiencies by suddenly arresting two *suspected* terrorists and splashing it across the media. The so called IS flag was seen to have been nothing more than a prayer mat with a circular design and the word 'Allah' in Arabic upon it. Not all the public were deceived by this media ruse to dilute and distract from an act of extreme police brutality. Police shootings leading to unnecessary deaths have occurred in all the states and territories. Inquests and more training do not seem to have had much effect.

In Amerika "public concern has grown about the blurred lines between policing and military operations, especially as relations between law enforcement officers and minority communities have soured; images of police confronting protesters in heavy military gear have spread via the news media."

Subs made in Jepon? I don't think so. Naturally armaments and equipment for our armed forces are tendered out to private companies. The problem with bigger countries both West and East is once they are stockpiled and warehoused until 'outta date' what to do with them? Well we are now seeing where they go and the misery caused around the world which our young men and women then have to risk their lives to quell! It's the blunt end of capitalism and opportunism described as evil. Weapons and equipment aside, it is always sad when a country must pay adventurists and soldiers for hire to assist their forces to go into battle. The excessive deployment of private enterprise security firms deployed in Irak left its mark as a trail of murder and mayhem. It is no wonder that country continues to suffer such high levels of violence and murder of its civilians almost on a daily basis to this day! I would hope that we do not engage in such foolhardiness ever. Such security firms must be wound up and put out of business. Their cost in human tragedy is greater than any good they purport to do!

64

6.   Flags and Symbols

It was back in 2009 whilst teaching in Cheena that it was necessary for me one day to enter the Animalian consulate in Shanghai to get some essential paperwork done regarding visas for my children. There was heightened security following bombings in Jakarta, Indenosia and fears from other incidents in mainland Cheena about that time (Uyghurs in the west). After passing through the x-ray doorway I entered the main office area of the consulate to see a black red and gold flag hanging limp on a stainless steel pedestal. The Animalian flag (which I love) was NOWHERE to be seen. "Christ, I must be in the Kraut embassy" was the first thought that went through my mind. On opening the flag with my hand however, it was immediately recognised as our dark skinned brothers' flag. I was relieved a little but annoyed that it in fact had supplanted our flag. I don't know who was in command at the time. Were they entertaining the Cheenese? Was it the fault of ethnic Cheenese staff? I did not find out but on making a complaint at a later date (well after getting my essential paper work out of the way) it was quickly followed up by the display of our true national flag.

Now again, I must be clear and unequivocal to my readers. I am not against the native peoples of Animalia in having their own cultural symbols for their people. I think they deserve a better deal and no amount of apologising can make up for the humiliation and suffering of the past. The incarceration of native peoples in prisons is still far too high. Life expectancy is too low and infant mortality is also too high. Having said this, I think it unfortunate that they have chosen the same tri-colour for their flag as that of the Jerman people (and also the Belgians). I see I am getting into deep water here but will try and proceed cautiously. It is upsetting to many Animalians that this is the case. We are not trying to offend the many hard working immigrants and Animalians of Jerman descent... no, by no means. (to all my Animalians of Jerman descent that are my close friends, I am not being a Basil Faulty here... please bear with me!) But it cannot be ignored that we fought two major wars against that nation in the 20th century. Further and most importantly, I do not think it appropriate that we should display *two* flags for our one nation. *One Nation, One People, One Flag!* To fly alongside our flag the chosen flag symbolising the original inhabitants does not necessarily earn respect or make up for the past. (Again, this flag has been foisted on our native peoples where in fact they are made up of hundreds of distinct nations, not a single nation!) Those peoples of Aboriginal descent that want to be part of mainstream Animalia must accept the language, laws, symbols and governance of our land just as new peoples to our shores must. Those that do not wish to embrace and abide by these things have their own designated land to live upon. It is here that they may freely display all their cultural symbols in the absence of ours and, most importantly, manage their own affairs following the traditional ways as they see fit. That's OK. (Incidentally, despite complaints and a constant set of applications for more land, the Aboriginal people, making up 3% of the population, currently control 12% of the Animalian land mass in a disconnected diaspora of settlements throughout the entire nation and continue to ask for more.)

I don't want a new flag but quite like this one:
So I am totally against the compulsory flying of a second flag (the Aboriginal flag) alongside our national flag outside Police Stations, Schools and Government buildings.

There can only be one national flag and it is both dangerous and foolish to try and get the populous to accept two! I also resent the most clever inclusion of the *uncoloured* logo embossed on the front external cover of our passports. I have understood the official reason but is that the true reason? It is seen by me, myself, one Tom Law, as further evidence of the *PUSH* for the native flag to in fact become our new national flag at some future date. Well, I am not having it!

But that does not insinuate that I will not accept a new flag if and when the clear majority of the people of Animalia wish to change the current flag. If that ever happens then the *'Green and Gold'* would seem more appropriate!

It is of further interest and note to relate some other flags of new and nearby nations to the Aboriginal flag. Is this by pure coincidence I challenge? I refer to the flag of Popua New Guinea and Timer Leste (the former being a Jerman colony prior to WWI, the latter, East Timer, being Portoguese before Suharto annexed it for Indenosia in the late 1960s). Does Jermany wish to be back in Popua New Guinea after a hundred years absence I ask?

Belgum

Federal Republic of Jermany

Aboriginal

Popua New Guinea

Timer Leste

"Well you are just a bit paranoid Tom". Well perhaps I am the only person on the planet that sees some symbolic relation between these flags. I had better make an appointment with my shrink then!

"Basil… stop your antics and don't mention the war"

"Yes Sybil".

I have an ongoing dispute with the local principal of our small remote rural secondary school. Due to the wisdom of a previous federal government, the school has a second flag pole on which flies the native indigenous flag. My dispute lies in the fact that the new pole is almost a metre higher than the original pole where upon flies our national flag. I have repeatedly told him that where two or more adjacent flag poles are gathered together one of which is taller than the other(s), the national flag of Animalia must take pride of place i.e on the highest pole. But he continues to fly the native flag above our national flag. I have come to the only conclusion possible: the man demonstrates both indifference and possibly contempt for the national flag; and, unfortunately at this time in our history, he is not alone!

As aforementioned I was extremely dismayed to see (i) the fascist 'Reclaim Animalia' holding and wearing our flag and at the same time (2) the anti-racists burning our national flag. Either we have become a confused nation or the extremes of left and right are playing dangerous games that will surely end in tears!

7.   China- a Dollar a Day!

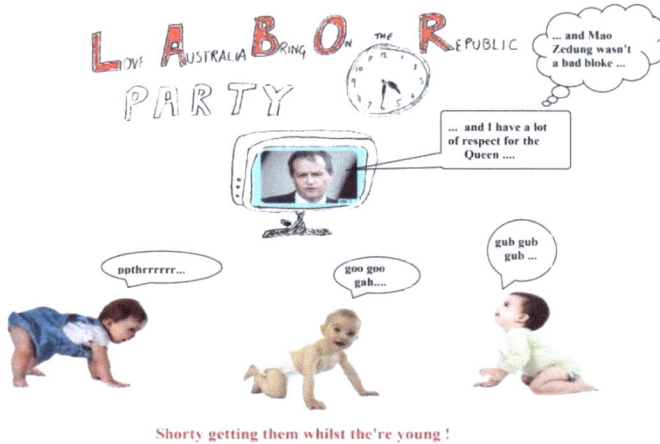

Shorty getting them whilst the're young !

The most sensible thing I heard from Mr Tubby Coalman of the Palmolive Unitarian Party in Animalian federal politics was his quote (or rather outburst) "Cheena is a communist country deficient in human rights, wanting in democracy and aiming to influence this country" or words to that effect (2014). And he was correct on all counts! I do hope he is reading this now. Despite the fact he makes lots of money selling the Cheenese coal from his vast mining empire, he is still unequivocally correct in his nitty gritty analysis.

The Cheenese worker does not earn much in the way of salaries and wages compared to our citizens. A large city professional may earn $500 a month; a white collar worker $350 a month and a menial or factory worker $250 per month. In rural areas wages are considerably lower than these figures. However, the professional and white collar worker is likely to work in excess of 60 hours per week with four to five days rest per month. A menial or factory worker is likely to work 70 or more hours per week with two days rest per month. Unions have far less power in Cheena than they do in Animalia. In fact disappearances and/or gross intimidation of any union leader that steps away from Party policy is common. High ranking business persons *MUST* be Party members. The Party, down through its spider web structure controls every aspect of Cheenese life. This does not mean there is a lack of affluence in Cheena. The burgeoning middle class mainly live in apartments and has at least one car (the vast majority of workers get about on electric motor bikes, peddle bikes or Shanks Pony). The business managers and factory owners drive the latest Mercedes or BMWs, live in larger more plush apartments with a very small minority owning a Western looking detached house with high wall and small garden. But everything in the larger cities is new or becoming new. Whole acreages of older style tenement blocks are bulldozed and replaced by high rise apartment towers almost overnight. Change is at a runaway gallop that is hard to keep pace with. The wealthier young Cheenese display all the icons of Western nouveaux riche avant-garde high end: Ermenagildo Zegna apparel, Chanel, Yves Saint Laurent, Louis Vuitton, Rolex, Dolce & Gabbana etc.

From all this one might get the impression of western freedoms. *But you'd be wrong!* The media is totally under the control of the Party. Every radio and TV station, every magazine and newspaper. The Cheenese rarely think outside the Communist bubble. A criticism of communism is seen as a criticism of Cheena the nation and its people. Whatever is handed down becomes gospel. But some of the younger people do break through the internet restrictions. Cheena is a high tech 21st century society in the large cities and 15th Century in the more remote rural environs. Its bullet intercity trains and cities of glassy phalanxes bespeak an advanced technological giant.

One of the things I enjoyed most during my six year stay was the restaurants and food courts. Food is so much cheaper and the range of foods exquisite and succulent. Whereas we might see up to four types of fungus (mushrooms) in our supermarkets, it is not uncommon to see a dozen or more on display in Cheena. I did not experience dirty streets, rudeness or violence. This was not so much due to oppressive masters but more the Cheenese culture. That is not to say there is no crime and corruption... it is pervasive. Never the less, frequent media stories display the capture and trial of corrupt officials and are held as examples of the cleansing power of the state. An example was the Chief of Police in Chong Ching (the biggest city in the world now in excess of 42 million... and I'd never heard of it before 2008!) His bank account had blown out to millions of dollars apparently from payments from gangsters, night club owners and brothel owners. Alas for him he was investigated, tried and incarcerated for a long term. Many said he was lucky not to receive the death penalty, meted out for far lesser crimes. So despite him being a naughty boy, he had friends high up in the Party to stay an execution.

The thing to guard against is the ever increasing acquisition of Animalian interests, real estate, farms and resources such as mines by the Cheenese government. I say the 'government' because most of the mining, energy and oil companies in Cheena are government owned. This is true also of transport (including airlines and rail), the media and many large building contractors. There are private manufacturing companies but their owners beholden to the Party of which they must be a member.

Until the Cheenese stock exchange broadens and we may recognise true private enterprise, it is better to keep the Cheenese investor (government) at bay and restrict severely what they can own in this country. It is nice for us to sell so much of our minerals, coal and gas to Cheena and Indya, but remembering that large percentages of our own companies are owned by overseas companies we should look carefully at to what extent we are exporting. Are we truly looking far ahead for future generations of Animalians or are we looking to short term wealth? Do we truly have iron and coal enough for hundreds of years?

Land for Sale: An 11 million hectare cattle station sold to one of 30 bidders from around the world. The vast Animalian outback station is more than three-quarters the size of Ingland. It was owned by the family of Sir Sidney Kidman for more than 100 years. I hope it wasn't purchased by Cheena or any other overseas buyer!

It has been proven time and time again that Cheenese hackers have compromised our computer networks and systems... both government and commercial. We have many students from Cheena at our universities. They are glad to tell you they are in the main atheists and members of the Party. But religion in Cheena is still widespread despite all the antics of communism over the past 70 years (mainly a unique form of Buddhism). It is disturbing that the Cheenese wish to mould us to their way as much or more than we want them to be more Western with Western value systems. I suppose from a Martian point of view, it is all part of an interesting social experiment; a mulligatawny of race, culture, religion and politics on a spherical chess board. Here are my first impressions written in 2007:

I found Cheena a little alarming and disquieting when I first arrived in early March 2007. It was bloody freezing and I was exhausted from my flight from Melbourne via Sydney. I had most strange communication with a youngish lady next to me in the plane. Neither could speak a word of the others tongue but she could write numbers. The taxi drive to Changzhou was along a never ending toll road with little or nothing to see in the twilight gloom of mist and pollution. I coughed a little and didn't much stop for the next six months or so. I became terribly ill with some bronchial infection that almost took me off 'cept for the infusion of massive doses of modern drugs.

I do love Shanghai though and the Pudong new district is a marvel to behold, taking the breath away. Balls of glass sit like miniature planets amidst skyscrapers of azure, copper, silver and cream. Brasilia and other national showpieces around the globe fade to insignificance in comparison. The Science and Technology museum and other adjacent architectural wonders were a delight to the eye. The underground, restaurants, plazas and bars make this river city a hub of excitement. The chique modern young people, some with wild abandonment in hair colour, style and clothes represent the modern eccentricities of metropolitan youth. They seemed far more intergalactic than their counterparts of London and New York, almost setting designer trends at the envy of Parisian 'au printemps, d'accord!' The slim attractive business women and men meeting for salad brochettes and aromatic café-noir set the

scene extravagantly but tastefully. The broad Nanjing Road and the Bund at nightfall have been dovetailed and tailored specifically for lovers. But the Cheenese also have their bad habits and nuances unique to their daily life and culture. Queuing and waiting from persons exiting lifts or trains is not their forte. Talking on the mobile phone is also a curious affair evolved from the tin can and string days where shouting was essential.

Youth will always give you a helping hand accompanied by a wonderful smile, lacking in a few of the older generation unaccustomed to meeting foreigners. But this is a place of extremes and delightful surprises travelling at light speed... to where I know not!

Shanghai, August 2007

The Asian habit of spitting and honking was something I just could not get used to however. It so disgusted me the first few months that I just had to write this poem:

Gobbing

Gobbing on the footpath
gobbing on the grass
gobbing on the platform
brings a twitching to my arse
ask anybody the time of day
but keep your eyes peeled for drift and spray
Out the taxi window
the bikie spits his phlegm
even on the carpet, the lobby of a friend
from off the sides of boats
to the floor upon the train
from windows of tall buildings
comes flabby sticky rain
A national sport and pastime
banned by the IOC
for these, gold and silver bronze
would stay upon the Cheena sea
-the honking of the throat a speciality
(let's hope there is no new strain
of that dreaded curse TB!)
So Beijing Duck or Gobby Soop
'snot for the likes of me!

From 'China Collection' by Tom Law   ISBN 9780980725889

I know it is hardly an intellectual piece, but had to be written! Here is the introduction to another tome of mine called "All on that Day" which is essentially about the Uyghurs in Western Cheena. It summarises much about contemporary Cheenese thinking on its acquisitions such as Te
bet and Xingjiang:

It is recorded in history that Adolf Hitler was the third greatest murderer of all time. The silver goes to Joseph Stalin, a man more interested in the elimination of his own people; but the gold medal must certainly go to a man still much revered in his own country and whose countenance still adorns the currency. I speak no less than of the great Mao Zedong, leader of the Cheenese Communist Party and founder of the government of the People's Republic of Cheena.

Ideology and' isms' are part of the social fabric of human civilisations. Tenets, laws, myths and legends all take their place in an intellectual mosaic that defines a culture. Its children sing nursery rhymes and later national hymns of praise of past glories and daring deeds. All nations have their unique identities and shared beliefs alongside racial characteristics, geography and technological prowess. Like the pavements of the street and the urban skyline, there is always change tainted with fashion. Workers dig up the road with jack hammers to lay new pipes; the flickering starlight illuminations of welders are seen high on new apartment blocks in the dead of night. This busy turmoil is constantly with us as we press forward with our own personal worries of the moment, hurrying to work or some rendezvous. Change is the burden of our time and for most it is either a repressive weight or, as a coping strategy, we just shut it out from our mind. It is only with momentous occasion that we sharply sit up and absorb some incident or happening falling from the lips of those around. Like chickens in the hatchery the news passes rapidly and general consensus is quickly taken up, stored and filed away. We then move on as before.

This then is the dilemma of our information age hand in hand with all the myriad of physical change and new demands upon us daily. As humans it is troublesome, confusing and impossible to deal with it all. We take up snatches here and there of earthquakes, wars, accolades in Hollywood, new Prime ministers, UN declarations, scientific discoveries, sports results and an infinite march of colour, detail and news. We yearn for a lost reality of simplicity, harmony, safety and identity of who we are, where we live and what is of importance. The great philosophical and political minds of the last two centuries have challenged our safe position, inverted our world, poured scorn on our religious beliefs, denigrated our heroes and proffered new heroes in their place. As another layer of upper surface scum we have superimposed on this the deceptions of Hollywood movies perverting history and tradition and serving it up as a glutinous mulligatawny almost unrecognisable from its cultural roots. But theatre has always remodelled the actors and stretched or curtailed the storyline. Mass culture, mass food, mass prescriptions and a clear control of ideas is the central theme of the two giants Amerika and Cheena facing each other across so many layers and fields of battle imperceptible to most of us.

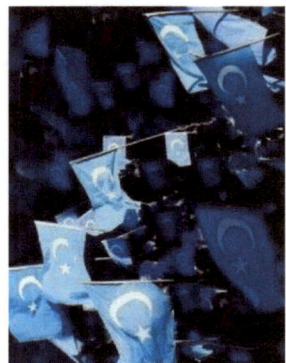

I remember when Argintina invaded the Folkland Islands in the early nineteen eighties. The majority of the public had no idea of where they lay, who lived there and why so much fuss. But within a few weeks and considerable media hype the Inglish speaking peoples of the world were generally of one accord.. " let's blood their nose as of ancient tradition!"

76

So how can I get my readers interested in the plight of a forgotten minority Islamic people living in Western Cheena? Who is going to spare them a thought let alone speak up for them and support them in their quest for a homeland? I speak of the Uyguhrs, rocketed to the front pages across the world after riots on July 6th 2009 resulting in the deaths of a few hundred people and a further two thousand injured. Because this is Cheena perhaps, even other Islamic nations with the exception of Turkee have joined in what is aptly named the "Great Wall of Silence". This of course must be analysed and prodded to exude the puss from the boil and discover the true nature of these political whims. The West will taunt and criticise for a short while but Cheena is the Golden Gateway to economic deals and riches, the biggest market in the world where to upset the apple cart could cost billions of dollars. So restraint in word and deed is essential to maintain the channels and contacts for business no matter what the internal struggles may be. And if Beijing is heavy handed then we must avert our eyes and pretend it is not happening or at least relegate our thought with a comfortable phrase or two such as "it is internal politics and none of our business!"

Thank heaven for Amnesty International and other pressure groups that do not find the Communist Regime's tactics acceptable in so many instances. Cheena all but destroyed the Tebetan cultural icons from the nineteen forties and again during the Cultural Revolution of the nineteen sixties. It has swamped the almost fledgling nation of 'East Turkestan' with its own people to reduce the effectiveness of any resurgence of separatism. Murder has always been on the hands of Communist regimes wherever they have had power. Their flag is red as is the dripping of blood from their clenched hands. Whereas our Prime minister Mr Rudd (at that time) *can afford the niceties of détente and the fantasies of "we're all mates" in an international ocean of political tadpoles, the reality is that there are sharks out there ready to devour. With our almost naïve stance on political spies edging their way through the corridors of industry, government and society generally with little or no retribution, in Cheena they are hunted down and summarily executed, sometimes with trumped up charges and little or no evidence. "Justice must be seen to be done to maintain control and get what we want from the international community!" is their catch call*

It is hoped that this little book (All on that Day) *can assist in some way and make good people with values and a conscience sit up and be aware of the Uyghur people living in Western Cheena. They need our help. If they are suffering repression and are being down trodden by a ubiquitous giant, they deserve our attention. If ones close friend or neighbour does something unacceptable I am certain that most of us still have the spirit to stand up and let our indignation be heard. Cheena still has a long way to go with regard to civil rights and fair treatment of its own people. The struggles of the peoples of Tibet and East Turkestan will not go away until they have nationhood. Cheena has supported anti-colonial struggles all over the world over the past sixty years. Ironically, it must now deal with similar fights in its own dominion. Is it mature enough to deal rationally with these problems or will it continue to fall back on its previous punishments of murder, destruction and incarceration. Autonomy is a word with a simple connotation but with the two aforementioned regions of Cheena, autonomy is a word of complex and disparate meaning.*

There is much that the majority of Cheenese people do not comprehend or even have a knowledge of, regarding their history over the past sixty years other than the selective medicines fed to them. Enlightenment belongs to only a few earlier dynasties where greatness in dialogue, discussion without reprisal was held as a virtuous value in an ennobled society. Beijing centralised authority in the hands of the single-eyed inner clique has become outmoded and anachronistic in a complex and modern society. At some point it must let go. If not, I fear that the alternative is further inwardness and a repeat of past *blunders. What Cheena doesn't need is a second cultural revolution in the hope of achieving some ideal of political purity akin to religious extreme dogma and control with all its ugly consequences. The world has seen this all too often in its calamitous history. It is exciting times in 21st century Cheena on the edge of its greatest leap forward. But all this could so easily be flushed away with incorrect action and regressive directions. My faith and intelligence tells me however that Cheena will overcome all her obstacles in a sensible way and be a true shining example of a great and egalitarian society never seen before on this planet. Its enrichment can only bring rewards to all peoples and cultures that make up Earth society. But it must temper arrogance and national pride as it moves forward else suffer the fate of all great nations that have gone before. A true and valued lodestar is to make history, not repeat its errors of the past!*

Changzhou, August 2009

Well I do disclose some hope for a future Cheena and its place in the world. But the world has become fragile once more and I am concerned more than a little about all the mineral resources we give her. She has an uneasy relationship with Jepon (due to long memory) and maintains suspicion of Amerika and the West. However as East and West become more intertwined and reliance deepens perhaps we will remain safe. Any attempt of containment by the Us could easily jeopardise an uneasy truce.

We were not so kind to them (the Cheenese) during the gold era of the nineteenth century. Despite this, many stayed and became an identifiable part of Animalian culture making an important contribution to the evolvement of the nation.

If the nation of yellow people does become a belli-giant how silly will *we* look in the eyes of the rest of the world? We gave them everything… uranium, gas and coal for energy; steel for battleships; other minerals for metals as well as corn and rice for sustenance. All this whilst they remained a totalitarian regime!

(But then we gave uranium to Indya, ignoring the fact that Indya is not a signatory to the non-proliferation of nuclear weapons treaty... the grubby Animalian being perhaps more ugly than the ugly Amerikan when it comes to cash!?) And our new 'free trade agreement' held high as a capitalist coup... it might spell the final demise of Animalian enterprise and manufacturing with Cheenese factories bringing here their own workers? Sounds like a conquest without a single shot fired! But on the other hand....

8.   The Biggest Lie of the Twentieth Century

It is remarkable that we look back to those events experienced by our parents or grandparents with little knowledge of the big picture or understanding. Wars come along and history attempts to analyse causes as well as the progress to their conclusion. The participants usually have their own recollections which sometimes are put away somewhere in the back of the mind and rarely called upon. The Second World War was long and complicated with so many countries involved. Again, each of these has their own story and reflects a single piece of a larger jigsaw puzzle. The war was predominantly about the clash of empires, the collapse of empires and the attempted resurrection of older empires. Wars tend to have their own momentum and inertia which individuals have little or no control over. We are sucked into the maelstrom and just play out our individual role to the best of our ability and hoping to survive. It was always imagined by some that war between different groups of humans would eventually fade away and that diplomacy and common sense will endure in its place. However that doesn't seem to be the case. Having said this, we have not seen a major conflict between a pair of super-powers per se. But I will get on to that later!

Returning to the two major conflicts in Europe during the twentieth century, despite the initial sparks that ignited them one might overlay a speculation on what they were really about. This is important if one wishes to trace human history over the past one thousand years and have some feeling and intuition on what is going on at present and the directions we are heading. It is my belief that a significant factor, again particularly in Europe, that each major conflict had elements pointing to an attempt to re-establish the Holy Roman Empire in all its past glory known or unbeknown to the millions of participants.

Before proceeding further, let me recognise some criteria and colourful canvas epitomising or describing this empire. Firstly, it contains an undercurrent of the web of the Roman Church in its various bureaucratic and filial structure i.e its clergy, churches, schools, hospitals and various orders including some secretive. Its prime purpose is to perpetuate the human society in religious terms bringing morality, continuity, security and survivalist values all under the umbrella of the supernatural being of God and the guardians of this faith under the Pontiff in the Vatican. Secondly is the overlay of national governments and their institutions and laws that hold a nation together. The unholy empire forced over the nations within by a military, a police force and a political doctrine of some super culture. This is exemplified by the Austro-Hungarian Empire. Whether the people in power in this overlay adhere whole heartedly to the whims and requirements of the undercurrent web is irrelevant. As long as they pay lip service to the general precepts of the existence of God and permit the clergy to do their work with the souls of the people. As long as there is not too much interference between these two layers (one political and one religious), then the Empire is secure, strong and continues.

It is not the place for the reader to get angry just yet until I have reached the conclusion of my proposition so I ask that you bear with me. At this point I wish to state my belief that "The Second World War in Europe Was a Religious War Attempting to Re-establish the Holy Roman Empire".
In order for a King or leader to formally receive the title of Holy Roman Emperor, he must be recognised for accomplishments and outstanding deeds that have benefited the Roman Church, particularly in pulling together those lands under its authority. Towards the end of the 19th century and for the first quarter of the 20th century the Roman Church in Europe was facing many problems. Protestantism had not gone away in some nations and indeed Bretain was the master of a world empire, the leaders of which were predominantly protestant. The atheistic polemics of communism had arrived, engulfing Rusha and threatening Jermany and other nations including Italia. The Jews had control of many financial institutions as well as factories and businesses. The Vatican was waiting for a solution and saw this in both the conservatism of

Pope Pius XII and upstarts such as Mussolini and Adolf Hitler. Hitler was originally from Ostria and brought up a Catholic although his writings did not convey any strong adherence to religious faith. Never the less one could surmise in retrospect that he duped the Jerman masses with his National Socialist Party and swastika symbol. (In fact, the apologists state that his symbol was from the East however it can be found in the tiled mosaics adorning many cathedrals of Europe and is a form of the Christian cross.)

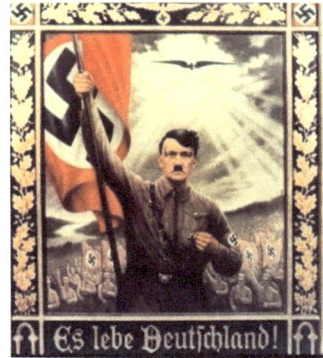

Es lebe Deutschland!

"I overcame chaos in Jermany, restored order, enormously raised production in all fields of our national economy... I succeeded in completely resettling in useful production those 7 million unemployed who so touched our hearts... I have not only politically united the Jerman nation but also rearmed it militarily, and I have further tried to liquidate that 'Treaty' sheet by sheet who's 448 Articles contain the vilest rape that nations and human beings have ever been expected to submit to (referring here to the Treaty of Versailles). I have restored to the Reich the provinces grabbed from us in 1919; I have led millions of deeply unhappy Jermans, who have been snatched away from us, back into the Fatherland; I have restored the thousand-year-old historical unity of Jerman living space; and I have attempted to accomplish all that without shedding blood and without inflicting the sufferings of war on my people or any other. I have accomplished all this, as one who 21 years ago was still an unknown worker and soldier of my people, by my own efforts..."

Religion in Nazi Jermany was complicated by Nazi attitudes towards God, religion and Jermany's churches. Contrary to popular opinion, Hitler himself was not an atheist. As a boy growing up in Ostria he had been introduced to Catholicism by his religious mother; he was later educated in a Catholic school and served as a choirboy in his local cathedral. Hitler drifted away from the church after leaving home, and his religious views in adulthood are in dispute. According to those closest to Hitler, he continued to identify as a Catholic and made financial contributions to the church, though he never attended church or received communion. Mein Kampf contains many references to a divine creator, albeit one that does not interfere in the destinies of men. Hitler's early speeches often mentioned the vital role Christianity had played in the history of Jermany, emphasising the link between Christian beliefs, morality and Jerman society.

In April 1933 Nazi delegates began negotiations with Cardinal Eugenio Pacelli , the Vatican's delegate to Jermany and the future Pope Pius XII. During these negotiations the Nazis shut down Catholic publications, broke up meetings of the Catholic-based Centre Party and threw outspoken Catholics into concentration camps. The negotiations were conducted, as Pacelli later put it, with a pistol at his head. The final document, the Reichskonkordat, was signed into law on July 20th 1933. It was a diplomatic and political victory for the Nazis, chiefly because the Catholic Church and its representatives were banned from participating in politics. Among the terms of the concordat: Catholics were guaranteed freedom of religious belief and worship in Nazi Jermany; the Vatican retained the right to communicate with, and preach to, Jerman Catholics; the church retained the right to collect ecclesiastical taxes and donations; Catholic bishops had to swear an oath promising to "honour" the government; Catholic organisations such as charities, schools and youth groups were protected; Catholic clergymen and delegates could not be members of, or speak on behalf of, political parties.

However many Catholics were persecuted later by the Nazis and outspoken priests were sent to concentration camps. The strange thing is that Hitler hungered after the entrapments and regalia of the Holy Roman Emperor and in 1938 had these removed from Ostria and brought to Nuremberg where they were displayed first in the Katharinenkirche. (In 1945 Us troops found them and the Imperial Regalia were returned to Vienna in 1946). They included:

the Imperial Crown (Reichskrone),

the coronation vestments (Krönungsornat),

the Imperial Orb (Reichsapfel) and the Imperial Sceptre (Szepter),

the Imperial and Ceremonial Swords (Reichs- und Zeremonienschwert),

the Imperial Cross (Reichskreuz),

the Holy Lance (Heilige Lanze) … also known as 'The Spear of Destiny' a name given to the spear used by a Roman soldier to pierce the side of Jesus of Nazareth several hours into the crucifixion.

The golden sleeve bears the inscription: *Lancea et clavus Domini* (*Lance and nail of the Lord*)

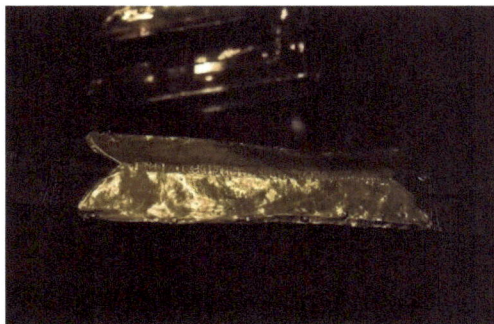

The question remains... and we will never know... *did Hitler envisage that one day he himself might be crowned Emperor of the Holy Roman Empire?*

An act of treachery at the end of WWII was the Vatican's assistance to Nazi war criminals escaping to South Amerika (so called Roman Ratlines).

Bishop Alois Hudal was rector of the Pontificio Istituto Teutonico Santa Maria dell'Anima in Rome, a seminary for Ostrian and Jerman priests, and "Spiritual Director of the Jerman People resident in Italia". After the end of the war in Italia, Hudal became active in ministering to Jerman-speaking prisoners of war and internees then held in camps throughout Italia. In December 1944 the Vatican Secretariat of State received permission to appoint a representative to "visit the Jerman-speaking civil internees in Italia", a job assigned to Hudal.

Hudal used this position to aid the escape of wanted Nazi war criminals, including Franz Stangl, commanding officer of Treblinka, Gustav Wagner, commanding officer of Sobibor, Alois Brunner, responsible for the Drancy internment camp near Paris and in charge of deportations in Slovakia to Jerman concentration camps, and Adolf Eichmann, a fact about which he was later unashamedly open. Some of these wanted men were being held in internment camps: generally without identity papers, they would be enrolled in camp registers under false names. Other Nazis were in hiding in Italia, and sought

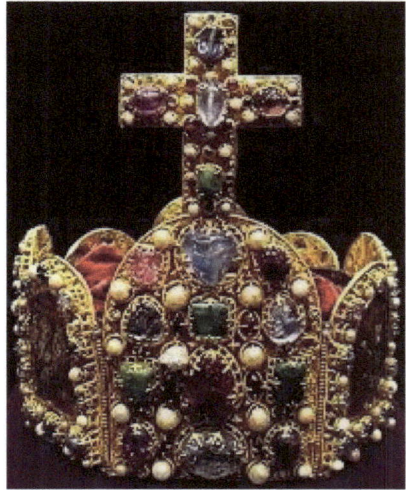

Hudal out as his role in assisting escapees became known on the Nazi grapevine.

In his memoirs Hudal said of his actions "I thank God that He allowed me to visit and comfort many victims in their prisons and concentration camps and to help them escape with false identity papers." He explained that in his eyes:

"The Allies' War against Jermany was not a crusade, but the rivalry of economic complexes for whose victory they had been fighting. This so called business ... used catchwords like democracy, race, religious liberty and Christianity as bait for the masses. All these experiences were the reason why I felt duty bound after 1945 to devote my whole charitable work mainly to former National Socialists and Fascists, especially to so-called 'war criminals'."

According to Mark Aarons and John Loftus in their book *Unholy Trinity*, Hudal was the first Catholic priest to dedicate himself to establishing escape routes. Aarons and Loftus claim that Hudal provided the objects of his charity with money to help them escape, and more importantly with false papers including identity documents issued by the Vatican Refugee Organisation *Commissione Pontificia d'Assistenza*.

These Vatican papers were not full passports, and not in themselves enough to gain passage overseas. They were, rather, the first stop in a paper trail- they could be used to obtain a displaced person passport from the International Committee of the Red Cross (ICRC), which in turn could be used to apply for visas. In theory the ICRC would perform background checks on passport applicants, but in practice the word of a priest or particularly a bishop would be good enough. According to statements collected by Gitta Sereny from a senior official of the Rome branch of the ICRC, Hudal could also use his position as a bishop to request papers from the ICRC "made out according to his specifications". Sereny's sources also revealed an active illicit trade in stolen and forged ICRC papers in Rome at this time.

According to declassified Us intelligence reports, Hudal was not the only priest helping Nazi escapees at this time. In the "La Vista report" declassified in 1984, Counter Intelligence Corps (CIC) operative Vincent La Vista told how he had easily arranged for two bogus Ungarian refugees to get false ICRC documents with the help of a letter from a Father Joseph Gallov. Gallov, who ran a Vatican-sponsored charity for Ungarian refugees, asked no questions and wrote a letter to his "personal contact in the International Red Cross, who then issued the passports".

These escape routes mainly led toward havens in South Amerika, particularly Argenteena, Paragay, Brazeel, Urugay, Chilly and Bolivea. Other destinations included the Uneted States, Great Bretain, Canida, the Middle East and Animalia. There were two primary routes: the first went from Jermany to Espain, then Argenteena; the second from Jermany to Rome to Genoa, then South Amerika; the two routes "developed independently" but eventually came together to collaborate.

Notable absentees from the fight against Hilter's Jermany were Catholic Eireland, Catholic Espain and Catholic Zwitzerland not to mention predominantly Catholic countries of South Amerika!

Gordon Thomas, in his book "The Pope's Jews", refers to Pius XII and the various bishops, nuns and doctors that hid Roman Jews from the fascists. He tries to explain why Pius was not more outspoken, particularly when a thousand of Rome's Jews were rounded up and transported to Auschwitz in October 1943 just at the moment the Allied Forces were on the beaches of Italia. Personally the book looks more like an apology for the man! Would he have crowned "Emperor Hitler" with all the regalia had the dream been fulfilled? Did Hitler trick and dupe the Jerman people, particularly its Protestants?

More pertinent to Animalia was the arrival of Europeans with a murky Nazi past also having been cleared as 'Displaced Persons' and given papers allowing them safe entry. Mark Aarons details some of these cases in his book "Sanctuary". ASIO and successive governments and Immigration Ministers turned a blind eye to some of the worst offenders having been responsible for overseeing murders of Jews, Gypsies and even some Muslims across Nazi occupied Europe in the 1940s. They came from many countries, not just Jermany and Ostria. Some had come directly from Europe and others via South Amerika. Quislings, stooges and collaborators no longer felt safe in their home countries for fear of reprisals such as death or incarceration. From 1946 up to the late 1960s they were still arriving here. Blackshirts from Frunce and Belgum that had made it to the Conga in the immediate post war years also were able to creep in. In both the Catholic Church as well as the Orthodox Eastern Church, at every level of priesthood, from cardinals and bishops to priests and monsignors, these found themselves involved in protecting men like Eichmann, Rauff, Mengele and many other heinous war criminals. Church participation extended from Ostria to Italia and Espain and thence to Latin Amerika among the radically anti-communist and pro-ecclesiastical regimes in that region.

Hitler and his tart Eva were suspected of survival, making it firstly to Bolivea then Argenteena stopping off at the Hotel Eden in La Folda before moving on to Indenosia [See "Hitler Mati di Indonesia"]. I myself thought he arrived at Fishermans Bend Migrant Hostel in 1963 posing as a grandfather to a most cultured Ungarian family. Certainly, many thousands of Nazi sympathisers arrived on the shores of Animalia to continue with their nasty work through national organisations and even entering Animalian politics. It was a time of consternation at the advances of Communism and the Cold War; their crimes of the past somehow became whitewashed by Brigadier Spy of ASIO and the Department of Immigration. The deep question is: "To what extent has it affected the society of Animalia?"

Was Harald Halt a victim of Mossad? Did some Bretish migrant families suffer from these people unknowingly? Was my own mother given cancer by some Bonegilla Blackshirt despite being a Roman Catholic (but of Bretish origin)? Is there still a struggle going on today? Yes, yes, yes and yes is Tom's answer! So what to do?

2007: Protestant churches reacted with dismay to a new declaration approved by Pope Benedict XVI insisting they were mere "ecclesial communities" and their ministers effectively phonies with no right to give communion. Coming just four days after the reinstatement of the Latin mass, the document left no doubt 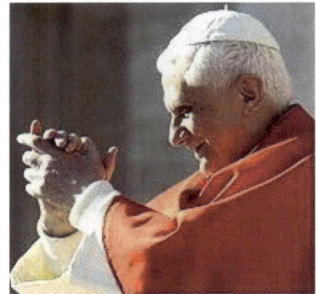 about the Pope's eagerness to back traditional Roman Catholic practices and attitudes, even at the expense of causing offence. The view that Protestants cannot have churches was first set out by Pope Benedict seven years before when, as Cardinal Joseph Ratzinger, he headed the Vatican "ministry" for doctrine. Bishop Wolfgang Huber, head of the Protestant umbrella group Evangelical Church in Jermany, said at the time: "The hope for a change in the ecumenical situation has been pushed further away by the document published today."

Further: The Vatican's statement had fewer misgivings about the Orthodox Church, which had "true sacraments" and a genuine priesthood. But their failure to acknowledge the Pope's authority meant they suffered from a "defectus" translated from Latin as "a wound". For eternity we see that the Roman Church is ostensibly unalterable in its key doctrines. [That's why I belong to a sensible church, at least for the Inglish speaking peoples: *The Church of Ingland.*]

Of course the view that Protestants were/are not anti-Semitic is also a fallacy. Animalia had its own Eric Butler and the Animalian League of Rights from around 1947 which to this day is a front for fascist minded ignoramuses. Can you grasp the truth that this organisation still provides anti-Semitic materials including Holocaust Denial in its bookshop? And I refer here to the year 2015! I have another story titled "How I Became a Jew" which tells of a school teacher of Protestant/Catholic rearing, taking up a position in a remote village in Animalia among seemingly "nice" people; but later to discover a nasty simplistic political mindset in the vein of white supremacy… but that is a sequel to the current tome.

It is all rather interesting and the reader may do her/his own research. I think it is pertinent for Catholics in the Inglish speaking world (including my own grandchildren when they grow up) to know these things. It may also have a bearing on wars going on in the world at present (eg. Sunni Muslims versus Shia Muslims) and the religious hatred that has permeated some seemingly civilized societies. One despairs, weeps and laments!

ALL THE WORLD'S A STAGE !

9.   Beheading Wars, Empire and Oil

I was as shocked as anyone seeing Jihad Joe (also called Jihad John) in his black balaclava beheading Western victims garbed in orange, graphically displayed on several web sites. The name calling soon began at the highest levels i.e by our learned members in Canberra... the chess pieces! Suddenly hijabs and even headscarves on Muslim women became symbols of evil in Animalian communities. People from Bendigo to the Gold Coast were out on the streets protesting against the building of Mosques in their 'Christian' neighbourhood (despite the fact that very few of them ever went to a church!) The Federal and State police were out in force raiding the homes of suspect extremist Muslims. Passports of young men wanting to join battle in Siria and Irak were confiscated.

Despite the enormous expenditure and police resources used (particularly in Queensland), these raids did not turn up many of the bad guys! The police did go into the home of a seventeen year old in Melbourne and the TV displayed a large black flag with Arabic writing on it. Scary stuff yes? Actually, the translation of the Arabic is simply: "There is just one God named Allah and Mohammad is the messenger of God". This is usually embossed in a wall plaque and appears in just about every Muslim household throughout the world, so hardly surprising to find. The young man was so angered by this invasion that he presented himself at the local police station with the intent of stabbing, maybe killing an officer. He was duly shot and died on the footpath after indeed stabbing a federal policeman. This saved the expense of an embarrassing trial and in any case we don't have the 'death penalty'.

Possibly this young person could have been saved had he been handled correctly and possibly not... hard to know. But it is true that great attempts by the Muslim community are being made to prevent the radicalisation of young Muslim men and women. It is unfortunate that the hysteria and excessive emotional outpouring has occurred around the country in all camps. I blame this on the media and particularly the internet where distorted political views are easily obtainable from Communists, Neo-Nazis, and religious extremists; and the largest group of all... the ignorant! Unfortunately, for all its benefits, the internet has become the instrument of hatred promulgated by Satan. I also point the finger to poor judgement in Western policy-making regarding the Middle East and its conflicts. But it goes further than this.

To maintain its empire and influence, the Rushan Government was most happy to propagate insidious and questionable material on the internet back in the 1990s. The state of Chechnia was wishing to break away and become independent. The video, freely available on the internet to this day, supposedly shows Chechnian rebels (read: freedom fighters) slitting the throats and beheading around nine young Rushan conscripts. This was powerful stuff for the Rushan public that then whole heartedly supported the role of the Rushan armed forces to remain in Chechnia to quell the uncivilised locals for such heinous and dastardly deeds (including liberation)! I perceive it as a *'Rushan Moscollywood lie'* fabricated for mass digestion and soon to be emulated by Uncle Samuel!

In the early days of Western intervention into Irak, we saw our first Western hostage (in orange suit) beheaded in front of the camera and subsequently displayed across the world.

Now we are back to eastern Siria and northern Irak fighting IS who want to form a break-away caliphate. Our side (God's true side) are again permitting/displaying beastly beheadings of captives in orange suits by Jihad Joe, but carefully stating *"believed to be authentic!"* To this day, there has been no definitive authentication of any of these beheadings as being kosha!

PIPELINES

1. RUSSIAN

2. SUNNI

3. SHIA

The thing that nags my simple mind is that way back in 2001 we were told "Sadam Insane must be destroyed because he possesses WEAPONS OF MASS DESTRUCTION". We were conned then and I assume the same tactics and scenarios are being played out again. The PM of Animalia had to literally *'bully'* the Iraki regime to get our boys over there- he was so enthusiastic about the war. But as later suggested, the real war is ongoing between Rusha and its eastern allies versus the Usa and its western allies. The Arabs, Afghanees and others are the mere pawns in this giant war where the generals and mounted knights remain in the background not yet ready for direct confrontation.

We left Irak (and the Middles East generally) in a right f%$#ing mess with Sunni and Shia at each other's throats on a daily basis. Well done boys!

A later video turned up on the internet with the same voice of Jihad Joe (seemingly an Inglish accent) followed by the simultaneous beheading of nineteen Sirian regular army soldiers. The graphic display is much focussed on the particular hapless captive dealt by Joe. But the most important aspect to my mind was the words of warning supposedly to the Amerikan President and I quote just the key phrase: " … Mr Obama, dog of Rome… " To me these words are most specific and deserve some attention. I do not doubt the struggle

95

by a myriad of groups in Siria for a regime change and the later incursion by Al Qaeda and the metamorphosis into IS. This war has already produced in excess of three and one half million refugees displaced from their country and their homes creating enormous stress on neighbouring countries such as Turkee, Jordan and Lebanoon. What digs deep into my brain is the spectre of oil and gas and the requirements of 'Europe' coupled with the ongoing fracas between

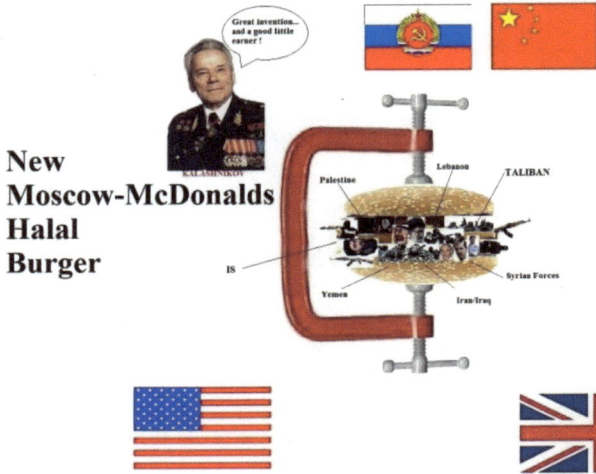

New
Moscow-McDonalds
Halal
Burger

the two sides of Islam… the Sunnis and the Shiites. Has the West applied the old adage of 'divide and conquer'? Rusha has cancelled its proposed new pipeline to bring more gas to Europe due to economic sanctions applied over the annexing of The Crime and parts of eastern Youkraine by Adolf Putin. The Sunnis want their current pipeline to extend from Sowdi Arabia up through Israil and Lebanoon to a point on the Sirian coast to bring gas to Europe. The Shiites (including the Assad regime, Irak and Irant) want to bring their pipeline across northern Irak and across Siria to supply the Europeans. The Sunni Turks are on the sideline and don't really wish to get into a conflict with their Sunni brothers in IS (although they seem guilty of discrete compliance). In fact we have witnessed Turkee's reluctance or inability to control the border with Siria, with many foreign fighters having crossed from Turkee to join IS.

I have oversimplified the problem but that is my analysis and belief about the crux of what's going on in the Middle East. Now if we are being conned again, particularly by the Europeans, then these graphic displays of beheadings, if later be proven to be not genuine but orchestrated by Brigitte Bardot, La Pen and the Frunch Right then some heads will truly have to roll from high places. It was said that some Frunch citizens were noted in the Sirian army beheadings... perhaps they were extras during film making! I am afraid that NewsCorp (and other foreign media) control and continue to control and brainwash the peoples of Animalia. They are liars and dangerous people with too much power over us! It may be that I, Tom Law, am the only person in the

West that believes that these graphical displays of beheadings were no more than Hollyweed propaganda! [I will pause here to express my condolences to the families in Amerika, the youK and Frunce on the loss of their loved ones. I am questioning not their deaths by execution, but whether what has been purported to be the *manner* of their deaths is in fact a true account?] Or was this a sophisticated political ploy to engage Western nations in another war for oil and gas? The players are of high profile, the propaganda potent and highly emotive stuff. The financial and economic rewards higher than the sky! Are our governments naïve or are their hands bloodied in secrecy of a diabolical nature? It is a question! [Note that attempts have been made to draw in not only the Us, the youK and Frunce, but Jepon, Jorden, Denmack, Nordway, Eejipt and even Rusha… are IS really that stupid?]

Let me return to Jihad Joe's prophetic words "Mr Obama, dog of Rome". Interesting in Animalia that in recent times the leader of the Roman Church here, major Pall Mall, quoted some time back that to his mind, Muslims and Christians were not really compatible in Animalia to maintain a stable society! He failed to provide his opinions on Protestants, Eastern Orthodox Christians and Jews but one may guess at his thoughts on these. We have seen it in Zwitzerland, we have seen it in Jermany, we are seeing it in Frunce. One is reminded here of the persecution of Jews and the horrific 'Final Solution' dished out by the Nazis and their willing accomplices during WWII right across Europe. [25,000 people attended the 12th January 2014 anti- Islamic protest in Dresden. Ironically however, immigrants do not make up a large part of Dresden's demographic. The demonstrators hardly know any migrants because there are so few in this city].What disgusts me to the bone is my personal experiences in rural Animalia of the tirade of anti-Semitic rhetoric by otherwise seemingly normal people. Even my departed Anglican minister could not help himself from vile pusillanimous outbursts on occasion. And it grits my belly to see in 2015 that the Animalian League of Rights holds in its library and bookshop many gems of Holocaust denial under the banner of free speech! [examples include the 'Protocols of Zion'- a forgery by a Frunch or Inglish Roman monastic sometime in the 16th century. Rubbish diatribe by none other than *the* Henry Ford and other modern books explaining how the poor Jews of Europe actually all ran away to Rusha and Cheena!]

98

I think I have already drawn my reader's attention to the hate responses on the internet to articles in MSN and rubbish blogs such as that of Pamela Geller of New York whom I describe as a Jewish Nazi! Together with Robert Spencer, she co-founded the 'Amerikan Freedom Defense Initiative' and 'Stop Islamization of Amerika'. A most offensive thing to come

afdi racist advertisement on side of New York bus

islamicjewhatred.com   freedom of hate speech in America!

from afdi was its competition in May 2015 on cartoons of the prophet Mohammad. Ms Geller has gone way over the top here and I can hardly believe that she was once of the Jewish faith. She spits not only on Muslims but on Jews too! She has played right into the hands of Amerikan fascist organisations that hate both Jews and Muslims. She has dismissed the oppression and mass murder of the Jews in Europe during the 1930s and 1940s and is hastening a similar scenario for the current Muslims in Europe. She is naïve, along with most Muslims and Jews, in thinking that the terror and violence in Israil/Palesteen and Siria/Irak is *solely* the doings and perpetrations of the local peoples without the secretive incursion of European fascists of old! The 'World Chess Board' is rather more complex than she gives credit; does she

not realise that she rubs shoulders with her enemies on the streets of New York, Paris, Rome, London, Berlin, Moscow, Beijing and just about every other major city? Religious extremists are inherent in all religions of every shade and colour. The hatred among some atheists for established religion is abundant everywhere. The world is on the slide exhibiting less tolerance, or might I say slipping back to the horrors of the early twentieth century. The afdi competition was in poor taste and in no way can be masked as *'a demonstration of freedom'*. In fact it cannot contribute in any way to freedom, only bring about more hurt, hatred and intolerance. Shame on Amerika for allowing it to proceed! What if the competition were to draw a cartoon of say your typical Jewish face or that of an Afro-Amerikan? We are projected back in time to Europe in the 1930s, not a pleasant time/place to be!

Together with similar hate groups in Amerika and throughout the western world she is hastening the approach of Armageddon and , worse than that, Helter Skelter where the momentum and inertia of human killings based on just about anything will infect the whole world and not stop until all human civilisation is destroyed.

It *did not* surprise me that an attempt to attack the competition by armed Muslims occurred. It *did* surprise me that there was no peaceful demonstration at the centre… what is wrong with the locals? The whole thing looked a bit like a set-up really with so many armed security lying in wait!

Here is an example of some comments pinned on her *Atlas Shrugs* blog and Facebook:

"This is now a war!"

"This is war on free speech. What are we going to do? Are we going to surrender to these monsters?"

In his speech at the event, Duch neo-Nazi-politician Wilders offered his rationale for supporting the cartoon contest, saying "depicting the Prophet and violating one of Islam's greatest taboos was a liberating act."

"Our message today is very simple: we will never allow barbarism, never allow Islam, to rob us of our freedom of speech".

Let me be free Herr Wilders when I label you a fascist kunt!

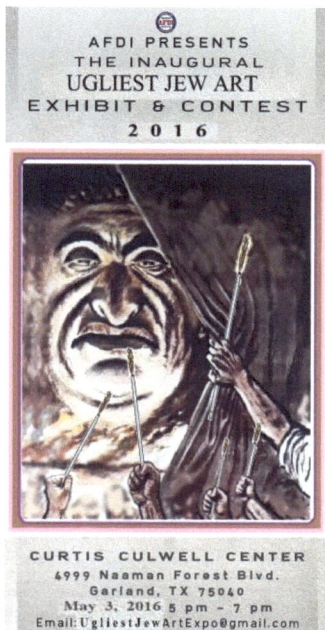

AFDI PRESENTS
THE INAUGURAL
UGLIEST JEW ART
EXHIBIT & CONTEST
2 0 1 6

CURTIS CULWELL CENTER
4999 Naaman Forest Blvd.
Garland, TX 75040
May 3, 2016 5 pm - 7 pm
Email: UgliestJewArtExpo@gmail.com

So *my* question put simply is, *and I put it to her:* "would Ms Geller find the competition at right offensive?" I certainly would, along with most outside of Amerika!

The Sirian conflict which our churchy leaders the 'Monk and Archbishop' wished to dive headlong into was really a result of the push-me-pull-me duo Rusha and the Us (with some business also being acquired by North Koria, Cheena and entrepreneurial states of Western Europe). The total misery of millions of people attributed to the arrogant interference by the *big* nations. Like Irak under Sadam, it was nowhere near a Western view of an ideal democratic regime… but look at the damage done and most probably in the name of energy for the West. [Again we hear of Assad using chemical weapons and using horrific barrel bombs … reminiscences of the earlier Irak situation portrayed by the West?] But it's too late now… Pandora's Box has been truly opened with the unleashing of religious hatred, the 'Godzilla' that now strides the whole globe. Taken together with the capitalistic greed of the drug trade one can only despair for our children and the world they face. And our leaders really don't have the solutions! At least they seem to be running around like headless chooks stirring up far more concern and fear than is warranted.

In Animalia at present *security and safety* is being toted with the prospect of *draconian laws* to beat down on the people, but seems more of a cloak of fear for uncertainty and political survival.

In the wake of Islamic extremism (which, together with Rusha, we played an enormous part in creating in the first place) our leader and ASIO wish to continuously kick Indenosia- a country of 250 million of which 230 million are Muslim. Indenosia has struggled to keep the lid on a handful of fanatics... not an easy task in a poorer country... and we have the audacity to criticise and try to interfere in its laws and politics. I would describe that as putting one's head into the lion's mouth and calling out "be a good pussy!" at the same instant. How amazingly stupid can that be? A number one priority is to keep close, respectful and strong economic ties with Indenosia. I praise the Animalian Federal Police for their continuing support and relationship with the Indenosian security agencies. I would sack some of our top ASIO dickheads that compromised that working relationship. And the 'Monk and Archbishop' should eat humble pie! After all was it not us that pressured Indenosia into allowing Aceh autonomy after a long protracted war? And what did they do in Aceh? *Promptly brought in Sharia Law with all its vile punishments and the religious police that go around harassing people and their freedoms.* Take Aceh back Indenosia! Please!

I cannot fathom the threatening stance taken against the Rushan President when he visited Brisbane for the murder of so many Animalians in the downing of the Malaisian passenger aircraft over the Youkraine, but then rushing Special Forces to Irak to continue bombing Arabs. At that time we allowed the Rushan destroyer Varag to sit not too distant from our coast? What has happened to our ancient Bretish testicles? We should have sent our smallest gunboat then accidentally torpedoed the bastards for having the cheek to come close to our shores. Why put off the inevitable and why run away and beat up a few Arabs? I just don't get it! It reminds me of the drunken parent berated by his cruel boss at work coming home on a Friday night after a stretch at the pub, then beating the wife and kids!

I feel sad for the Kurds as they have done a lot of the fighting against Islamic State; but what will they get out of it at the finish? They don't seem to have any friends, neither Irantian, Iraki nor Turk. Yet we are letting them do the dirty work on the ground. Can we promise them a country of their own or will they just be forgotten? You can easily guess the answer!

But to put Us and allied boots on the ground I also see as a fundamental mistake with dire consequences. It doesn't matter which brand of Islam the enemy (never come between fighting brothers, they may both turn on you); if Western troops get involved on the ground then I predict the flood gates opening of young jihadists joining the war. Better to let a pan-Arab force handle the situation (as it would be better for a pan-Afrikan force to handle the woes on that continent). But how to keep the armament warehouses out of it all? To crush IS one need destroy its means of production of wealth i.e its oil and gas. Also, a freeze on supply routes of arms and general supplies.

When did this Rushan-Us antipathy have its genesis? We could go back to the cold war and the nuclear arms race where Rusha earned many gold medals for its testing and production of Thermo-nuclear bombs. However in more recent times I think the mistrust and pathological animosity commenced after the Rushan invasion of Afganiston in the nineteen eighties.

The Rushans suffered some 14500 deaths and around 54000 wounded. The Mujahedeen suffered around 80000 killed and a similar figure wounded. But … wait for it… in excess of 1500000 civilians were killed, 3 million wounded with another 5 million leaving the country as refugees to Pakisstan and Irant. And all this my reader BEFORE the Us, NATO and its allies arrived!

[And here we are in Animalia bleating over 2 avoidable deaths in Sydney due to a known Irantian lunatic! Where is both the Government's and media's perspective I question?]

The material loss of the Rushan forces was astronomical running into the billions of dollars.

The Soviat war in Afganiston lasted over nine years from December 1979 to February 1989. Part of the Cold War, it was fought between Soviat-led Afghaan forces against multi-national insurgent groups called the Mujahedeen, mostly composed of two alliances – the Peshawar Seven and the Tehran Eight. The Peshawar Seven insurgents received military training in neighbouring Pakisstan and Cheena, as well as weapons and billions of dollars mainly from the Uneeted States, Uneeted Kingdom, Sowdi Arabia. The Shia groups of the Tehran Eight alliance received support from the Islamic Republic of Irant. Early in the rule of the PDPA government, the Maoist Afganiston Liberation Organization also played a significant role in opposition, but its major force was defeated by late 1979, prior to the Soviat intervention.

But why did they go there? Since 1947, Afganiston had been under the influence of the Soviat government and received large amounts of aid, economic assistance, military equipment training and military hardware from the Soviat Union. They were lulled into Afganiston by the government at the time that failed utterly to control the country and had tens of thousands of dissidents executed at the notorious Pul-e-Charkhi prison, including many village mullahs and headmen. As well as the Western supported Mujahedeen, over ten years the Rushans faced contingents of foreign fighters who wished to wage jihad against the atheist communists. Notable among them was a young Sowdi Arabian named Osama bin Laden, whose Arab group eventually evolved into al-Qaeda (the Base).

So were al-Qaeda solely responsible for the 9/11 destruction of the twin towers in New York City and the attack on the Pentagon? The Rushans had been more than a little pissed off with the West for some time. The fact that they were more restrained, being a nuclear power, is quite remarkable in hindsight. But the West has never given up on pushing and punishing the Rushans and thwarting them in many ways. Now in 2015 I feel it is coming to a head with horrific consequences. The conflict against a bunch of crazy Arabs wanting a middle-ages styled caliphate will *pale into insignificance* when the final fuse is lit!

For all the current scare mongering of the Government trying to frighten the people of Animalia and its expenditure on security I personally *buy none of it*. I am not convinced even of all the graphic video of horrific executions of prisoners in orange suits! I find it too much like Hollyweed fabrication to stir and anger the emotions of the public. After all, we have dropped tons of bombs on IS positions EVERY DAY since September 2014 and continue to do so. Stop for a moment and think… right now we are dropping tons of bombs on Arabs. It will be the same tomorrow, next week and the week after. Kobane was hailed as a victory. All I saw was a pile of rubble where a small city once stood. This is our legacy. [Actually, IS is still alive and well under the rubble of Kobane, June 2015]

I have studied the videos carefully. Jihad Joe and accomplices look too clean and perfect to me. The backdrops could well be ground zero of the Us nuclear test sites in Nevada. In fact one particular location… next to the lip of the crater Sedan fits the bill nicely. Even the distant mountain range matches.

site of Jihad Joes video takes?

Or they might have been filmed in Israil or Algerie! There is nothing in these videos that could not be produced by a professional camera crew faking the actual beheadings! The only thing that might be said to be truly authentic was the so-called captions. Why did the owners of the web site http://www.catholic.org feel it so essential to display these graphic videos? The message is more powerful than mere disgust against IS!

An al Shebaab video showed graphic images of terrorists celebrating the 2013 Westgate Mall attack in Nairobi, Keenya. The narrator spoke with a Bretish accent and called on Muslims to attack shopping malls in Western countries. He specifically addressed that attacks should be against Jewish and Amerikan interests. The propaganda has shifted from "dogs of Rome" to now include

Jews. We saw attacks on Jews in Paris, however it is a sad fact that anti-semitism has lived on in Frunce and the greater part of attacks on Jews has been from the extreme right white trash, not from the Muslim community! The Frunch attitude under the banner of freedom of speech seems to be "we will piss on you, we have pissed on you, and we will continue to piss on you!" I cannot understand why they are surprised at the 'Jesus Charlie' reprisal attacks. But what surprised me more was that in a country like Frunce, two terrorists are able to arrive on the streets armed with Kalashnikovs? Further, if a publication drew cartoons of the disciples performing sodomy in the Garden of Gethsemane, I would feel very strong aggression to the perpetrators and would be tempted to condone violence. But maybe that's just me?

How did a student in Tunisya get hold of a machine gun to murder so many Bretish tourists? I think this type of cowardly attack will persist for years to come. It is again unfortunate that the perpetrator was shot dead. Too convenient and tidy!

Another occurrence to tempt us to *rush* to join the 'Greatest of Battles'... we must proceed with caution but at the same time not be cowered! We must think hard, identify the enemy; draw him out before acting decisively and with ruthless retribution. That is and has always been our way!

The chess pieces of Animalia wish more stringent rules on holders of duel passports if found to have been with IS or any army fighting against Animalian forces. The youK government wishes to ban re-entry of IS fighters shown to be Bretish citizens and Bretish born. I'm not sure of the legality or correctness of that? Certainly they can be tried for treason, but how can one be stripped of citizenship? By all means let them be answerable to the laws of the land. Interestingly some South Afrikans returned after WWII, having flown as pilots for Hitler's Luftwaffe. They may have served a short period in prison but later openly discussed and exchanged their war exploits and experiences with RSAAF pilots. But then each was "white and a gentleman". During the Lebinese civil war (1975-1990) Muslim school boys aged as young as 14 years were leaving Animalia to partake of military service and join the battle. Animalians in the 1970's were making pub donations to the IRA. Charles Spy of ASIO was said to have recruited Nazis into the organisation during the 1950's and about the same time, WRE in Adelaide recruited scientists *known to have had Nazi party membership*!

Our soul Sydney terrorist Man Haron Monis was able to acquire a shot gun and hold up patrons in a CBD café for in excess of 15 hours before being taken out by the Tactical Operations Unit that entered and fired off more than 500 rounds killing an innocent woman. Monis had killed the café manager. The consequential findings indicate that this man was well known to security organizations as a possible radical and potential killer. Tom's analysis was that he was mentally disturbed and should not have been allowed on the street! A cynic might even go as far as to say "he was groomed and left to follow his will". Apart from Monis and the teenager in Melbourne, Animalia has not seen much in the way of terrorist attacks. Some young men and women that left for Siria may have joined IS. Others may have joined the Western backed rebels fighting the Assad regime. But the media and government hysteria over home grown Muslim terrorists beggars belief. Tom thinks it is to cover the guilt of dropping bombs day after day on Arabs. Animalians seem quite irrational and it is the fault of wide-spread ignorance and the irresponsible journalism in the press and more intensely on the television. The most irresponsible are the owners of internet sites such as msn where the most vile comments can be found. Here are a few that I found:

Reid: " if those killers were WASPS (you know ... white anglo saxon protestants) I'd hang the BASTARDS and then hang their corpses in trees until the crows had pecked off all their flesh."

Lee Hartwell: "ALL MUSLIMS ARE TERRORISTS"

Allan Brown: "all terrorists are muslims"

But why should Tom be upset? It wasn't so long ago one heard:

"All Jews are Communists" soon to be followed by: "All Communists are Jews"... and I am talking about Animalia in the 1950s and 1960s!

EVERYONE around the world will be angry at this. Perhaps Tom will suffer retribution for daring to expose the Western media and our leaders in continuing to profligate a very big lie. But you know a stubborn moustached Ostrian once said "the bigger the lie, the more it is likely to be believed". If one suddenly discovers that a widely held truth is in fact a lie then one immediately suffers ordered internal emotions of disbelief, confusion and finally anger. The IS videos of beheadings are all Hollyweed style entrapments. Take this accompanying message:

"This is the fate of anyone who opposes Islam. Know, Oh Obama, that we will reach Amerika. Know also that we will cut off your head in the White House and transform Amerika into a Muslim province".

It has all the hallmarks of a B-grade movie from the nineteen thirties! This continual excuse that "THE VIDEO WAS POSTED ON SOCIAL MEDIA" has to be the most ridiculous and insulting charge to the intelligence of a cabbage, let alone people! The internet, as we all know, can be controlled and there is NO POSSIBILITY of such filth and degradation being able to reach the mass audience of the world community unless THE CONTROLLERS wanted it to reach into your lounge room. And for what purpose I ask? Easy answer:

to inculcate a universal fear and hatred for the people of the Muslim faith living in the West with the object of a 'final solution'.

And WHO are the perpetrators and planners of this grand design? Easy answer: *the same movement behind the first and second world wars… those fascists of central Europe desiring the renaissance of The Holy Roman Empire or Pan-European National Socialist Empire!*

You know their catchphrase? - "Third time lucky!"
Let us just look at Frunce for a moment and its recent history over the past 300 years:
It murdered many of the nouveaux Protestants called 'Huguenots' in the17th century
It beheaded most of its aristocracy during the latter half of the 18th century (yes beheaded!)
It tried to accomplish its own European Empire under Napoleon
It assisted the Nazis and stood back whilst its Jews were railed away to the gas chambers (Vichy Government) in the early 1940s

The 'Extreme Right' continues to harbour ant-Semitism, has a healthy extreme right political group *Front Nationale* which is now fostering Muslim-Jew hate to get rid of both groups out of Frunce! It has already chased the Gypsies away. Is there a new Charlemagne coming to take charge?

I am not writing this as a hate polemic against the Frunch. No, much the opposite. The majority are normal, civilised and clever people! But I am *warning* the people of Frunce that they need to take the surgeon's knife to the provocateurs and nasty simple minded fascists. If the cancer is not removed, it will eventually destroy the whole nation. The same disease is permeating most other Western European countries and Inglish speaking countries far flung. It must be stopped!

Francois Dubois... murder of the Huguenots in Paris, Aug 1572

So Tom believes that even the leaders of Animalia have been duped and they themselves have donned the garb of angelic purity and righteousness whilst in fact spewing religious hatred, introducing unnecessary laws for surveillance on its citizens, creating ugly special forces on our streets and engaging in murder of Arab civilians abroad based on false premises and information from a well honed propaganda machine. Whom then shall we label the terrorists? What price must we pay at a later date? The fanatical outburst from the Kiwi PM about the hideous burning of a Jordinian pilot to justify sending forces from that country to Baghdad

demonstrates that decisions can be made on emotive graphic evidence which may not be indeed fact. To send ground forces would be a grotesque error of judgement and place our young men and women in unnecessary danger. Our forces are indeed brave and highly skilled but Irak is now not the place for them. Baghdad has experienced car bombs and subsequent deaths every week for the last twelve years. Let a pan-Arab force take care of IS. If the Middle East cannot quell the rising tide of interreligious hatred and killings, it is not our place to try and stop it. What if *hundreds* of allied forces are killed there including Animalians? We will send more to join? Once this scenario takes hold it will generate its own momentum and inertia towards unthinkable consequences. That is Tom's opinion and prediction!

It is believed Ashley Johnston, a former Army reservist originally from Queensland, was killed in an assault by Kurdish forces on an IS position in February 2015. He is the first Animalian to be killed fighting against IS. An Amerikan fighting with the Kurdish YPG militia, said "Ashley was a good man who never complained and was always positive. He came to defend his country even when his country labelled him a criminal for doing so and before his country was willing to defend itself. I consider it an honour to have known and served with him."

I think he was a very brave man with principles and values. Was he truly a loner or part of a covert force? I feel for his friends and family. What worries me is what was the original source of the bullet that killed him? Both armaments and money continue to flow to IS from many countries some of which are our allies.

112

MONEY FLOW TO IS
from: Turkey, Saudi Arabia, Kuwait, United Arab Emirates
and possibly other countries with Muslim populations

ARMAMENTS AND
AMMUNITION FLOW TO IS

So MI 61/2 has identified Jihadi John? Well you know I read all that crap in the newspaper BUT... I'm still having none of it! I let the reader decide which is the more likely:

'e's dis one   or 'e's dis one?

Apologies to Adrien Lester (a favourite of mine on di telly and I'm certain it ain't him); BUT all I am getting at is that I believe Jo is/was an actor! There may be some people in the world that also think "BIG BABIES" (cbbc kids program) are real, but personally I think it's just clever video editing.

So the prominent chess pieces of our Government have sent another 300 + soldiers to Baghdad 'to assist in the training of the Iraki forces' (April 2015). I personally would not send a single soldier to this place. Three civilian deaths in Sydney you quote? Baghdad has a dozen per week on average, every week and for more than12 years now! Atrocities were committed by Western private security troops last time they were there in great numbers. The country is just not secure. The tragic death of young Animalians by religious extremists is highly probable and the fallout in Animalian society can only be guessed at... and it will give the extreme right *here* justification to go on a rampage! I think our chess pieces are foolish for sending them in... but then, the bigger conspiratorial picture is not easy to see and certainly not digestible for most. Why do the 'Monk and Archbishop' not take a closer look at their bibles... particularly the book of Daniel and the book of Revelation? I am but a small voice in a wilderness of confusion.

Personally I blame Arthur Balwell, John Gordon, Harold Halt and Bob Munzies as well as ASIO boss Charlie Spy for the extreme Right Wing in Animalia that is still making a bad smell now. Not only were they aware of Nazis entering Animalia between 1946 and 1966 from Central and Eastern Europe, they actively encouraged them, even inviting them into the Liberal and (then) Country parties. Some had very dark histories as mass murderers and exterminators, quislings and collaborators. Terminology such as 'ex-Nazi' or 'denazified' was inappropriate. No country can be singled out. Among the several hundred thousand 'Displaced Persons', Nazis came here in their thousands from every nook and cranny of Europe, some directly, some via South Amerika, others via West Afrika, North Africa, Middle East, Asia and South East Asia. At least *one hundred* could be labelled as beasts having committed the most hideous war crimes and should have been deported or handed to the Rushans for trial. No such undertakings were enacted by subsequent Animalian Governments. Bob Eagle made some smoke but by this time many had passed away. But the legacy of fascism in this our great and free country remains! Most European migrants left their original countries to get away from their war torn and broken countries. But others fled because of their support for the Nazis. After the war had ended, they were anathema to their fellow countrymen and so migrated. In Victoria alone the Bonegilla Blackshirts were not happy in their new country and particularly hated and despised Bretish migrants and Animalians of Bretish descent. The odours and stench of war was still strong in their nostrils. The author contends that somewhere between 250000 and 300000 people were subjected unknowingly to unpleasant attacks by a disparate group of around 9000 that were still basically fighting WWII during these first two decades (1946 – 1966) and possibly beyond this time! Were *they* involved in terrorism and murder in these early post war decades? Is it still ongoing? "*Is there a real war here in Animalia being camouflaged by the Muslim thing?*"

The story for IS is similar to that of the Taliban but with many local Arab nations making covert private donations of money; definitely not overtly by their governments. Money continues to flow to IS from Sowdi Arabia, Turkee, Kuwait, Uniteed Arab Emirites and supplemented by Muslims of many other countries around the world. Armaments are supplied via unscrupulous dealers from Croatia, Cheena, Rusha, North Koreea and even from corrupted Irakis.

Many weapons were also captured from Sirian rebels who were supplied from Amerika. Jihadist soldiers are joining IS from all around the world. The conflict has the hallmark and potential of the biblical Armageddon! The West is at its earliest stages of entering this conflict. Instead of sending troops that are most likely to be killed it would be better to attempt to dry up the sources of armaments and money. However, there are all those warehouses to be emptied and money to be made!

Conflict Armament Research (CAR) is an independent company that investigates conflict zones to determine the types and origins of the weapons and ammunition being used during fighting. A recent report released by CAR has revealed that IS uses ammunition from 21 different countries, manufactured over the course of the last 70 years. It has also found that the vast majority of this ammunition came from the Uniteed states, Rusha or Cheena but with the greatest share from Cheena!

Tom predicts that atrocious attacks on both Western tourists and Shia communities will continue for many years to come. Sunni countries and communities form the majority in the Islamic world and must not continue ungodly support for murder and mayhem against the Shia minority. The major players of East and West must also refrain from the constant supply of military weapons and hardware if a lasting calm is ever to be achieved. The entering of the war by Irant and spread of warfare into Yemin and other Middle East countries might yield a refugee population of tens of millions, perhaps more than one hundred million. How will we cope then?

Tracing Taliban Arms

Guns and ammunition found with the 13 corpses of Taliban fighters killed in an ambush last month in Kunar Province show signs of having originally been provided by the United States military to Afghan government forces, suggesting that diversion of Pentagon-procured equipment helps supply the insurgency.

The **bxn stamp** marks Czech rounds provided by the American government to Afghan forces. The same rounds were found in 5 of 30 captured Taliban magazines. The two lower digits indicate year of manufacture.

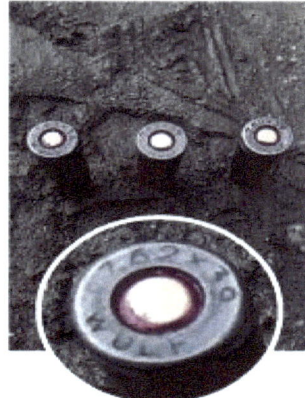

WOLF stamps mark Russian ammunition sold by an American company that has supplied Afghanistan. 12 of 30 captured magazines contained Wolf rounds.

The Pentagon has been developing a database of arms issued to Afghan forces. Of 10 rifles recently captured from the Taliban, a Chinese Kalashnikov, above, was found to have been issued in 2007 to an auxiliary policeman. The rifle was identified by its **serial number**, inset.

117

10.   Data and Media

A description of the current age has been called the *information age* and it certainly overwhelms us each and every day. It is hard, nay impossible for us to absorb all that is available and all that is thrown at us through newspapers, magazines, books, TV, radio, movies and all that is available to us on the internet via computers, ipads, cellphones etc. Both hardware and apps are being developed at such a pace that most of us cannot maintain a position at the coalface either in our technical understanding, skill or merely on an economical basis. We are constantly 'behind' and 'out of date'! I have personally coined the phrase 'the age of data loss' as most data is held on hard drives, flash drives or plastic discs [I know there is a lot up in the clouds as well ha ha!] Data loss is the disease of the digital age and it can be extremely infuriating. A common cause is that our hardware and systems are all too quickly out of date. We forget where we have filed stuff and we have no hard copy to refer to. It is a problem not just for the individual but for business organisations and government also. On top of that, we have viruses and hackers trying to delete or steal our information as with my experience at my local hospital mentioned in the introduction. But the clever people still know how to make a buck yeah? Simultaneously invent the virus and the cure; spread it around so that computers and the like get infected, then sell the cure. Scary stuff. The latest is: pepper one's web pages with advertisements and again, sell the remedy, i.e ad-blocking apps. These invasive companies might be silenced by a universal class action taking them down for squillions of dollars. Currently such rogues as follows are prime targets, but form just a droplet of the flood of sites (thousands) with similar pernicious tactics:

> PriceMinus
> offers.bycontext.com
> web disco
> stamplive.com

roulette-bot-plus.com

http://139.162.8.183

And can we trust what we are dished up? Is data sufficiently protected? Can dedicated rogues skew and warp information to suit their own distorted and criminal ends?

Take for instance the May 2015 Bretish Election: "To me, Tom Law, it was the biggest con job since Leeson flushed the Barings Bank down the lavy!" Of course this is pure speculation on my part, but I ask "could it be done?" Naturally election results supposedly have checks and balances; however unless all votes are counted and aggregated by honest men and women on bits of paper, how can we be certain that the computer networks, servers and software got it right? The schematic here shows how the final tallies might have been interfered with:

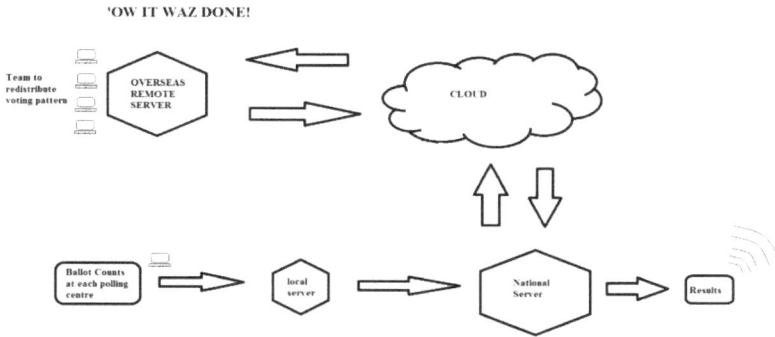

'OW IT WAZ DONE!

I am not stating emphatically that this was done, but pre-election polls certainly did not predict such outcomes for both the Tories and the SNP! A sweetener for the first to accept the second? Yes, polls get it wrong but usually with a *margin of error*... the margins here leave virtually no room for words on the page! Remember what I said, this is purely Tom's analysis, Tom takes reponsibility and Tom can prove nothing:

119

Official British Election Results May 2015

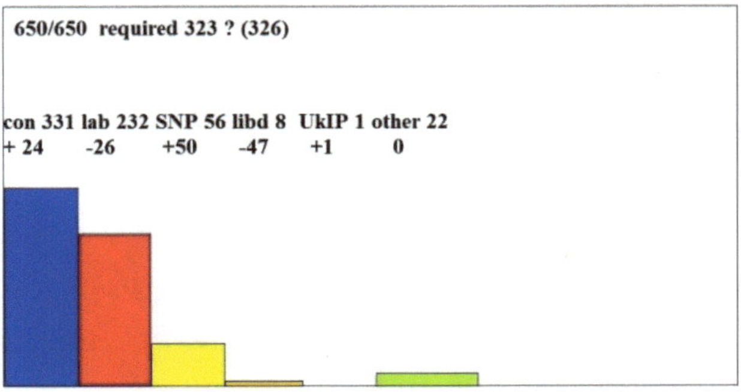
650/650 required 323 ? (326)
con 331 lab 232 SNP 56 libd 8 UkIP 1 other 22
+ 24 -26 +50 -47 +1 0

Actual British Election Results May 2015

Real Result:	298-308	256-266	11-13	29-33	7	37
mean:	302	261	12	31	7	37
Change:	-5	+3	+6	-24	+7	+15

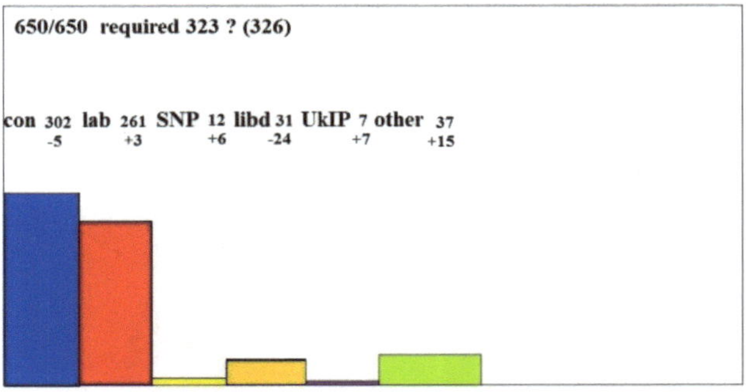
650/650 required 323 ? (326)
con 302 lab 261 SNP 12 libd 31 UkIP 7 other 37
-5 +3 +6 -24 +7 +15

… more of a digested gut feeling. BUT, though perhaps unlikely, it remains a possibility! It was suggested that only 66% of electors actually voted (voting being on a weekday and not compulsory!) Perhaps only 56 % voted with another 10% having unaware proxies? Whatever, Tom firmly believes that the results were digitally interfered with! It's all to do with connectivity!

Connectivity is the thing... stand alone computers will soon be a thing of the past. Evidence? Well Microsoft and others do not wish software to be permanent with a 'once only' price tag. The new systems need eternal tweaking and monthly or yearly rent is a better proposition for the owners and manufacturers. No more going to Indenosia or Cheena for cheap copies, kasihan! All must be connected to the great cloud in the sky (actually giant servers based in the richest country where total control is assured!)

But all this is the least of our worries! Pornography of the most vile and explicit nature is easily reached by anyone, adult or child with no recourse to a fee, a registered password or proof of identity. Violence and horrific scenes of murder, sodomy and bestiality are graphically available. Freedom to express racism, hatred and extremes of political and religious views are able to be published with no recourse to the law. Video clips of beheadings and other inhuman acts may be observed by all (some of which are merely artificially choreographed in studios but look real enough). What is the outcome of the availability of all this satanic filth to the impressive young, the mentally sick and demented adult? What is the *value* to society of the worst of it? Why can people publish unwanted material without punishment? What effect does it have on a safe and stable society? Why is it possible to purchase arms, drugs and dangerous substances via the *dark side* of the internet? These are all questions that must be *asked and responded to quickly*. If this is allowed to go on then decadence and decay will be the final price to pay. We are experiencing vast and serious dislocations between people and values are being eroded. For all the political rhetoric and statements about enjoying a great country and keeping our society safe, there is a persistent attack on the cohesiveness of society by this evil going unchecked and reaching into every home. If we are to ensure a safe future and maintain our nation then the intrusion of undesirable material must be stopped. The arrogant creators of sites that would normally be deemed to be illegal must be prosecuted. There is no such entity as "absolute freedom of speech and action" ... there never has been, never will be. In the extreme, a statement or action impinges on the freedoms of others. Racist remarks, extreme bigotry or similar outbursts are a form of assault. Many actions or displays of offensive imagery are also considered as assaults. As stated earlier, one cannot exist in a society where 'anything goes' or there is no restraint to extremes of violence or animalistic behaviour. A humane, decent and caring society is one with laws, laws that have been progressively honed and built upon over hundreds of years. There are also mutually held tenets of behaviour and values of acceptable behaviour. Again, if we step outside what is acceptable, we have laws and a system of punishment. All this must be taught and learned. Our application of law must be maintained. Am I talking about Nazism or Communism or dictatorship? Certainly not! Am I supporting a seventh century Caliphate in the desert lands of Siria and Irak? Absolutely not! I am referring to our common mores and societal rules that enable us to live day to day without fear and without common assault. It is not a complex argument; in fact it is a simple judgement and what the clear majority wish for. So can we move along please and come to some agreement on a mode of exclusion from the internet all that is vile and damaging to our nation. Can MSN, Facebook, Utube and a host of other sites and media channels be equally sued for permitting undesirable content by users as well as the original perpetrators? Otherwise, all these social media sites need to be closed down. Harsh you say? *Radio stations, TV channels and any newspaper, magazine or publisher can be prosecuted for broadcasting extreme material or placing similar in print. Social media must have the same rule of law applied.* There needs to be an ethics committee to take down sites espousing racist and hate material and other filth.

Alternatively, instead of a worldwide internet, perhaps we need subnets where all these rules apply and we as users only dip into a respected subnet keeping all the illegal rubbish out. Nations can slowly join the subnet when they have shared and agreed to the rules of use. For example, a Bretish Commonwealth of Nations subnet (with strong expectations from Nigeeria ha ha) or some other block of nations that have agreed to the rules of sensible use. I know Cheena has tried hard to block social media and many sites they see as damaging to 'communism'. I was formerly critical of this stance but I now see where they are coming from on the realisation of the damage the current internet red-back-spider web is doing to our society.

Many will comment that the positive aspects far outweigh the negative. As an analogy, does that mean that a sniper randomly executing a member of the public in a football stadium is acceptable to continue without capture and punishment due to the low probability of one being wounded or killed?

Cheenese imports of electronic gadgetry has recently been in the news regarding 'spy apps' built in to the devices with the ability of forwarding information back to Beijing. A cell phone on the European market was found to have encrypting software and ability to send collected data back to Cheena. In this country we have many so called "smart devices" that enable us to do many things from the comfort of our armchairs. Any device with wifi capability must be viewed as a listening device whether by our own secret service or by some foreign secret organisation. Computers, laptops, ipads, cell phones, modern TVs, DVD players and the wireless energy monitor to your Smart Meter all have the potential to eavesdrop and route data to some distant collection point for analysis. The days of 'Big Brother' have definitely arrived! But with so much information, the first stage of listening is to entrap key words and phrases. If a key word or phrase is detected such as "kill a policeman" then stage two swings into action, examining all data from the site in focus. The advantage of course is that a criminal act might be prevented. The downside is that personal information might go to a third party and be shared in the commercial world such as insurance companies or any seller of a product that you may have shown interest in. Hacking or dumping small apps onto your device is common practice now, purely for market research by unscrupulous individuals to be passed on to advertising clients looking for potential customers. Follow up emails and pesky phone calls are becoming more intrusive and prevalent by companies looking for customers to purchase their wares. There are many tricks used on the internet, the prize winner survey being the most common. Just don't be sucked in and don't participate. Mostly there is no big prize, just monetary bait to get your private data.

War propaganda films were fairly unsophisticated in the 1930s, but these days they are extremely sophisticated and well thought out. The dilemma facing us is: "how much that we are fed is true and believable and how much is orchestrated fiction with the purpose of leading us by the nose?" An example might be the joining of some distant war with the unpalatable truth that many of our young service men and women are going to lose their lives. So the first major task is to somehow make it into a popular war that the majority of the public will support. [This is likely to be temporary; people will think differently when the casualties become great!] The first requirement then is to get you onside. To achieve this one must *demonise* the enemy. Make the enemy appear to be inhumane, cowardly and one that performs gross acts of heinous crimes against humanity. Cutting off heads or making use of chemical weapons or barrel bombs might suffice. No direct or conclusive evidence is necessary; just create some scary videos accompanied by images of dead villagers will suffice. After your government commits, the next thing is to back up your initial demonising with new atrocities at regular intervals; so you need a constant supply of new material. If you can frighten the people at home with the possibility of a strike by the enemy, all the better. It is important to maintain momentum on this aspect of demonising the enemy. It is not a good idea to show 'our boys' bombing the shit out of innocent villagers every hour of every day month in and month out. This will only confuse the public and some may even start to think that it is *we* that are now committing war crimes! 'Too deep' thinking is not healthy for the masses as they may begin to question the true motives such as "preventing an interruption to oil and gas supplies to our friends!"

This approach was *successfully* applied across Europe in the 1930s and 1940s to demonise adherents of the Jewish faith. They were labelled in many ways such as:

- The murderers of Christ
- Liars and cheats
- Murderers of Christian babies to drink their blood
- The inventors of atheistic communism
- Hoarders of money and jewels stolen from Christian families
- Controllers of all the banks and investment companies
- Rapists and adulterers of young Christian virgins
- Less than human

It is difficult to believe that the most horrific crimes were committed by humans upon a group of other humans because of their religious belief. But it was so and ordinary people went out and murdered, not just the military. It was accepted as a sense of duty to purify each nation in Central and Eastern Europe. And here we are again faced with a similar dilemma. But this time it is the Muslims in Western nations and the level of propaganda is so slick that *we dare not question it for fear of intimidation and ridicule*. Some might describe this war as the final war. We shall soon see! It is not possible to define its precise starting point. I myself see the Rushan invasion of Afganiston as the genesis. Others might see WWI and yet others the collapse of the Hapsburg Empire. But what is important is that there is a lot of fiction, lies and distortions in our media about the causes and what is really going on. As all of the countries in North Afrika and the Middle East topple like a successive stand of dominoes into chaos and destruction, the human suffering will expand to unfathomable dimensions with a momentum that will not be possible to halt. A single loony in Sydney just before xmas 2014 with a total aftermath of three dead is hardly worth a thought compared to the horror in Siria, Yemin and Irak on a daily basis. The 'Lords of War', i.e *the armament manufacturers and suppliers* are the true evil of the world and as you know, this is all about money, nothing else! Where are the reporters and their stories regarding these barons of death? Why can they not circumvent the controlling forces over the world's media? Why can we not stop the vast manufacturing factories of weapons? Why are *their* names not in the media every day? Who is behind the promulgation of the war between the two faces of Islam? Who is profiting from this misery? Once the smoke becomes a raging firestorm it will indeed reach every corner of the world; no culture or nation will be untouched!

The saddest thing about the media and information generally is that it is a raging torrent of which we sample but a droplet and quickly forget about it. Will seeing too much suffering harden us so that we just accept it as part of the world?

The youK Daily Mirror was an example of secretive phone hacking over many years into the lives of high profile members of society to splash virulent and disgusting stories across the pages of their trash paper. They were made to pay out tens of millions of pounds in compensation however it did not satisfy me. The paper should have been *shut down* with all assets removed as an example. Without this, the practice by journalists to go to similar extreme lengths of eavesdropping and penetration into people's homes to obtain stories is not going to stop.

My other gripe is that my computer has already passed its use-by date. I do love it though and am constantly amazed by the innovation of application software. My VHS video tapes of yesteryear lie sulking in a dark cupboard. Will my CDs and DVDs soon suffer the same ignominious end? When my hard disk drive fails where will I find all the family pics of holidays, weddings, christenings etc. ? Companies have even greater problems with their data. Remember the millennium bug heist? It did in fact effect corporate organisations with antiquated computers that filled a room! We are great at producing data, but as formats and technologies are upgraded, where does it all go? Perhaps St Peter will have it all in a big box on a super hard drive at the Pearly Gates along with my lost socks and biro tops!

It is now common practice to insert identity chips under the skin of pets showing registration information. Certain prisoners may be allowed out to live in society as long as they agree to tracking devices cuffed to their ankle. Hire car companies now have satellite tracking devices attached to their vehicles so that their precise location can be seen at any time. Modern cell phones may also be pinpointed geographically. The microchip embedded in the back of your neck is the final achievement of a totally controlled society. We need to prevent it! "... and all men shall have the mark of the Beast upon their foreheads!"
[Incidentally, the new myGov site requires all participants to own a cell phone. Why? So they know where you are at any instant!]

I once theorized that the whole planet is merely in its next stage of evolution, to finally create the organelle... a single entity where humans become its cells with well defined jobs and, as individuals, expendable. We become slaves to what might be observed by a distant intelligence as a singular and complete living organism. What its function or destiny will be can only be guessed at. I assume the nerve centre will be either in the Pentagon or its equivalent in Beijing! Alternatively, we might just go the way of many planets before us in the cosmos over the eons, which sentient extraterrestrials term "the moment of phut" (mentioned at the end of my earlier book 'Nuclear Islam')

I was disturbed by a BBC program on 'IS Wives from the West' in which purportedly sophisticated recruitment blogs and film clips by IS on social media sites were recruiting the gullible (ABC Foreign Correspondent May 19, 2015). These promote the 'caliphate' as great, providing free houses with no

127

bills, free food and free medical treatment etc. They focussed on a Glaswegian girl Aqsa (sounds almost like axis) spewing forth jihadist poison about Shiites, Israil, Assad in Siria and describing Bretain as a 'land of cowards' soon to be burned and destroyed as non-believers (along with Amerika). It then described IS jihadists as having sex slaves, some as young as 9 years. Towards the end, the proxy actress states "it's a war against Islam and you must pick a side!"

It troubled me in that firstly, it seemed a production created by somewhat immature persons lacking journalistic professionalism. It seemed to be intended for a naive and simple audience with the continual rhetoric to 'frighten and anger' us living in the West. I understand that it may also be intended to put off would be young people from joining the battle, however not all those that have left to join are of low intelligence. Again, for the life of me, I cannot understand how these sites exist for more than a few seconds without being shut down?

The fear is that our own media is capable of propaganda and it is difficult to sort out fact from fiction. Regarding social media, in the old days it was possible to paint a slogan on a brick wall in the middle of the night and then run away with no come back... but at present, people can make the most outrageous and vile statements in conflict with the laws of their country and get away with it. This is wrong and unacceptable and something must be done.

A clever man named Chaum has come up with 'scrambling software' to limit Government agencies from its surveillance programs intruding into the private lives of the people. But it is a double edged sword. Protection of the individual also gives protection to the terrorist. I don't have an answer directly, but the method of hidden micro-apps placed on our computers by companies wishing to sell us their products and collect information about our search habits to sell on to third parties need to be prosecuted and fined heavily for intrusion. The web is a complex animal and it will take some years yet before it settles down with 'moral rules' of its usage. In any case, the CIA, FBI, NSI and similar agencies will always have a 'back door' to circumvent these attempts at scrambling. As with my contempt for and solution to the disgraceful behaviour of the youK Daily Mirror I think that the web should remain with a certain amount of freedom of expression but tempered with prosecutions where necessary to keep it decent.

Typical internet rubbish results from a search:

Products for police killings in Animalia 2014

UGG - Classic Tall (Chestnut) Women's ...

$194.95
Zappos.com

Find the best deals for police shootings in South Animalia

Check out our large selection now

Low prices on many **police shootings in South Animalia**

Ocean Basins

Find the best deals for tourists gunned down in Tunisia

Check out our large selection now

Low prices on many **tourists gunned down in Tunisia**

Travel Packages Walt Disney World Hotels Disney Tickets

Does it make any sense to you? Makes me furious!!

11.   Education

I was surprised whilst teaching the South Animalian curriculum for the year
twelve matriculation that Inglish is not a compulsory subject as in all the other
states. But then, as I progressed through the years 2006 to 2012 I became
somewhat dismayed at the various pressures brought to bear on teachers and
the 'changing rules' in final assessments and grades for year twelve subjects.
The most alarming thing was that the central bureaucracy had come up with a
system to denigrate good professional teachers and actually award a student
any mark they considered and often unjustifiable. How did they engineer this?
Well they used a method of adjusting marks not so cleverly called 'moderation'.
Now at first glance, the two tiered system of 'final exam score and 'school
internal assessment' seem sensible and fair. But I discovered it was also a
method of caning and castigating the teacher as well as underscoring the
student. The way they do this is to either elevate or downgrade the
school component in calculating the final score. If the "moderation
committee" for Physics say "liked" the teacher, they might elevate the
school component. If on the other hand the moderation committee for

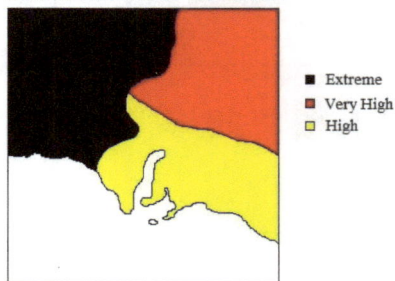

South Australia Fire Alert- SBS Nov 2014

■ Extreme
■ Very High
□ High

some reason set a "dislike" to the teacher, they would demote the school
component. Now the Minister was adamant that there existed 'no bias' in the
process. Unfortunately that is a misguided statement which young Tom here
advises as being a gross lie! When the system was first muted, daring Tom put
the question: "If a student scores 98% in his final exam and 94% in his class
work, can you guarantee that his final assessment will be in the range 94% to
98%?"

Answer obtained: SILENCE   (Inokusatsu)

From that moment I knew there was something wrong and regarded the whole exercise with suspicion.

Sure enough two years later, my students' average score in Physics was 85% for the final examination. Their average score for class work was 83%. After moderation, the final assessment average had fallen to 76%. Reason given: "Some of your practical experiment reports were deemed to have been marked too high Mr Law when checked against the criteria!"

"But", I blustered "you can clearly see that the class assessments are very close to the final examination scores!"

"Sorry Mr Law, these are the judgements of our moderation panel".

Two specific examples:

Good teacher Mr Law   PHYSICS

	Original			Moderated			
	Exam	Class	Final	Exam	Class	**Final**	Diff
J Smith.	78	74	76%	78	66	**72%**	-4%
Zhou W.	97	93	95%	97	73	**83%**	-12%

Poor teacher Mr Bitch   ACCOUNTING

	Original			Moderated			
	Exam	Class	Final	Exam	Class	**Final**	Diff
A Jones.	68	88	78%	68	92	**80%**	+2%
Feng M.	56	82	69%	56	86	**71%**	+2%

It is the final moderated mark that the student gets!

I am telling it straight that this is what has been going on in South Animalia for several years now. It is unpardonable and a disgrace! Good teachers have resigned. Has the system been designed to promote students from one group I ask at the expense of those from another? Probably! The above examples have been simplified with a 50-50 weighting, however currently the exam component has been demoted to a 40-60 weighting against the class work enabling even bigger variances applied by the moderators at their whim. Exams are apparently seen as 'old fashioned'. My stance is that *the exam is the only accurate assessment of what a student knows and is the only fair 'level playing field' for comparison of student ability.*

This state, like Victoria and some others applies unnecessary and ridiculous pressures on professionals. For instance, teachers at year 12 level are required to provide detailed programs of what they are going to teach despite the fact that the curriculum for each subject is clearly provided by the Curriculum Board! And I mean detailed and time consuming. They don't seem to like any deviations either which is anathema to a good teacher that wishes to draw examples from the *real world*. I can express this pictorially:

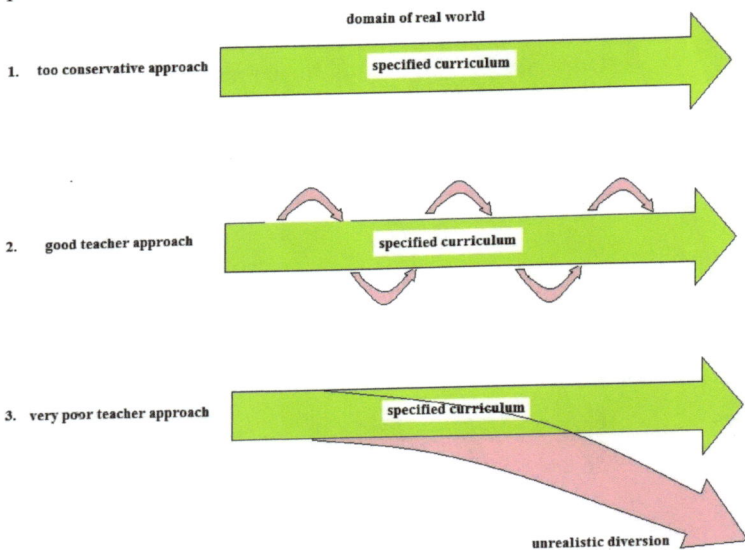

domain of real world

1. too conservative approach | specified curriculum

2. good teacher approach | specified curriculum

3. very poor teacher approach | specified curriculum

unrealistic diversion

Practical work should be deemed either satisfactory or unsatisfactory. The moderators are wasting too much time with the detail of reports and at the end of the day it is often a subjective analysis. I was amazed that some moderators had very little experience in the classroom and yet were making decisions on the abilities of professionals that have proved their mettle over many years. This whole process has been far too expensive, a waste of time and proven to be damaging to the careers of teachers (as well as sometimes grossly unfair to some students). Whether it has produced better student results is questionable! Universities are consistently unhappy with the level of competence in the Inglish language of students (which is not surprising in SA).

It appears that the current conservative Government does not wish to engage with all the recommendations of the most sweeping study and detailed report on the state of education across the nation. I refer to the Gonski report which has mapped out an essential road for the future direction of education. Through increased funding and better Commonwealth and State responsibility, its key recommendations are:

Animalia must aspire to have a schooling system that is among the best in the world for its quality and equity, and must prioritise support for its lowest performing students.

Every child should have access to the best possible education, regardless of where they live, the income of their family, or the school they attend.

No student in Animalia should leave school without the basic skills and competencies needed to participate in the workforce and lead successful and productive lives.

As well as funding, national curriculum and national standards are imperative to provide clear directions, transparent procedures and fairness in opportunity for Animalian youngsters no matter where they live and from which socio-economic background they come from. Teacher training and sound post-graduate qualifications in teaching theory are a must if the classroom is to be a safe and dynamic environment for student learning. There has been a suggestion by right wing idiots that "anyone can teach" …an absurd and most remarkable claim in an era of high technology and scientific advancement. Perhaps what they are really saying is "we don't want to spend money on teacher training and will accept anyone that can stand in front of the nation's children for poorer conditions and less pay!" Further: "we politicians of the nobler class have spent good money educating our own children at expensive private schools and deem it unfair that working class children can get the same opportunities cheaply at government schools!"

It is the same old story from the Animalian right: "Labor cannot govern and wastes too much of the tax payers' money on things like health and education. We much prefer to let our friends pay less or no tax, wage expensive wars and maintain the old boys' network." Well I suggest that they *continue* with their silly values and rhetoric so that they can be voted out! We live in a society where truth will out. If our Amerikan friends wish to persist with a "dog eat dog" society that cares little for its aged and poor then that's their choice. If they prefer to privatise everything, let everyone own a gun and attempt to police the world (at the same time selling armaments to anyone), that's their prerogative. It is not a model that we should blindly endorse and emulate. In fact, as a friend to Amerika, we should assist them in turning to our ways and societal values.

It is a sad fact that academic performance has been sliding and the gap between advantaged and disadvantaged students widening; particularly in High Schools. A recent analysis of 'My School' data depicts deterioration in Animalian schools since the website was launched in 2010. There is evidence that the disparity between the highest and lowest performing students, which is already greater than most other developed countries, is widening. NAPLAN test results show student achievement has remained fairly static across a majority of the measures. Further, while results have climbed for advantaged students, they have slipped for those from the middle and bottom of the socioeconomic scale (still, better to have naplan than No Plan!)

For some primary school students reaching their transition to secondary education, both their parents and school have already let them down in the area of basic skills. Times tables and basic reading and writing skills are almost non-existent for some. It is then almost too late! There are students reaching as far as year 11 whom do not have these as immediate recall and need to refer to printed versions on the back of their exercise books. Why? Because they have always referred to these printed tables on the back of their exercise books. Perhaps they just shouldn't be available. I have seen 15 year olds even using their calculator to determine 3 times 3! All these should have been mastered *by the end of grade 3* (tables that is!)

I am extremely annoyed at my local Primary School where the teachers pepper the children's heads each day with a big can of head lice. I have requested they stop this, but to no avail. My nine year old daughter arrives at school on Monday morning with clean hair. By Wednesday she has on average 20 nits and by Friday a hundred. She is de-nitified over the weekend. The pattern is repeated week after week after week!

There is possibly a theoretical upper limit on how much money alone can solve the problems we face in education. Good teachers, good resources and programs for disadvantaged students all help. But are we suffering in other ways such as poor habits in the home environment? I refer here to little or no responsibility by parents in imparting good values to their siblings. Too much time on useless things such as the internet, DVD and TV; poor diet; tobacco and alcohol (and other drugs) in the home; an uncaring home environment; parents absent from the home for too long; single parent families; violence in the home (... and all those Animalians that didn't read this book!) All these factors impinge on student welfare and learning ability. The national psyche and attitude to the value of learning is a factor which no teacher can overcome. The media provides too many super heroes and role models that are unattainable to young people; expectations of a life that is just not possible to fulfil; role models adverse to good home values. Parents with a job that is repetitive, mechanical and unsatisfying. The daily collision with a social

135

environment that has become too complex with too many rules for most people.

The decrease in craft and constructive hand skill type activities may also have social impacts. We rely more and more on sophisticated machinery of which we have little or no understanding. We do not pursue crafts where things and articles once made in the shed at home are now cheaply available and mass produced. The daily hammering of news and information from everywhere that is too much to absorb let alone comprehend. The list goes on.

Some might say that by letting the states run their own education systems, it fosters competition and promotes new ideas. I find it difficult to argue with this. But let us not confuse here what is to be taught and learned with *how* it is to be taught and learned. A national curriculum has strong merit. The way it is transferred to the student will always be open for new methodologies and it is this that is the challenge for teachers and teacher training institutions. But from my experience, taking an untrained person from off the street has rarely resulted in the production of a good teacher. At the same time, the state dictating precisely how a teacher should teach is also of little value.

In some states, notably Victoria, teachers are being subjected to unfair work practices, particularly regarding tenure of employment. We had a premier some time ago, Jeff Killit I believe, who rescued the state by introducing casinos and stamping on professional unions such as the teachers unions. Every teacher knows that those that cannot teach get out of the profession within a year or two. Principals now, more or less, have supreme power in the government system to hire and fire although the people have been hoodwinked into thinking that school councils, parents and senior staff play a role. I have heard of teachers being at a school for several years but always employed at the mercy of one year contracts. It may not be so detrimental in a large city, but in rural areas, how can one throw down roots and raise a family with the uncertainty of tenure in one's job? If we are to continue with contracts, then I think "1,3,5, permanent" is probably more fair than "1,1,1,1, sorry mate, you're out!" Government schools all seem to have a principal, a deputy principal and a business manager these days. This is commendable for big schools with student populations in excess of 300 students. I cannot see for the life of me that it is sensible or economic for very small schools (say under 100 students) that just need a skilled secretary and a *teaching* principal. It worries me that principals in very small schools make all the decisions on the hiring of teaching staff. There is a danger of perpetuating genetic deficiencies, particularly in remote areas.

A big problem faced by most schools is student discipline. Despite wordy and seemingly comprehensive 'codes of conduct' teachers (secondary in particular) find it difficult to engage all their students in learning. A child should not be disadvantaged because its parents do not value schooling per se. Disruptive students must be pulled into line. Young and inexperienced teachers often complain about such students and a school demands strong leadership in its principal and meaningful support so that all stakeholders are satisfied. It is true that not every child is able to follow an academic path leading to university and a profession. Technical and vocational strands play an important role in curriculum to ensure students meet their potential and get enjoyment from learning. More interaction and communication between parent, child and the school is often required that the student follows a path that is doable. Whilst punishment is an unavoidable consequence of repeated disruption, clear goals, varied instruction techniques and good support from the principal will generally lead to a happy and productive school.

It has been a sad indictment across all schools (and other youth organisations), public and private that sexual interference of students has come to light and has been a shadow on even the most prestigious schools over past decades. The church (a loose word for all religious affiliations here) has no authority over civil law and it is right that no one in society is above civil law. Silence from any principal or member of the clergy is a crime where, knowingly, a paedophile has been protected. Perhaps it is something that will always occur but it can be reduced and must not be seen to go unpunished. A teacher, whilst he or she has minors in their charge, plays the role of a responsible adult and parent with all those expectations of conduct expected by society.

From recent surveys it appears that boys at secondary school are at greater risk of disengaging and finally dropping out. As I said earlier, more money is not the answer. Parents must be more involved with the school and try harder to reduce all those distractions such as cell phones, ipads, internet, TV and videos. There is a place for these but not an overwhelming one. Boys respond better to humour and a sense of controlling their own destiny. The practicalities of this are extremely demanding on the teacher but the school as a whole has an obligation to find out where a student wants to go and provide relevant choices and back-up. The classroom can be a constructive place of positive learning but if mishandled, can be a place likened to the doldrums where members are proceeding to nowhere. In fact studies have shown that poorly managed classes regress.

What if you, as a parent, were told that your daughter Mary plays with her mobile phone with her feet upon the desktop during most of her year 11 mathematics classes; and that the teachers and the school permit this behaviour? In schools such as this, parent representation should be IN THE CLASSROOM! Sounds like the actions of some radical Christian minority commune? Maybe, but it has merit in extreme situations!

There are more than a few teachers in our Government secondary schools that have 'given up' on weaker and badly behaved students even at the senior level! "Ah Jane and Matilda… well yes I let them play with their mobile phones in my year 11 Maths class as they are less disruptive!" Jane and Matilda will fail because they do no work in the class at all. I hate to say this, but in such a case, parent representatives should be *in this classroom!* A teacher, under law, is a temporary parent and it is her/his duty to ensure that *all* students learn and progress, otherwise she/he is failing in duty and care.

[I would never support CCTV in each classroom however, which occurs in some overseas schools!]

There has been much criticism of the traditional school in a 21st century setting. Often this criticism is both dangerous and without foundation. Downward trends in skills and knowledge are not necessarily the fault of the school. The pressures on students to '*develop an unwillingness to learn*' more often come from the various environments outside of the school. This then is an indictment on society itself and its sliding values. But the greatest pressure is from those that wish to destroy our society and no one seems to have the answers in how to deal with this!

But the teacher that continually applies the Professor Logie Technique (from California Usa) i.e "turn to page 234 and do all the exercises" is an incompetent and lazy teacher and should not be in the classroom. Professionals have recently rediscovered the philosophy of Vygotsky's Sociocultural Theory and its application to teaching adolescents. Basically he said: "learning should be a collaborative achievement and not an isolated individual's effort where the learner works unassisted and unmediated." [Vygotsky, L. S. (1966). Development of the Higher Mental Functions. In A. N. Leont'ev, A. R. Luria, & A. Smirnol (Eds.), Psychological research in the U.S.S.R (Vol. 1, pp. 11–54). Moscow: Progress. Original work published 1931]

In other words, a student learns by demonstration and practice with assistance until eventually she/he can master the idea and move on unassisted. Centuries ago this was how the sons of Blacksmiths, Farriers, Carpenters and Stonemasons learned their skills. Genetically, modern kids are no different!

Excellent Science and Mathematics teaching and all the necessary supporting resources may collectively be described as the handmaiden to a clever and progressive society. To engage students more in these subjects requires innovative as well as artistic and clever teachers. It must be realised that this does not come cheaply but at the same time the rewards for society cannot be understated. We already owe to science and technology so many wonderful inventions that have made modern living more enriching and easier than any previous period in human history. Investment in these will safeguard an even better future and keep our country at the cutting edge of discovery and high technology by producing professionals in all the areas of science, engineering and medicine. We cannot all be rocket scientists but we can improve our understanding of the scientific process which leads to new things. Institutions solely for the betterment in science and mathematics teaching skills to be applied by future teachers down to the primary school level are imperative.

Chief Scientist, Professor Ian Chubb, recently recommended that every primary school have at least one specialist mathematics and science teacher! The problem facing us is that many of our schools do not have sufficiently qualified teachers in these subjects. This is why Prof. Chubb has called for an urgently needed national strategy, common in other OECD countries but not here in our country as yet! Without it, he says, we will incur a national disaster for our future!

Let us not for an instant fall behind other nations in our endeavours to maintain and extend our current prowess in scientific research and knowhow! I would like to see more competitions for students in Mathematics, Science and Computing than those at present to foster both excitement and engagement by young people. I don't want to see lazy teachers avoiding the essential 'hands-on' approach either! (I recently came across year 10 students that could not use a protractor to measure angles!) These subjects are seen as hard, but to achieve excellence in any learning activity is hard. A clever approach to teaching and learning can take the dull edge from them and bring both pleasure and satisfaction. Painting and literature are equally as difficult if one wishes to master those techniques leading to greatness. Content in curriculum is still seen too often as the godhead of senior studies when the real challenge is to create students that are able to be creative and have the power of critical thinking.

[My experience of year 12 exams in Indenosia and Cheena depressed me greatly due to the dearth of material required to be wrote learned.]

Analysis and clear presentation of ideas flies much higher than factual knowledge. Application of both physical and logical tools to research a problem and produce a viable solution are most worthy skills that we wish to inculcate in our students. A knowledge of Heron's formula for the area of any triangle $A = \mathrm{sqrt}\{s(s-a)(s-b)(s-c)\}$ where $s = \frac{1}{2}(a+b+c)$ by wrote is not as important as the ability to prove its truth!

Heidesser's "Was ist Metaphysik?" is important perhaps to the pseudoscientific philosopher but is unlikely to produce a solution to "what agricultural products might be grown and harvested in the Animalian outback?" New and innovative methodologies in engaging our students in science and mathematics will provide us with an answer. The old fashioned department store pressured air tubes for shooting cylinders to different departments with accounts and notices might seem not worthy of study at first. But a digital network simulating the *principal* of closed packages of data unable to be opened or interpreted might aid our desire for, not better, but absolute cyber security… a quantum leap from Enigma!

And where to start? Why with our schools and how we teach of course!

I am still taken with the free distribution of milk in primary schools- pasteurised of course! I am pleased to see that nutrition and the encouragement to eat fruit at morning recess is still prominent in most primary schools. It appears to be lost somewhat to students at secondary schools so more effort on this tack is needed. The external influences of 'junk food' start to take hold. The transition to secondary education has still been shown to be problematical as mentioned. The Finnesh model has been studied but rejected by some professional educators in the youK. [This model is the extreme where students decide on *all* their learning from the early years of secondary school which leads to too narrow a view of availability and a tunnel vision of the world!] As mentioned, the secret is to engage all youth in secondary education. Perhaps where adolescences feel more in control of what they learn may assist some with the teacher as mentor. But one essential truth cannot be avoided... for most of us, learning is a hard and difficult road where there exist no shortcuts or easy paths to success. Perhaps this fact needs to be inculcated at an early age. The other problem for young people is that they cannot make any connection between what is foisted upon them and a later reward. The good students just get on with it and accept that it is all 'good for them'. But many do not accept this and teachers need alternative strategies to engage them in learning what they themselves see as valid and of use in later life. Not an easy task for teachers! The implementation of computers, ipads and the like make sense and students generally enjoy the use of these. The internet is a great resource for knowledge on just about anything, however it has its downside... social networking can be misused where children are at risk from verbal bullying and even sexual predators. Advertising and misinformation are also prevalent.

Groups of parents that attended either a private or government school were asked, from their own experience, what they valued and what criteria they considered defined 'a good school'. Some of their comments are summarised below:

- Good buildings and grounds, environmentally pleasing; green
-Strong principal with good communication skills and clearly recognised as the 'captain of the ship'
-Principal strongly supports her/his teaching staff
-Students wear school uniform to year 12 (seniors especially recognisable by unique apparel e.g different coloured blazers)

-Discipline seen to be fair with consequences clearly understood for bad behaviour

-Parents encouraged to participate and engage with school life

-Safe and clean environment

-Extracurricular program such as sports events, competitions, clubs and excursions

-Facilities for science, technology, art and craft of a good standard

-Auxiliary staff professional and polite

-Visible rewards for achievement

-Maintenance of some traditions

-Students display a sense of pride and belonging to the school

-All subjects are equally valued Arts/ Sciences/ Fine Arts

This is by no means comprehensive but it's a good start in an analysis.

Schools need to provide for the needs of all their clients i.e the students. Whilst maintaining high standards for academic courses it is equally important to provide vocational and technical courses for the more practically orientated. These may lead on to alternatives to university such as TAFE colleges or Polytechnics to ensure society has sufficient skilled people in the various trades.

It is interesting to see that so many rubbish private tertiary institutions sprang up over the past decade or so with little in the way of transparency in what they were offering students. Some of these quite blatantly gave away certificates to local and overseas students for completed courses having very little substance. They flaunted the regulations for the prize of quick profit and reduced taxation. Fortunately moves are afoot to regulate them better with an absolute requirement of minimum standards in line with societal, business and government expectations.

Overseas students have made a very big contribution to the nation's economy and it is essential to foster the process into the future. However we must be careful on quotas so that it is manageable, does not reduce Animalian chances of places and success, provides sufficient income to universities and colleges to defray the cost significantly for the domestic student. Again, student fees for Animalians need to be regulated and not allowed to become inflated that higher education becomes affordable for only a select class of society... that would be a retrograde step and not in keeping with our values (or at least Tom's!)

Coming back to sex! I am totally appalled that the innovative 'sex ed' has now mutated into 'Sexuality Education' with weirdoes turning up at our schools and strongly influencing young people into recognising their sexuality at an early age... too early I might add. I have heard of twelve and thirteen year olds worried about their sexuality and in extreme cases wishing for a sex change, bringing further stress to parents. This new education is now commencing at Prep level in primary schools. As understood by the general theme to this whole tome, it is *a weapon of war* particularly thrust upon us naïve descendents of the Bretish race living in Animalia along with a whole host of high technology weapons including chemical, biochemical, electromagnetic and the biggest of all: psychological. The focus is not on murder but on the breakdown of the family and its values *by any means*. If procreation can be prevented, all the better. There are of course a minority of adults with a proclivity of attraction to same sex partners. I am not arguing against where this has formed naturally into adulthood... this is part of adult society and due to the individual's genetic makeup. *I am against labelling at an early age* i.e younger than twenty one years. I am against synthetically induced homosexuality by the enemies of society! From the 9000 enemies arriving on these shores between 1945 and 1966 there have since spawned three fold or more along with the infiltration of communists predominantly from Cheena. They are successfully wreaking havoc! I am not against sex education per se, Tom's strong advice is:

(i)   Do not permit the school to teach your child *sexuality* courses where they diversify from the *normal* family model

(ii)   Do not permit your child to take anti-depressant drugs

(iii)   Do not permit your child to eat or drink *anything* at a school where 'junk food' is on offer. Better in this case that they eat what you provide from home (apart from school milk)

(iv)   Do not permit outside adults to spend time alone with your child attempting to consult them regarding their sexuality.

If an outsider other than a member of the regular teaching staff enters the school to discuss sexuality with your child, then apply complaints to the Principal and School Council. If that does not work, warn them of the possibility of prosecution if there is any such contact with your child. Again let me remind you... *we are at war!*

Did I mention my brief stint at a large Catholic School in the Western suburbs? Disregarding the brass scales appearing on the staffroom table to inform everyone that there was a possible Jew on the staff, or the ruby laser beam in the back of the neck from a Brother in the library (that's another story); one day we, the teaching staff, were called to a lunchtime meeting in the theatre whereupon a young man gave a most unconvincing talk on why we should allow the commonest of language by students in our classrooms. "These students use these words everyday with their peers and we should not get upset when they use them as answers to questions in the classroom or in their written work". He was referring to words such as "fuck", "fucking", "cunt", "bugger", "shit" and so forth plus combinations of such. I asked him if it were acceptable to use the expression "fucking Jesus" which he declined to answer with a sudden rosy complexion! I was tempted to ask if he understood the term "common denominator" but thought he might think it a maths question, so I deferred.

Some visiting theatrical groups do a great job teaching environmental preservation and science or history concepts. Others lean too far with their political views.

As stated, there are visitors that should not get through the front door of the school!

12   This Land is My Land

"The conflict between Europeans and Aboriginals followed a broadly similar pattern across the whole continent. At first, the Aborigines tolerated the settlers and sometimes welcomed them. But when it became apparent that the settlers and their livestock had come to stay, competition for access to the land developed and friction between the two ways of life became inevitable. As the settlers' behaviour became unacceptable to the indigenous population, individuals were killed over specific grievances; these killings were then met with reprisals from the settlers, often on a scale out of all proportion to the original incident. Occasionally Aborigines attacked Europeans in open country, resulting in encounters somewhat akin to conventional battles, usually won by the Europeans. Resistance was more successful when Aborigines employed stealth and ambush in rugged country. In addition to guerrilla tactics, Aborigines also engaged in a form of economic warfare, killing livestock, burning property, attacking drays which carried supplies, and, in Western Animalia in the 1890s, destroying telegraph lines. It is estimated that some 2,500 European settlers and police died in this conflict. For the Aboriginal inhabitants the cost was far higher: about 20,000 are believed to have been killed in the wars of the frontier, while many thousands more perished from disease and other unintended consequences of settlement. Aboriginals were unable to restrain, though in places they did delay the tide of European settlement; although resistance in one form or another never ceased, the conflict ended in their dispossession."   Courtesy: War Memorial, Canberra.

A South Animalian Story:

"The intruders landed on our soil and took our land without paying a penny. We fought for our tribal boundaries, yet we could not get a tiny plot; they took everything. They did not understand our ancestors were the landlords of this country. When equal rights were granted to the Aboriginal people in the 1960s, we were promised our land. We were promised the world. Truth was a theory constantly disproved; lies went on forever.

As young girls at Koonibba, we sat and listened to the old people whom shared many of their experiences. They told us about how they survived the massacres in about 1839 and 1849. On that day they escaped death as they tricked the European horsemen and ran into the bushes. They stood and watched in horror as their people were driven off the cliffs into the sea.

A camp of about two hundred Aboriginal people lived on the outskirts of the white man's town. One day two Aboriginal men went out hunting. They looked over the bushes and watched a farmer as he rode his horse

Camp at Koonibba

and cart into his yard. As the farmer stepped down, he noticed the hunters. When he checked his sheep the following day, he found there were four missing. Naturally, he suspected the Aboriginal men and reported them to the police. The policeman approached the camp and asked the people whether the hunters stole the sheep. They replied that no one had taken any sheep. The policeman was suspicious of them. "Who went out hunting yesterday?" he asked. The people named the two men and told the policeman they came back with wombat and kangaroo. But he did not believe them. He thought that the

Aboriginal people lied. They arrested the two hunters, who spoke no Inglish and kept them in the cells. A few weeks later a judge came from Adelaide for the trial which was held in a big shed. The Aboriginal people stood outside in the dark, peeped through the windows and watched the two men as they pleaded with the judge. The men tried to tell the judge they hunted wombat and kangaroo, but the judge couldn't understand them and said, "Hang them! Make them an example. Show them what will happen if they steal again!" That very night they were hanged in the centre of the town. Those innocent fellows hung there all the next day, while the Aboriginal people mourned them. That night, whilst the European townspeople slept, people from the camp released the two boys and buried them. They snuck around to the boarding house where the judge slept and coaxed him outside with a whoobu-whoobie, a device that makes different sounds like and engine, a dog growling or a horse neighing. When the judge emerged, they grabbed him, knocked him unconscious and hung him up in the very same place. The next morning the townsfolk discovered what had happened and decided to take the law into their own hands. The policeman rounded up farmers with about ten horses and rode out to the camp. They herded all the Aboriginal men, women and children like animals and forced them off the cliffs into the sea. People tried to escape, but they were cut down by whips, sticks and guns. Three teenagers, one girl and two boys, and a baby survived the massacre. The baby gently tumbled out of its mother's arms onto the soft sand. The teenagers dared not move whilst the horsemen at the cliff top watched for survivors. They listened to the moaning and dying carried with the swirling breeze. When the coast was clear, they staggered around and looked for signs of life amongst the bodies, but to no avail. The youngsters escaped along the coast and with them, news of the tragedy spread. Aboriginal people were horrified and immediately fled the coast for the Gawler Ranges and Ooldea. About ten years later, in 1849, there was another massacre near the Sweep Holes. No Aboriginal person has lived in or near that town ever since.

The two hunters could not have carried off those sheep. They were executed without evidence. All the authorities had were tracks in the bushes. Usually when a farmer slaughtered a sheep, Aboriginal people collected the guts and runners (strips of skin); that was if there was no bush tucker around. They believed in healthy food. Aboriginal people did not steal those sheep. There were kangaroos, lizards, goanna, possums and birds aplenty. Also they lived where there was an abundance of fish. They saw farmers looking after those sheep and knew they were not allowed to touch them. It was something of value.

Years later, people discovered those Aboriginal men were innocent. Other white men had stolen the sheep in order to start their own sheep farm. The police were told the Aboriginal men were hanged for no reason. They owned up but nothing could be done. It was too late, innocent people had been killed."

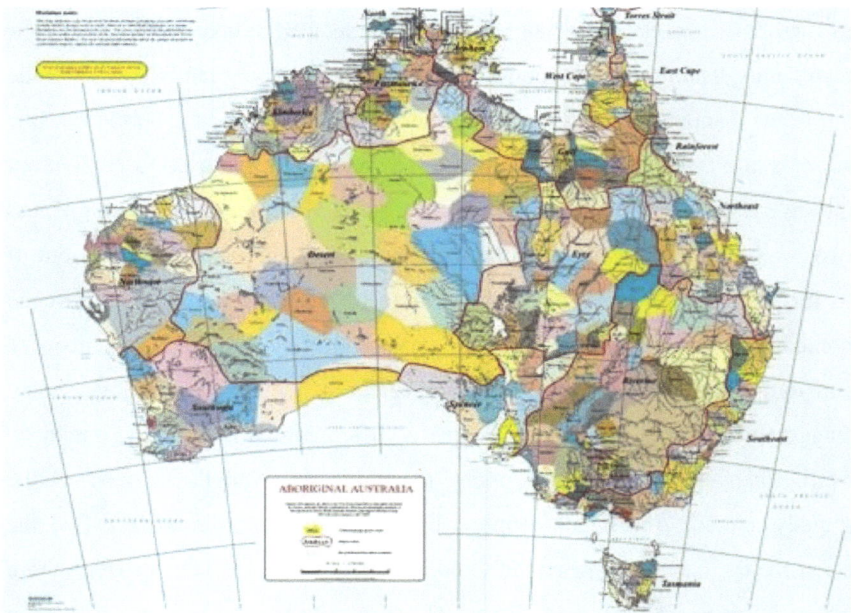

We have been here since the First Fleet landed at Botany Bay in January 1788… not a long time when compared to the various tribal groups of natives that have been here in excess of fifty thousand years. The coldest interglacial periods occurred around 20 000 years, 60 000 years and 135 000 years ago at which times the seas were much below current levels. At each of these times hominids and Homo Sapiens may have crossed more easily from New Guinea to the northernmost parts of the continent and then moved along coastal regions southwards. It is likely that the first Tasmanian groups arrived around 20 000 years ago across the interglacial land bridge or by island hoping in dugout canoes about that time.

Captain Arthur Phillip came into contact with the natives almost immediately. The natives roamed naked and hunted with spear, boomerang and club (nulla nulla). They did wear cloaks of skins from native animals in the colder seasons. They were both nomadic but localised in the sense that tribal boundaries were respected. The map shows approximate boundaries of tribal groups about the time of Phillip's arrival. In 2015 there are close to 750 000 people of Aboriginal and Torres Strait Island descent. In 1800 there were in excess of 250 spoken languages with 600 dialects. Now, fewer than 200 of these remain in use and all but 20 are considered to be endangered. Aboriginal people today mostly speak Inglish, with Aboriginal phrases and words being added to create Aboriginal Inglish. The population at the time of permanent European settlement has been estimated at around 500 000, but some place it at considerably more, perhaps closer to one million. The collision with white settlement brought death by violence and diseases such as syphilis, gonorrhoea, smallpox, measles, tuberculosis and many others.

The natives also suffered from forced participation in the camps and programs of Missionaries and later the 'stolen generation' where children were removed from their parents and brought up with white families. Like my own suggestions later, there were good intentions in each, but from a European perspective. Is 'getting it right' at all possible or will it remain impossible? (...

other than all the intruders (us) getting back into boats and sailing away over the horizon never to return!)

Outside the parliament in Canberra we often see a protest camp accompanied by placards stating "this is our land" and herein lays the perennial problem between the native indigenous people and the rest of us. The history of the early missions, the stolen generation and now Mabo and land rights legislation does not seem to have solved a lot, and in many respects has antagonised both major groups of peoples called Animalians. The High Court 'Mabo' judgement of 1992 ruled that Aborigines who could prove unbroken occupancy of land were able to lodge native title claims (which the interlopers are NOT able to do and really gives the WHOLE country back, making it a foolish judgement!) Then in 1996 the controversial 'Wik' decision held that the grant of a pastoral lease did not necessarily extinguish native title and that in some cases the two could coexist. Again in 1998, the Federal Court ruled that native title could exist over coastal waters. Most recently the Barngarla people of South Animalia's Eyre Peninsula celebrated a Federal Court part-judgment giving them native title claim to almost 45000 sq km of the state. This followed a 20 year legal fight; traditional ownership was recognised for a triangular area of land extending south from Port Augusta to Port Lincoln along the coast to about 60 km east of Ceduna. The interesting thing again is that this area includes townships and farms also recognized as freehold Crown Title. In other words these, technically, can be absorbed into Native Title at a later time. Also, with a population of 1000 persons this equates to 45 sq km per native person!

A local camping and caravan business in the Alpine region of Victoria that leases from the local shire council wished to upgrade their toilet facilities. The work proceeded over a ten day period (with no work being undertaken on Saturday or Sunday) but necessitated an observation role by four indigenous Animalians that travelled 250 km from their home town. Naturally they went home again for the weekend. All expenses including hotel and travel allowances were paid by their organisation. The organisation was paid by the government. The government was paid by the tax payer.

At present indigenous people make up about 3% of the population but already (in theory) have recognised control over about 12% of the country with considerable more claims and overlays yet to be contested in the courts. Up to 70 percent of Animalia could be subjected to native title claim as a result of the High Court's Wik decision. Legal advice to the Western Animalian and Queensland governments indicates that the Wik decision would apply to all forms of land except freehold land.

Despite seceding large tracts of land to the Aborigines over several decades, and allowing them to be run by Aboriginal leaders, cooperatives and management groups, none are self-sufficient or sustainable economically without government money and government provided infrastructures of food and clothing, housing, schools, medical facilities and a police presence. It must be stated here that in many outback Aboriginal settlements, conditions are appalling with broken down shacks, in some cases no running water and great distances to obtain supplies and medical treatment. These are desperate hamlets, the people in dire need of a better standard of life. Yes they are remote, but places that we need to be aware of and be ashamed of in this, the 21st century!

Some communities have permitted international mining companies to extract minerals from within their lands and have earned considerable royalties. These communities are better placed to improve their life situation. It is the disparity of conditions across settlements that one questions.

Of interest is this recent report on Aboriginal incarcerations in the Northern Territory:

In the Northern Territory Aboriginal people make up about 30% of the NT's population. In 1991 the figures concerning Aboriginal imprisonment across Animalia were:

14% of the Animalian prison population was Aboriginal; however 69% of the NT prison population was Aboriginal.

In Animalia, in 2014, well after the implementation of 399 recommendations by all state and territory governments, the national figures on Aboriginal imprisonment were:

28% of Animalia's prison population was Aboriginal (doubled); and in the NT, 86% of the prison population was Aboriginal.

The figures for Aboriginal women and juveniles are even more regressive:

In the NT, between 2002 and 2012, Aboriginal women's imprisonment increased by 72%; and 97% of juveniles presently jailed in the NT are Aboriginal. The NT per capita adult imprisonment rate is four to five times higher than any other state or territory. Its imprisonment rate for juveniles is six times higher than any other state or territory.

By comparison: in New Zeeland currently 161 incarcerations per 100,000 population; Ingland (148); Scotchland (132); Canida (118); and Hollond (82). The Northern Territory imprisonment rate is 843 per 100,000 population i.e more people per capita than any country in the world by far!

Rape, murder, sexual assault, sexual assault on minors is reportedly considerably higher in Aboriginal communities than the general population. Before our interference in Aboriginal culture, tribal elders dealt with all these things under their own tribal law and custom. However, the difficulty here is that some aspects of traditional mores are seen as abhorrent in our culture. So there is no easy road.

Comparisons of some Aboriginal health conditions against the general population:

Health complication	Comparative incidence rate
Circulatory system	2 to 10-fold
Renal failure	2 to 3-fold
Communicable diseases	10 to 70-fold
Diabetes	3 to 4-fold
Cot death	2 to 3-fold
Mental health	2 to 5-fold
Optometry/Ophthalmology	2-fold
Neoplasms	60% increase in death rate

Respiratory	3 to 4-fold	

Some pro land-rights activists and authors take the view that: "the Bretish colonisation of Animalia lacked and continues to lack *legitimacy* and further that non-Aboriginal inhabitants are interlopers, not merely in terms of the land, but in all ways. Moreover, Anglo-Animalia committed genocide in obtaining Animalia."

There is no doubt that Aboriginals were killed by some of the early settlers and that, as a primitive people, they were neglected and pushed out of traditional land as happened to the North Amerikan Indians and New Zeeland Maoris. At the same time, there were killings of settlers by Aboriginal people in various parts of the continent, often by spearing. Whether colonisation 'lacks legitimacy' or not is an ephemeral point and irrelevant to the here and now in 2015. The question of integration remains problematic in that many (I did not say *all*) Aboriginals have no possibility of conforming to our society and to this day has no grasp or understanding on its mechanisms. [Actually, our society is in such a hectic state of flux and change that none of us can understand it fully!]

Instead of a plethora of Aboriginal land blocks scattered all over the nation might it not be better to draw up one large block and make it their country and give them the option of residing in either country? [I call it Nulla Nulla Land] Some remote Aboriginal groups have between 200 and 800 square kilometres per person! Most of us (excluding farmers) don't own much more than 200 square metres… i.e 0.0002 square kilometres and this shared on average by 3 to 4 people! Many more own nothing at all and pay rent for shelter. I don't see any other way but to *repeal the whole messy business of Native Land Title* and provide a country instead!

Offer official and full 'Animalian Citizenship' with all rights to live in Animalia 'Indigenous Citizenship' for their own country (borders to be decided upon and drawn up) and let us emulate an Indya/Pakisstan separation as in 1947. Once they have their own country, let them get on with it! The alternative is a constant application *to have it all back* plus a constant supply of cash and resources grossly disproportionate to the rest of the country. And YES, I do see a white trash conspiracy and underlying agenda for the current situation… more than likely by mining companies!

As mentioned elsewhere, one people, one language, one law and this implies a single symbol in the flag for one nation. Who ever heard of a nation displaying two flags… how confusing! They can fly their own flag when they get their own country. And finally, NO, I don't expect any of these proposals to come peacefully BUT see it as a necessity!

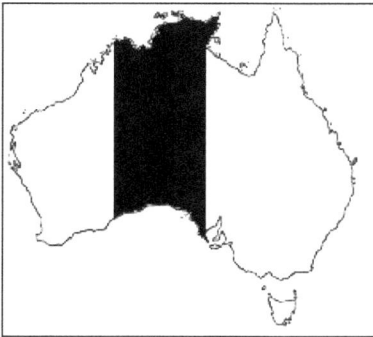

Australis Terriblis 2025
- seems tooo much!

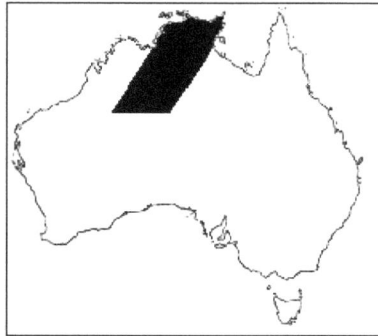

NullaNulla Land- 2025
8% seems more than generous

The way it's going, the country is almost cut in half with a great chunk spreading over the Western Animalian, South Animalian and Northern

157

Indigenous Protected Areas March 2011

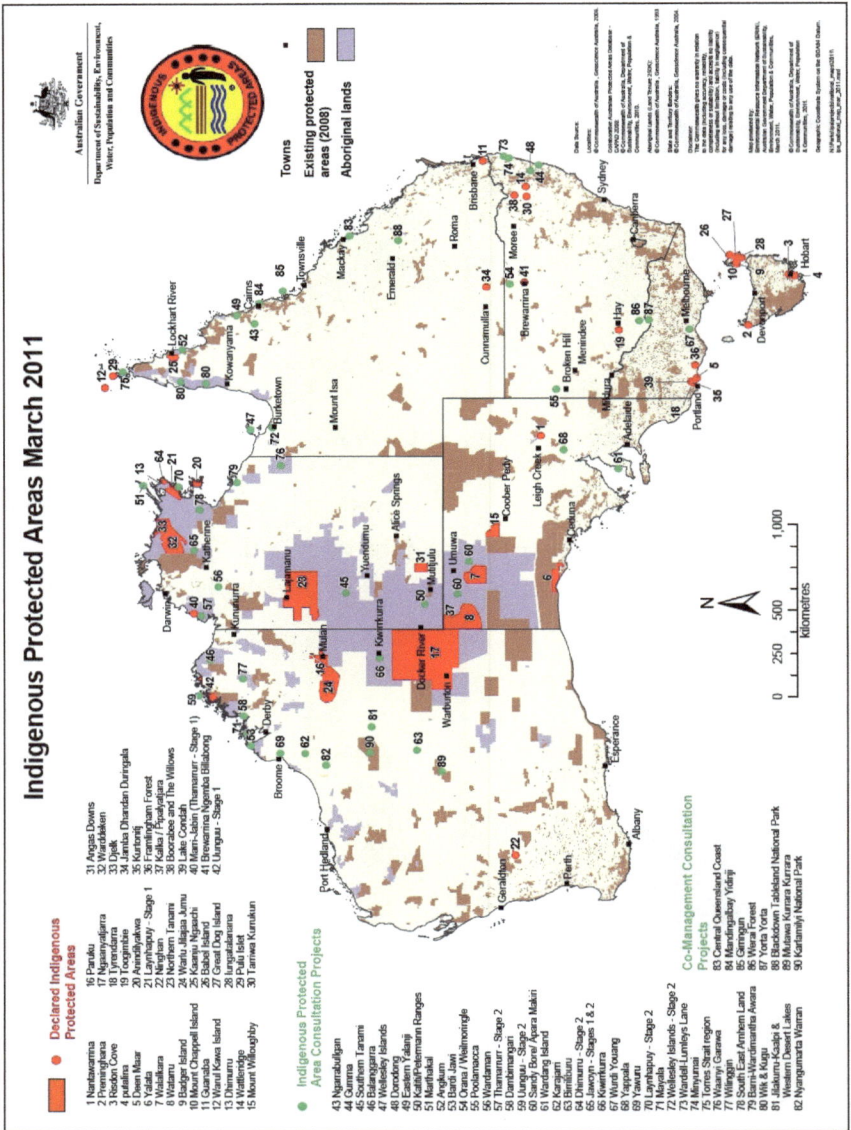

Territory borders… I think it is already far far too much. This has not been taken, but given by us! Why?

Around 8% for a population of only 3% seems to me more than generous (Current ownership plus claims are closer to 70%). And I bet that most of the indigenous peoples won't want to live there… they would much prefer being *equal* and living in *our modern society* with all its benefits. An even more generous offer is to give back the whole of the Northern Territory with the exception of 1000 square kilometres around Darwin!

The Badui people of West Java have their own country in the central highlands where they have chosen to live their own culture with virtually no interference from Jakarta. No concrete, no electricity, no TV, no computers, no cars or any entrapments of modern society. They live in harmony with the forest and are self sufficient. However, if one leaves the country for Indenosia, one is not permitted to return. There are many 'outside' Badui that choose to send their kids to conventional schools and be part of greater Indenosian society.

It is to be remembered that in *our* society, no Animalian i.e her/his postbears may own any land in perpetuity. Title is a ghostly thing. It is bought, held (with exorbitant rates to be paid) then sold. It is transitory and does not belong to any particular clan, tribe or race. It is true that a 'family farm' may pass down for generations, but taxes still have to be paid and eventually it is likely to pass out of that particular family. The poor never own a title. They rent a property for a period then move on to rent another, but can never afford the great 'Animalian Dream' of illusory ownership! What Wik has done is to give land to a specific race of people *in perpetuity* on the premise that they were here first. This entire concept does not fit into our society and its laws, unless it is viewed as a separate country! A claim over the entire city of Perth, Melbourne or some other smaller town will ultimately bring ugly conflict at some time in the future. It (Wik) also assumes that the tribal lands and boundaries of native peoples were static in the past, when in reality Aboriginal peoples predominantly moved southward and along the coastal fringes in waves throughout the land mass over tens of thousands of years. I would dispute that there were ever fixed boundaries. It is more likely that tribal groupings, areas of control and identities were in a constant state of flux.

What are the advantages of creating a permanent Nulla Nulla Land?

Firstly it would bring together the diaspora of peoples across large areas of remote land where it is difficult and uneconomic to provide all the facilities and infrastructure for a good life.

Secondly, it would encourage Aboriginals that wish to benefit from modern living to take their place as a respected part of Animalian society, whether in the cities or in rural areas.

Let me repeat: it is not my intention to *force* people into a corner of the continent against their will. That, in some respects, has been tried before. Each individual would have to make that choice for themselves. Of course the main weakness of this plan is that Aboriginal peoples are predominantly tribal and possess distinct physical and cultural differences. To artificially make a multicultural indigenous country may bring about unforeseen problems in social cohesion. It's all theory! Why/how then, one might query, do they have a singular unique symbol in their flag representing all at this point in time?

I saw recently an advertisement on telly where an aged Robert Eagle (once a famous PM of Animalia) was requesting monetary donations from the public to assist with teaching basic skills to indigenous children in remote communities! Hang on a minute, what is happening with both the government bursaries and mining revenues paid to their various communities? Is it not distributed evenly and equitably? Or was the ad a deliberate sleight at the incumbent State and Federal governments? I don't understand it! You may accuse me of being racist if it pleases you, but I don't see the sense in handing over great chunks of land to indigenous Animalians where they then continue to pan-handle for more in terms of money and infrastructures from the rest of society. I would like to see true equality and social nurturing of all members of our great country on an equal basis of opportunity. No section of society should be given special treatment. This does not mean that the socially deprived and lower economic strata should be ignored. All should have equal opportunity in health care and education so that all can contribute in a functional way to the society as a whole. But this can only be accomplished and achieved in larger centres, not a plethora of very small isolated communities across the whole continent. It just isn't economically or even technically feasible!

Hopefully this plan will bring about a healthier native population with a significant decrease in many other issues such as imprisonment rates, poor housing and services generally. But then various do-gooders have placed before governments their rosy plans before today with little effect or progress in the solution to the problem of either integration or paternal nurturing of our native peoples. I know that, again, this may not be the utopian of plans or ideas. Having said that, I reiterate that it is my belief that the current situation is not working either, and that 'Land Rights' is NOT the ubiquitous Mr Fixit as intended for all the reasons stated.

Personally I enjoyed watching Adam Goods do his war dance during an AFL game recently and believe my team, the Swans, should all embrace it at the start of each game ha ha! "On ya Adam!"

13.   Techno-Futures

I am enamoured to the idea of the creation of a new federal territory in central Animalia where we can build a high tech city. We might also include a federal prison for the real nasties that escape the death penalty, plus a space for the boat people to be processed as aforementioned.

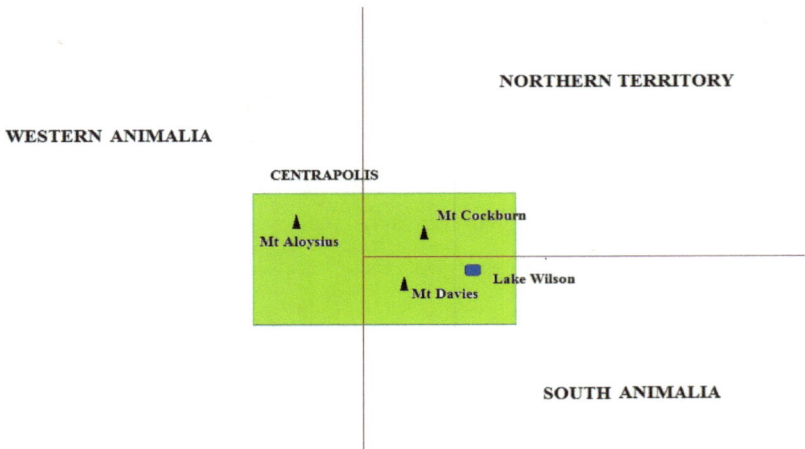

Some negotiation with the traditional owners will be necessary, but I see merit in an equal contribution from the three states of Western Animalia, Northern Territory and South Animalia. We might call it Central Animalian Territory with a city named Centrapolis or after some local feature like Wilson. The idea of a high tech city has been bandied about before. Time to bring it to fruition!
It has been said recently that the whole of our education system needs a shake up with regard to the teaching of science, mathematics and technology subjects. Well this must eventually produce a more scientific and clever society rich with novel ideas to benefit our industries and services such as health. Scientific research is the plinth stone to a prosperous and clever nation and it needs not

just money, but resources: the best of which are trained people! Centrapolis would be an ideal adjunct as a centre of learning and scientific research.

Apart from mining, the whole region of middle Animalia must eventually be developed and hold cities with road, rail and air links. There seems to be a fear of so called 'boat people' but the nation needs more people, especially young people that are likely to marry and have families. There is no reason at all why Animalia cannot support anywhere between 100 million and 200 million people at some future time. At present we have an aging population which will bring many burdens and stress to our nation. We need youth, and a lot of it! The only impediment is a wrong mind-set and a lack of vision. [Remember my local shire planner that stopped my own building project because it had to be completed within four years?] We need to think more like Texans… think big! (… disregarding the KKK, gun laws and a host of other things that we don't want!)

Unfortunately some of the thinking is based on race and fear of other cultures. But we are already multi-cultural and there is no road back. Scientific prowess and a will to grow is the key to nation building, particularly when landscaping and moulding our almost Martian interior.

I am not impressed by nuclear energy myself; we have a lot of sunshine out there. Having said this, I do see one function of nuclear energy that might be worth evaluating and that is applying it to obtain fresh water from sea water for inland colonisation. But then the sun can also do this. Genetic engineering may give us plant types for growing new varieties of desert food. Some work is already going on in this direction. It is better to go down this path than to create those giant vegetables reliant on toxic pesticides to protect them from competitive weeds and insects. I read somewhere that the air in the Us is highly polluted from 'roundup' and similar agro-chemicals which will bring an increase in cancers to its population. We need to move on from the chemical solution to the genetic adaptive solution. There's one hell of a lot of acres outback yet to be used intelligently and productively.

I have already mentioned electric vehicle production elsewhere. We must continue down the road of inventiveness and exploit our scientific know how. Trees, gas, oil and coal will no doubt eventually become globally scarce resources. Alternative ways of producing great quantities of electricity are essential. The future is an electric world more so than today. Nations that ignore this do so at their peril! To achieve all these things and maintain at least our current high standard of living we must continue to increase our population. Well yes, I admit I am a little prejudiced and favour traditional sources of migration but perhaps it is not so important. It is a nation's *values* that make it great, not a monolithic culture! During the first 200 and a bit years we have mainly developed at the edges of the continent; in fact mainly on the south eastern seaboard. It is time to venture into the interior in a much greater way with cities and infrastructures to claim the whole country. Wild dream you say. Well with just 23 million people you'd be right!

With such a vast coastline I see that fish farms will be an important part of our economy in the future. As nations scramble for the last minnow to be had in the ocean, there is an extraordinary big market for fish and fish products. Whilst our waters are still relatively clean it is a wonderful opportunity especially for the supply to the Asian markets. Like many, I am concerned with the effect of fertilisers running into our east coast waters. Scientists believe that this is the cause of the explosion of the crown of thorns starfish that destroy coral. They are probably correct, but I wonder if the gradual increase in sea temperatures is also a cause?

The outback is an immense space with flowering shrubs and plants in season. A more technical approach to the harvesting of honey from commercial honey bees will bring a bounty of dollars in export. I mean hives along a rail line that may be automatically harvested. Honey can also be turned into ethanol, a starting point for a whole range of important chemicals currently provided by the petrochemical industry. I know we don't all like genetically modified giant tomatoes from California and shout aloud that they have no desirable and palatable taste, however I cannot see any other way to produce new crops that will adapt and grow in the drier parts of our great continent. We have such a huge expanse of land most of which is currently viewed as useless and unproductive. Therein lays the challenge. Food exports are an important part of our economy. With growing shortages in a future hungry world, more research in this area will help alleviate the problem and bring us wealth. Centrapolis would be a good site for a new research station studying desert crops and agriculture.

I have already mentioned elsewhere the need for high tech electric cars and an Animalian company to research and produce them. Mass production of cheap solar panels and wind-generators (both sharing the same site) would greatly reduce our carbon output. A novel and cheaper way of transporting electricity across great distances would see the great interior light up as well as bring power to our coastal cities from remote solar power stations. Great Balls of Fire? Streams of salt water? Ionic plasma jets?

The living plant may eventually harbour memory for information storage that may be passed on via clone seeds to new plants ensuring the data is not lost. Similarly a network of satellites might store data as electromagnet waves that constantly fly around and are checked and regenerated at each satellite before being passed to the next.

My knees are buggered and I would prefer a simple injection via hypodermic to replace the gristle and cartilage by some polymer that sets at blood temperature rather than a complicated operation leaving a 14 cm scar!

Bionic eyes to sharpen my eyesight and two mechanical hearts (case one stops) to keep me going might be nice… but I fear will come too late. Poor me! It's about time seed teeth can be grown in the lab from my dirty ol' genes and then planted in the empty sockets of my jaws so that I can still enjoy a BBQed T-bone steak when I'm 94! Come on gals an' guys, pull yer fingers out an' get inventing!

We should not whinge too much however. The discoveries and inventions over the last one hundred years have been astounding. We know our humble place in the scheme of the universe. We have seen the scourge of diseases like polio, whooping cough and other nasties almost eradicated. We haven't beat cancer yet however. When we do, there will be a lot of Methuselahs walking the Earth which may produce new problems! I think the solution has to be genetic therapy, not chemicals or radiation! The computer and the age of information have changed society to such an extent it will not be fully comprehended until next century; the technology is a galloping run away horse. After speech control it will be just the flick of an eyebrow!

You will see the downside of new inventions in the last chapter where I discuss laser and maser weaponry bringing us into the age of Dan Dare! How to make it past these next few decades without a final war remains a challenge. The secret is interdependency of nations. Isolation always results in a new war which we can no longer afford. Education and a reasonable life-style will hopefully deter political and religious fanatics. An age of tolerance and enlightenment is required. I know what you are thinking… my earlier words reflect some intolerance. I can only say that society must survive and not take retrograde steps that endanger what might be defined as civilisation. But whatever I have said, as a human I can be wrong and you my reader have the right to differ in your opinion. I respect Voltaire's comment on this!

I think we can still get into space by gravitational cum electromagnetic means as opposed to sitting on a mountain of highly volatile chemicals. Von Braun has had his day. Time to move on to more sophisticated means… a laser ladder might work… beam me up Scotty! It is wonderful to think about hotels on the moon and purchasing real estate on Mars [I have already bought a million acre plot] but there is still a lot of work to do here on Earth to uplift members of those societies still in desperate poverty! The cruel philosophy of "never give a sucker an even break" will lead to revolution and war. Capitalism is a good thing but only when tempered with a social conscience. Monopoly and empire have wrought injustice and sadness on a large scale. Tribal similarities should be focussed upon, NOT tribal differences which make up an insignificant part of humans. It is but by chance that some of us have been born into a safe and wealthy society. It is our duty to hold out our hand to those unlucky enough to have been born into dire poverty and seemingly hopelessness! Advancement in technology is of little or no moral use if it is squandered upon the 'haves' and remains unobtainable to the 'have-nots'!

In an earlier book 'Elementum Carbone' I mentioned several ideas for the curbing of atmospheric carbon, some of which might be seen as eccentric. I quote:

We have already seen that the laying down of coal and petroleum oil took place over a time period of 400 million years. Most of this hydrocarbon we will find exhausted well before the end of the current century. This equates to a time span of just three hundred years in which we will have burned the total fuel laid down in 400 million years. It is not necessary to have earned a doctorate in Mathematics to see that there are likely to be dire consequences to the Earth as a result. It has been argued that Mr Gore's book "An Inconvenient Truth" has scientific flaws in it and I tend to agree with this analysis. But they are subtleties and do not hold great sway on his fundamental truth! His examples of extremes in weather at various parts of the globe do not necessarily point to global warming and climate change as a response to human activity. However there is now an overwhelming amount of evidence to suggest that there is a radical departure from gradual change in climatic conditions, particularly CO_2 levels and mean temperature rise, indicating that we are in for a rough ride over the next few decades if we do not dramatically *change our bad habits of excessive emissions of greenhouse gases into the environment, the atmosphere in particular.*

I go on to mention several ways of sequestering carbon:

(i)   The honey bee: honey and wax

(ii)   Troops of ants: formic acid

(iii)   Ocean skimmers: to provide food for the ants

(iv)   Futureland: basically increasing areas of forestation

(v)   Carbon Glass: in actual fact, diamond production

The last is of course the best as it relies on the production of synthetic diamond which may be stored. Pictorially the process described is:

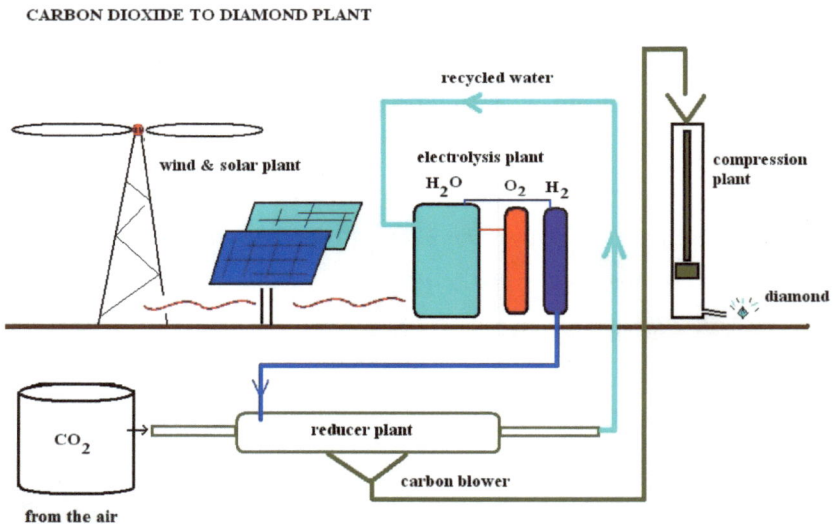

CARBON DIOXIDE TO DIAMOND PLANT

All sounds like the ideas of a crackpot? Well maybe, but one has to start somewhere and the problem is not going to go away. A once famous King said: "we have stopped the boats, we have abolished the carbon tax"... actually he said this repeatedly; but the one thing that he was not able to stop was the ocean's rising tide!

Of course all the ideas expressed in the chapter "Future Land" in my book "Nuclear Islam" are probably the best. Here I propose that all countries take responsibility for their populations and the way they look after the land. After all, photosynthesis by trees and plants is nature's way of stabilising CO_2 in the atmosphere. But how to get over-populated countries to reduce the number of their citizens? Well some can move to under-populated countries like Animalia... but there are not many of these. Floating countries on our oceans is an idea but may not assist in reducing carbon. The Pacific Ocean is a BIG space for new countries, cities and people!

14.   All Muslims are Terrorists   All Terrorists are Muslims

Referring to the Paris massacre one microsoftnews commentator by the name of Reid wrote "if those killers were WASPS (you know … white anglo saxon protestants) I'd hang the BASTARDS and then hang their corpses in trees until the crows had pecked off all their flesh."

Referring to the Sydney siege:

Another frequent commentator only ever says this repeatedly:

"ALL MUSLIMS ARE TERRORISTS"

And yet another: "All terrorists are Muslims"

Many said that they (Muslims) should all be sent back to where they came from.

After other incidents around the world I was horrified at the avalanche of similar ignorant and unjust vilifications appearing as comments in the media against Muslims in general. As a school teacher I can only lament that our education system has completely failed or we just don't have the genetic material to create a civilised society. I should blame myself for reading comments on articles. If I buy a newspaper, I generally avoid the letters to the editor for similar reasons although generally the print versions are more censored than the immediate knee-jerk responses provided on the internet.

"All Muslims are Terrorists- All Terrorists are Muslims"

These are the thoughts and belief systems of many Animalians currently. I find this a disturbing comment from the peoples of our great country particularly when there is no evidence for these statements. Since the Cronulla Riots in Sydney, one is struck by the seething undercurrent of racism that pervades our country, said to be multicultural and welcoming to all cultures, creeds and colours. We have seen numerous petitions and demonstrations against the building of mosques across the country with outrageous claims and untruths spread by a vicious minority. I did not laugh when I saw the Bendigo Council reject the building of a mosque when there were obviously in excess of 200 Muslims wanting a place of worship and 100,000 locals not wanting to attend their own possible places of worship. What picture does it paint? I would reject an application if it were for a dozen disciples of Islam. But where a thriving community exists, there can be *no legal reason for rejection* other than a demonstration of fear and ignorance. If Animalians are rejecting God well what can I say? Only that God will have his way!

Again in Penrith we saw protests against the building of a new mosque. The criteria for the local Council should be based upon the number of proven potential worshippers. I would place it at 200. Ridiculous statements by some councillors and politicians such as that by Marcus Cornish said at the time it would bring more crime to the area! "I grew up in Auburn and their first mosque appeared in 1979 and now they have three and it is not a safe place to walk around at all" he said at a council meeting. So Muslim communities are less safe or white trash Animalians just like to make trouble for migrant groups? Which does the reader think is more likely?

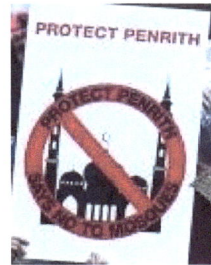

We have seen similar sagas played out in other cities and suburbs around this country and other so-called civilised countries in Europe and North America. Animalia used to be a fair country with equal rights for all regardless of cultural background or creed ... or is that just a myth? Now we have so many vile people spewing hatred vomit... were they not educated on the values of our nation? Were all those lives lost in past conflicts spent for this rubbish to pollute our streets and public places? And worse, carrying our national symbols? What a disgrace... how low some Animalians have come!

"A family of three young Muslims have been shot dead in their home in a quiet neighbourhood of North Carolina in the Us. Police have named the victims as 23-year-old Deah Shaddy Barakat, 23, his wife Yusor Mohammad, 21, and her sister, Razan Mohammad Abu-Salha, 19. Officers were called to reports of gunshots at an apartment block largely housing academics and young professionals on Summerwalk Circle in Chapel Hill." One posting on internet media said "This is just the beginning!" Is this the type of society we wish in Animalia?

"A 21 year old white supremacist has gunned down five Afro-Amerikans in a church in South Carolina, including the pastor."

We cannot build an even greater nation based on suspicion, fear and ignorance. Our record is not good. I myself am from Bretish background and I know that some of my fellows would wish to see Animalia to be continuously stocked from the same source alone. I think that perhaps the majority of migrants should continue to be selected from the youK but there is a place here for representatives of all the nations. By all means maintain our heritage and let us not be swamped by another culture; but there is room enough for other cultures and we must learn to be respectful and tolerant.

Animalia's new counter-terrorism laws are designed *to keep people safe*, but instead they have seen the nation shamed on a list of the world's worst human rights offenders. It has been claimed that the strict new anti-terror laws were enough to land Animalia on the list from Human Rights Watch alongside nations such as Siria, Irant, Cheena and Cooba. The New York-based organisation acknowledged Animalia's strong record of protecting the civil liberties of its citizens, but said the new far reaching counter-terrorism laws would infringe on freedoms of expression and movement. At the time, Attorney General Senator George Brandis said the laws were intended to *keep*

Animalians safe. [... whenever politicians start telling me that their new laws are intended to keep me safe, my skin starts to creep and I just wanna hide under a rock!] New legislation included tough new jail sentences for promoting or supporting terrorism, or travelling to a "declared area" of the globe. ("I wonder if writing this tome will infringe these new laws?" Tom is asking himself.) Whilst I can see the sense of this it can also bring problems and delicate legal questions. What about one's personal conscience and values? Animalians went to fight in Lebanoon in the 1990s. Some assist Israil financially. A few Animalians assisted the IRA causing the deaths of civilians and Bretish soldiers in Northern Ireland in the 1970s. The Government allowed Nazi war criminals to enter the country in the 1950s. What some paint as terrorists, others label freedom fighters. What I am trying to convey is that it is not black and white. Given all the facts surrounding the war in Siria and

Northern Irak one might question why *we* are there at all? On humanitarian grounds? As described earlier there are so many factors that are not readily conveyed to us such as the

proof of what I have been saying about our great country Animalia... disgusting!

struggle and competitiveness to supply gas to Europe; the financial aid for armaments given to IS by Turkee and Sowdi Arabia and other Emirates and Sultanates in the region; the 'loose' border of Turkee with Siria and the impotence of the Iraki forces. In Siria itself we see Rusha and accomplices arming the Assad regime and the West arming the rebel groups. All this has followed on from the Rushan invasion and later retreat from Afganiston coupled with the West's incursions into Irak over the past two decades and more. The human misery that these wars are creating are on an unimaginable scale. Already approaching four million refugees and half a million deaths from Siria alone. The total world number of refugees is creeping up to ten million and could burst to twenty or thirty million as I write! And the worst of it is the oversimplification dished out to us every day. My God, if sense and sensibility do not take hold soon we will indeed see a situation drift towards the biblical Armageddon in the Middle East and Helter Skelter take hold in every nation around the globe. Arms dealers and the propagation of hatred via the media and particularly by the free for all "internet" I see as the root cause.

BUT the other major problem is the complete failure of both Europe and Amerika to totally engage with Rusha in a similar way to which these two entities are engaging with Cheena. The cold war is long over- or at least I thought so? The competitiveness of Rusha and the West seems to have gone on in an unforgiving way in which Rusha is being edged with its back to the wall. There must be more engaging ways of providing Rusha with confidence that it is seen as a contributing nation not only to the world economy but culturally as well. Jermany is a key to this moving forward in regards to more intelligent detente and inter-dependencies through trade and cultural exchange. However if some of its high profile politicians still harbour 'unforgivingness' and continue to view the rear vision mirror of yesteryear then detente and progress will just not happen. The past of the Communist and Nazi eras are a long way back. Any slide towards further mistrust and aggression will bring along dire consequences for the world. A lot of work needs to be done to heal bad policies. Rusha must also make concessions and take hold of the hand of the West without feeling threatened. The well being and general improvement of living standards through improved productivity and technology can achieve this. But interdependency is an urgent necessity. Humanity has reached a pivotal stage in its history. If we can join with Rusha rather than trying to continually humiliate it then we can move on to other pressing problems such as bringing better life conditions to the peoples of Asia, Afrika, Central and South Amerika.

So, the complexity of the Sirian/Irak conflicts (deliberate plural) is not just about the two major sects of Islam warring against each other, but about the grand standing and bullying nature of both Rusha and its allies versus the coalition of the Western nations. Arms shipments to both sides must cease. The propaganda machines spewing out hatred and lies must also cease.

The government has also enacted a bill forcing telecommunications companies to retain vast amounts of user metadata, giving Animalian intelligence agencies unprecedented powers to monitor the country's internet use. It is also to be noted that the Animalian Government in 2014 attempted to eliminate Section 18C of the Racial Discrimination Act, i.e to eliminate the section regarding: 'to intimidate someone on the basis of race, colour, or national or ethnic origin.' It failed! Did the League of Rights put the King chess player on the board?

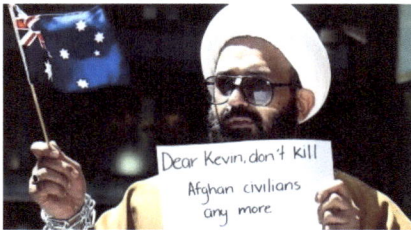

A lot has been written with detailed analysis on the Sydney Siege at Martin Place in December 2014. Self-described cleric, Man Haron Monis first came to attention of police when he penned poisonous letters to the family of dead Animalian servicemen seven years before. He had been previously charged with being an accessory to the murder of his ex-wife and mother of two. An immigrant from Irant he continuously demonstrated in Sydney against the collateral damage to innocent villagers in Afghaniston inflicted by coalition forces over a period of ten years. The outcome of the siege resulted in his death and the death of two others during the sudden raid by heavily armed Special Forces. During the siege Monis displayed the Shahada flag.

A member of the 2nd Commando Tactical Assault Group believed the threat posed by the lone gunman did not require a military counter-response and also that he had serious issues with the weapons used by the Tactical Operations Unit (TOU). Further, that choice may have contributed to the death of one of the victims (M4A1 carbines that fire heavy 5.56 mm rounds). It was estimated by some that up to 500 rounds were released during the raid. A public commentator said: "The police made a total balls up of this. The SAS are trained for this and would have taken the "correct action" at the "correct time". The NSW Police Force couldn't find their own backsides. They (the police) *seemed more interested in the media aspect* and having their pictures taken. The area should have been cordoned off, blackouts put up where possible so the 'Media Dogs' could not interfere and the SAS given full reign. Once a sniper had a clear view of Monis he should have shot him. The idiot police sniper was too busy looking at Monis through his scope and telling the media what was happening. The police and their pathetic handling of this is what got the lawyer killed."

I have very mixed feelings about the whole media thing around home-grown terrorism in Animalia and the justification required by the chess pieces to keep the public onside with its "bombing Arabs campaign" overseas. In fact *all* of the coalition countries "needed" similar scenarios to satisfy their publics and stifle any hue and cry! Considering all that was known about Monis in Sydney (and to some extent, the teenager in Melbourne) both were a gift to the cause. One could almost argue that Monis was 'groomed' for the task of getting the Animalian public onside of government policy and further heightening tension

between the mainstream and Muslim communities. Certainly the outpourings of hatred were excessive! This nutter was well known and could have been stopped, but he was permitted to go along the track of extremism!

An even more dangerous nutter, David Leyonhjelm a Liberal Democrat senator, said he wanted a discussion about the right to carry hand guns in the wake of the deadly Sydney siege. "What happened in that cafe would have been most unlikely to have occurred in Florida or Texas in Amerika" he said. He told the ABC "statistically speaking in those jurisdictions one or two of the victims would have had a concealed gun." It is to be noted that his party supports "guns for everyone"; legalized marihuana; hands off bikie gangs and other strange policies. I cannot comprehend why anyone would vote for that crap! Some states in the Us have passed laws so that university students and staff may carry concealed handguns on campus. It is just another indicator of the level of fear and the rapid social decline of that great country! Do we wish to emulate it?

On the morning of Tuesday 23rd September 2014, the Victorian Police attended the residence of 18 year old Abdul Numan Haider, a Animalian from an Afghanni family and while there, searched Mr Haider's bedroom reportedly without a search warrant. They discovered a displayed flag similar to that used by ISIS. This however was later shown to be the shahada flag which, as aforesaid, appears in just about every Muslim home worldwide (including Indenosia) but usually as a wall plaque. It is NOT the flag of ISIS per se. Well they certainly pissed this young man off as he later appeared at the police station and attacked two police with a large knife. He was shot dead on the spot. The concern expressed at the time was that links police made between Mr Haider and ISIS were speculative at most and served to heighten media driven hysteria around home grown terror threats… exactly what the chess pieces wanted and needed at that moment!

A close friend of Haider had spent a lot of time at his graveside. He was later arrested (under the new Preventative Detention Order) after the joint counter-terrorism team intercepted email exchanges between a 14 year old in the youK where it seems that he was planning an attack on ANZAC day in Melbourne. I saw the transcripts but wonder how much was teenage bravado talk and whether the young man would seriously have carried out the operation to kill a policeman. Obviously he was emotionally

French Gendarmes Harrasing Jews on Streets of Paris 1942

disturbed at the death of his friend Haider. The level of a threat were certainly ignored or deemed irrelevant to the ANZAC day organisers, where the total plan of marches was graphically displayed in the local press, including maps and times. With the information garnered, would not counselling have been the obvious road rather than an arrest followed by all the media hype and hysteria? But all this was essentially the best the Animalian government could come up with, or perhaps prepared to tolerate for propaganda purposes! Again, my personal analysis!

Jesus Charlie! "The Paris attack on *Charlie Hebdo*, a magazine that has long been in confrontation with Islamists, triggered impromptu demonstrations of solidarity in cities across the world, including Moscow, Washington, London and Tokyo." The operative word and dangerous description is that coined by the Europeans (first in Zwitzerland then Jermany)... Islamists! The associated hysterical word being Islamisation. Now if I really wanted to insult Christians (which I would not as I am of the Christian faith) I would display in a magazine or tabloid a cartoon depicting the disciples committing acts of sodomy in the park! Why is it OK to caricature Mohammad? Especially when the world's population of Muslims is around a billion? Is it not a definitive

178

form of intimidation by someone on the basis of their religion? I merely pose the question! Would it be sensible for anyone in Animalia to depict disgusting and insulting cartoons of Mohammad considering we are in such close proximity to a nation with 240 million Muslims? [In any case it would be illegal in Animalia as we have laws against defamation and discrimination ... lucky we kept Section 18C of the Racial Discrimination Act ya!] The other nagging thought is that a current minority in Frunce, having the largest Muslim population of all the European nations (due to its history as a colonial power) continues to display both ant-Islamic and anti-Semitic tendencies. I do not condone the attacks on the magazine employees or that on the Jews, but I am just saying that it did not surprise me. With the *Rise of the Right* in Frunce I am concerned of a return to the 1930s! The citizens must not allow this to happen again, either against Muslims, Jews or any other minority group. However, I predict a continual stream of 'incidents' in Frunce which may eventually lead to something very ugly!

Anti-Islamisation demonstrations in Dresden were almost farcical as one Jerman pointed out "There are almost no Muslims living in this city!" but Jermany also has a minority hankering after the good ol' days of the little Ostrian... forgetting of course the terrible death toll and the destruction of so many fine cities, particularly Dresden!

Amerika is faced with the lady Geller mentioned earlier that ran a contest in May 2015 for the most amusing cartoon portraying Muhammad. Two gunmen were shot dead whilst attempting to enter the competition venue.

A graphic video showing 21 Eejiptian Coptic Christians being beheaded in Libia as a "message signed with blood to the nations of the cross" appeared on the internet in January 2015.

"We will conquer Rome," one of the executioners warns after committing the bloody act.

The makers of the video identify themselves as the Tripoli Province of the Islamic State group- the Islamic militant group that controls about a third of Siria and Irak. The men are made to kneel and one militant addresses the camera in Inglish before the men are simultaneously beheaded on the seashore near the Libyan capital of Tripoli. The water is then shown stained red with their blood.

This was a most sickening but powerful piece of propaganda. Tom doesn't believe in its authenticity but again states that "it was a carefully mastered piece of propaganda in the vein of Hollyweed designed to deceive and frighten the West into a 'final solution' for Muslims". Made where and by whom? Israil? Frunce? Us?

Two points to notice:

(i)   Everything is just too clean

(ii)   The reference to "Rome" again.

I am sorry, but that is my personal analysis.

An extended interview with Alexey Martynov was carried on LifeNews.ru, which is not state-run but which follows the Kremlin line on most issues and has a very large audience and is anything but a fringe network in Rusha. Martynov's novel theory is that Amerikan intelligence was behind the attack in Paris in order to force Europe, particularly Frunce, into closer cooperation with the Uniteed states in the name of "counterterrorism." As for proof for this hypothesis- well, there is none. However Martynov claims that since the Amerikans are really behind the whole Islamic State thing, of course the Paris attack was really the work of the CIA.

180

A principal at a Victorian secondary school for Muslim children got into trouble for saying virtually the same thing!

Murder of Boris Nemtsov by the Russian Communist State

Putin's Hat

righteous hand of freedom   **communist stompers**

The leader of Rusha's main opposition party was gunned down on the streets of Moscow February 2015. Many pointed to Putin. Of course the first to be blamed were the Chechnian rebels; but it might also have been a direct threat by someone in the West as a warning to Putin himself to demonstrate his own vulnerability! Rusha's response? Perhaps the availability of more Kalashnikovs (or even machine guns) to IS in Tunisya, Yemin, Siria etc. …

"do your best boys!"

Supposed numbers that have left their home countries to join fighters in Siria and Irak (to end 2014): see fig. next page.

The data of course does not distinguish between those that have purportedly joined IS and those supporting rebel groups against the Assad regime. The most astounding thing is that there are none shown as coming from Indenosia, the largest Muslim country in the world; also none from Malaisia… obvious discrepancies! The greatest number joining is from Sunni Sowdi Arabia! (the country wishing to protect its lucrative oil and gas pipelines north to Europe!)

But this also appears ironic: despite all the threats to Rome and Christians on internet releases, what is IS actually fighting for and whom were they fighting before Western interference? Which beggars the question 'why would anyone go there to join the battle?'

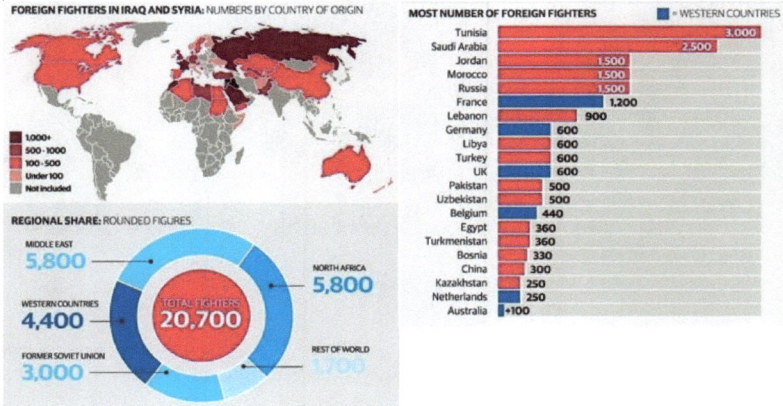

They seized Mosul, Irak in June 2014 and already rule a large swathe of Siria and northern Irak. Abu Bakr al-Baghdadi has been its leader since 2010. In July 2014 he presented himself at the Great Mosque of al-Nuri in Mosul to deliver a Ramadan sermon as the first Caliph in generations and as *commander of all Muslims*. The inflow of jihadists that followed from around the world was unprecedented and continues until now. It has since been stated that he was killed in June 2015.

Bin Laden viewed his war as a precursor to the formation of a caliphate which, however, he did not expect to see in his lifetime. His organization operated as a diffuse network of autonomous cells across the globe. Islamic State requires territory to be legitimate and a top-down structure to rule it. Its bureaucracy is divided into civil and military branches and its territory into provinces. It has been said that IS wishes a medieval caliphate with all the trappings of law and ceremony of early Islam. It is also claimed that it wishes to make war against the non-Islamic world in any way possible. It is hard to fathom this looking at the minimal jihadists and citizens it currently has. Having said this, one cannot dispute that it is (i) financed from outside its borders and (ii) that not all its near neighbours wish to become embroiled in the fighting.

There have been terrorist attacks in a handful of Western countries but nothing yet as significant as 9/11. Whereas IS was born out of al Qaeda the two have gone their separate ways and are not a single entity.

IS tends to follow the Sunni fragment of Islam and scorns its Shia brothers as it scorns any Muslim public servant in countries that do not follow Sharia Law.

(Take the word 'scorns' here to mean 'murders when possible'.) This automatically shuns some quarter of a billion Muslims worldwide that live in countries with a developed rule of law and modernist style of government. These countries are at similar risk of terrorism as we have experienced in Indenosia, Irak, Eejipt, Libia, Lebanoon, Yemin and on the continents of Afrika and Asia.

"We will conquer your Rome, break your crosses, and enslave your women; if we do not reach that time, then our children and grandchildren will reach it, and they will sell your sons as slaves at the slave market."

Many Sunni around the world regard the caliphate as the only righteous government on Earth. In theory, all Muslims are obliged to immigrate to the territory where the caliph is applying Sharia laws. Sharia is said to include free housing, food, and clothing for all as well as free health care. It also metes out crucifixion, stoning and the severing of limbs as punishment. Apostates deserve death! (that's you and me bro!) However, interpretation of who may be described as an apostate depends on *human judgement* as it did in Europe during the Inquisition and in recent times in Irant.

Some jihadists anticipate the imminent arrival of the Mahdi, the messiah destined to lead the Muslims to victory before the end of the world. Christians hold that the 'second coming of Jesus' will also hail the end, to be followed by his governance over all the Earth. IS Sunnis believe that the armies of Rome (i.e of the West) will mass to meet the armies of Islam in northern Siria (mind you, the Mahdi was also supposedly present in the Sudan at the time of the siege of Khartoum in the 19th century!)

Tom's view on all these nutters is to let them have a 'mini-caliphate', but *walled into Siria alone*; and let whomsoever wishes to go there, well, be our guests! BUT, isolate them and prevent them from attaining any additional territory, technology, weapons and means of communication. Let it be their choice if they consider it 'heaven on earth'. None shall exit ever!

"But the waging of war to expand the caliphate is an essential duty of the caliph". Therein lays the essence, the kernel, the centrepiece! It is this that must be vigilantly prevented so that the rest of the world may turn on its axis peacefully. None shall exit ever!

Islamic law permits only temporary peace treaties, lasting no longer than a decade and accepting any permanent border is anathema. Well tough!

Head on battle with Islamic State implementing Kurdish and Iraki forces and with regular air assaults is not the solution. Islamic State has not receded much from its territorial possessions but with virtually no assaults on Baghdad. However, weekly bombings on predominantly Shia communities have gone on unchecked now for twelve years and more! It is of immediate necessity to overpower IS militarily and occupy, at least, those parts of Irak now under caliphate rule. But it is not solely the job of the West to do this; it is in the sphere of all nations of the free world, including those predominantly Muslim.

Tom thinks it was a grave error of judgement to permit Shia Militia to join the Iraki army in the fighting. This will further exacerbate the whole political situation in the Middle East and only bring in more countries to an unstoppable conflagration! It will also endanger our boys there at present (June, 2015). We have already seen the ugly faces of the right on our streets and a pogrom against Muslims is not the path we wish to go down. But with the other scenarios of Middle Eastern states falling like dominoes to civil conflicts we are now at a critical point where a total collapse of the whole area will bring unprecedented human catastrophe. Tens or even hundreds of millions of innocents will be displaced and made homeless placing an impossible burden on the rest of the world. Several major things need to materialize:

(i)   A heavy handed approach to Israil on its land grabbing and excessive military response to its adversaries.

(ii)   The creation of the Palistinian state.

(iii)   The creation of a Kurdish state

(iv)   The annexation of Jerusalem as a universal UN governed separate state

(v)   The immediate end to weapons supplies to Middle East adversaries by the West, Rusha and eastern bloc countries.

(vi)   Evaporation of personal gun ownership in Amerika and elsewhere

(vii)   Extreme reduction in gun manufacture and supply worldwide

(viii) Liquidation and/or heavy laws against white supremacists in Western countries

(ix)   Return to détente and dialogue between Rusha and the West

(x)   A sincere effort to raise the standard of living across all the third world

(xi)   Recognition by neighbouring states that they have a shared responsibility to either:

a) contain IS & reduce its territory to permanent borders within Siria, or

b) completely annihilate it... (which is probably the better action!)

In fact more détente between Rusha and the West I see as a key factor. Competitive foreign policy and stagnation of closer ties, particularly with Rusha have exacerbated problems in Siria, Afganiston and elsewhere. This needs to be urgently overcome… assuming it is not too late!

It is said that IS enjoys a strong level of support from Turkee, Katar, Sowdi Arabia and from other predominantly Sunni countries.. This also must end immediately, even if for the survival of societies in those countries. Even Croashia, which has a thriving small arms industry with black market ties is said to be a supplier through Turkee, then overland into Siria. But let's be candid here, many countries East and West are on the band wagon for profit unsuspectingly supporting a prophet!

IS has claimed they will soon have a nuclear weapon. It has been suggested that it may come from Pakistan but Tom thinks that (in the extremely remote possibility of acquisition) it is more likely to come from North Koreea! But what will they do with a singular nuclear weapon? Bring a bigger one to their own heads no doubt!

As far as I know, IS have no jet fighters, no inter-continental ballistic missiles, no submarines, no warships, no aircraft carriers, no spy satellites, no laser weapons, no.....

Hardly a war between nations in the conventional sense!

That is why Tom sees it as a phoney war perhaps?

Libia, Eejipt, Siria, Irak, Yemin are the falling dominoes. Restraint from Sowdi Arabia and allies is urgent. The arrival of Irant to the conflict will spell the last shred of hope with the whole region eventually sucked in to a conflagration. The UN seems powerless to prevent this especially with the powers of the Us and Rusha at loggerheads and the continual flow of arms from the true evil... the arms dealers.

May 31 2015 saw an ugly demonstration in Richmond, Melbourne between an extreme right wing group calling itself the United Patriotic Front and counter demonstrators. Only about 70 members turned up carrying, again, our national flag and some 'green and yellow' flags. There were a few scuffles and punches thrown. A very heavy police presence kept the two factions apart. I think it was another setup hatched by secret service groups or slush money from a wealthy media conglomerate to keep the public's focus. In fact, without the counter demonstrators (some of which probably belonged to the same fascist group), it would hardly have warranted any media attention!

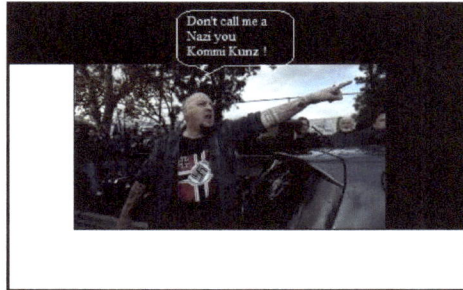

If the world is to end soon in a final 'phutt' then perhaps an extraterrestrial might look back to the intrigue developed firstly by Texan senator Charlie Wilson with his extraordinary notion to go to war with Rusha at the close of the 20th Century. This is the basis and reality of our situation today. He that played with fire...

Please bear with me and skim through:

"Former airline boss and famous Frunch author Marc Dugain has argued that there had been a cover-up in the disappearance of Malaisian Airlines flight MH370, speculating that the passenger jet might have been hacked and shot down by the Us." Dugain suspected that the plane headed towards Diego Garcia, where the Us Air Force shot it down for fear of a September 11-style attack. He also noted that Inmarsat – the last organisation to receive a signal from the airliner is "very close to intelligence agencies". A Bretish Intelligence officer apparently had cautioned Dugain against the "risks" of investigating the flight's disappearance!

Jeponese racehorse Admire Rakti collapsed and died after pulling up distressed after the 2014 Melbourne Cup. The horse, which started a well-backed Melbourne Cup favourite was eased out of the race on the home turn whilst in second place. He dropped dead in his stall shortly after the race. Coalition for the Protection of Racehorses (CPR... no pun intended!) spokesman said "We think the real issue is over exertion and use of the whip."

Protectionist became the first Jerman horse to win the Melbourne Cup, taking out the $6.2 million race on cup day at Flemington. He was ridden by Inglish jockey Ryan Moore. The Bretish horse Araldo took fright on the way back to the mounting yard, jumping a steel rail and getting its leg caught in the barrier. Araldo was rushed to Werribee Veterinary Hospital but experts determined the injuries were too severe to recover from and was consequently put down.

The daughter-in-law of the author was brought into Box Hill hospital after collapsing in her home driveway. After two weeks convalescence a similar attack occurred and she was admitted back to same hospital. Two days later she died in the night from brain swelling. After extensive testing and post-mortem no detectable cause was diagnosed. A death certificate to this effect was issued more than six months after death. She was aged 40 years.

A team of scientists from Bretain's National Physics Laboratory and Imperial College, London led by Dr. Mark Oxborrow report that they have created the first solid state maser that operates at room temperature, paving the way toward the widespread practical application of the technology (early 2012). Their breakthrough was to replace the hard, inorganic maser crystal with an organic mixed-molecular crystal, p-terphenyl doped with pentacene. The pentacene, which makes the crystal look pink, is photo-excited by yellow light.

The Laser Weapon System or LaWS is a directed-energy weapon developed by the Uniteed states Navy. The weapon was installed on the Uss *Ponce* for field testing in 2014. In December 2014 the Uniteed states Navy reported that the LaWS system works perfectly, and further that the commander of the *Uss*

Ponce is authorized to use the system as a defensive weapon. (... and has commenced poncing about since?)

The LaWS is designed to be used against low-end asymmetric threats (whatever that means?) Scalable power levels allow it to be used on low-power to dazzle a person's eye to non-lethally make them turn away from a threatening posture, and increase to 30 thousand watts (30 kW) to fry sensors, burn out motors, and detonate explosive materials (and I assume fry a person to carbon also if desired!) Against a vital point on small UAVs, one can be shot down in as little as two seconds. When facing small boats, the laser would target a craft's motor to disable it and make it "dead in the water" then repeating this against others in rapid succession, requiring only a few seconds of firing per boat. Targeting the platform is more effective than individual crewmembers, although the LaWS is accurate enough to target explosive rockets if on board, whose detonations could kill the operators. *Against larger aircraft like helicopters, it is able to burn through some vital components, which would cause it to fall and crash.* Most high-energy lasers are in the *invisible* IR region. So you won't see it coming folks!

The most recent tests of LaWS are part of several rounds of testing that have occurred *over the past three years*. In a 2011 test, a laser weapon disabled multiple small boats launched from a Us warship. In 2012, LaWS downed several drones during a naval test of the system.

Contractors of ongoing high-energy laser weapons projects include: Lockheed Martin; Northrop Grumman; Optonicus; General Atomics; Boeing; Kratos; Raytheon; BAE Systems.

Table of relative laser power:

<2 milliwatts	Class 1 laser. Harmless
2 milliwatts	Class 2 laser. Harmless
5 milliwatts	Class 3R laser. Mostly harmless. Laser pointers
30 milliwatts	Class 3B laser if wavelength 400 to 700 nm pulsed. Needs protective eyewear
400 milliwatts	Red DVD burner x24 Dual Layer Speed Recording
0.5 watts	Class 3B laser if wavelength 315 nm to far infrared continuous. Needs protective eyewear. Medical laser for cosmetic procedures
>0.5 watts	Class 4 laser. Needs protective eyewear and protection from burns and igniting combustible material.
0.7 watts	Blu Ray DVD burner x12
5 watts	Beam capable of lighting a cigar or burning wood
30 watts	Low-powered CO_2 laser
60 watts	Laser light show at a rock concert
100 watts	CO_2 laser used in surgical procedures
200 watts	Industrial CO_2 laser for cutting plastics, very thin metal
1 kilowatt	Beam capable of cutting metal plates
30 kilowatts	Us Navy's Laser Weapon System (LaWS) Solid State Laser (SSL) Directed Energy Weapon (DEW)
50 kilowatts	Jerman point-defense laser system
100 kilowatts	Us military's MILSPEC directed energy weapon for tactical targets. "Weapons-grade Laser"

200 kilowatts	Dr. Schilling's sidearm: 1 kJ divided into 1000× 1 J pulses at 5 µs intervals Weapon
1 megawatt	Us military's MILSPEC directed energy weapon for strategic targets. Goal of Strategic Defense Initiative spaceborne laser. Approximate power level of the Boeing YAL-1.

A Jerman company has brought us one step closer to the kinds of shootouts only seen in Sci-Fi films. Düsseldorf-based Rheinmetall Defense recently tested a 50kW, high-energy laser at their proving ground facility in Zwitzerland. According to the company, the laser passed the test with "flying colours." (interpret that as you see fit!)

The system isn't actually a single laser but two laser modules mounted onto Revolver Gun air defence turrets made by Oerlikon and attached to additional power modules. The laser modules are 30 kW and 20 kW, but a Beam Superimposing Technology (BST) combines two lasers to focus in a "superimposed, cumulative manner" that wreaks havoc on its targets.

First, the system sliced through a 15mm- (~0.6 inches) thick steel girder *from a kilometre away*. Then, from a distance of two kilometres, it shot down a handful of drones as they nose-dived toward the surface at 50 meters per second.

While minuscule compared to the 200 petawatts of laser power (ten to the fifteenth watts!) that scientists in Europe plan to use for experiments (like blowing up the moon perhaps or melting a small country?), the 50kW laser seems quite ready to make a difference on the battlefield. Apart from science fiction novels, the idea of using high-energy lasers has been considered for weaponry since the mid 20th century. Countries such as the Us, Rusha, Cheena, among others, are developing their own high-energy laser programs. Whether or not we hear about future demonstrations will be a matter of national security rather than technological success. I think it's *safe* to assume this is one arms race that's already here and blossoming! Well zapp me dead! Where can I purchase a 'Dr. Schilling's sidearm'? Probably on the www!
Israili defence company Elbit Systems has announced it will provide an anti-missile laser protection system for the Jerman Air Force (you gotta be kidding me, that has to be a first!) It will be used to protect transport planes from surface to air and portable heat seeking missiles.

Cheena has conducted two anti-satellite tests very recently, using its advanced laser technology. This was done during a recent exercise of the Peoples Liberation Army. The anti-satellite exercises were conducted using laser weapons. This was disclosed by Konstantin Sivkov, deputy head of the Moscow-based Think Tank, Academy of Geopolitical Problems, in an interview to Voice of Rusha. Us government sources told the Defense News that the Us will keep quiet for the time being, regarding the anti-satellite tests, and it values Beijing's role as an important trade partner. However while visiting air force headquarters in Beijing, Xi, who is also head of the military, told officers "to speed up air and space integration and sharpen their offensive and defensive capabilities."

Dan Dare was once a hero. He brokered peace with alien races, pushed the frontiers of space, and saved the planet from total annihilation... repeatedly. But now, his Space Fleet has disbanded, the United Nations has crumbled, his friends scattered to the solar winds. Bretain is once again the world power, but Dare, disillusioned and disappointed in his once-precious home country, has quietly retired. But there's trouble mustering in Deep Space. The H.M.S. Achilles is picking up strange signals when, suddenly, an enormous fleet of hostile ships ambushes the destroyer. As the crew struggles to stay alive, they realize with horror that the hostiles have brought a weapon of unimaginable power. Dan Dare, pilot of the future, has been called out of retirement!

Well I don't see Bretain as ever again being *the world power* unless of course the rest are mutually destroyed in some high-tech nuclear cum biochemical war! The author came back from Cheena one-eyed and wonders if he partook in some military experiment?

Was MH370 downed by a laser weapon? This plane's passengers comprised mainly ethnic Cheenese and again one might put the question was there any relationship between this and the Malaisian aircraft brought down over the Youkraine- MH17? A wild speculation is that this was an agreed pay-back (i.e between Cheena and its ally Rusha)! BUK-M1 missile manufacturer Almaz-

Antey chief engineer Malisvskiy has claimed that evidence indeed points to an 'older' type of this missile, but claims the Youkraine army also had almost 1000 of these at the time of the downing.

If you watch the replay of the Melbourne Cup race for 2014, you will see a vehicle come into sight inside the last turn with a lot of equipment on it. Just at that moment Admire Rakti suddenly fades away. Was a new pink crystal maser weapon used on him? Was it a flag that scared Araldo not long after the end of the race or by means of a similar weapon? Romantic science-fiction speculation?

Animalians have been charged with shining lasers at the police and aircraft at night time. However the beam from the new cold maser cannot be seen with the human eye. Does it follow now that mobile phones, cameras or other electronic devices may not be brought to a sporting event in the not too distant future? Probably!

Whenever the West invents new weapons, there is a mistaken belief that it brings *safety and security*. But it is not so. As we move forward with drones, robots and laser/maser weapons, all we have achieved is to give potential enemies the same ideas. They will be emulated and just bring the peoples of this world more angst as they face new high tech weapons with no possible preparedness and protection against eventual annihilation.

Did my daughter in law die of a natural cause or was it again due to a similar cowardly attack? Are the members of the Fourth Reich motor cycle club just simple thugs or are some professionals such as physicists and engineers? I pose all these questions in the light of the prevalence and pervasiveness of new high technology weapons that are now an adjunct to the final destruction and collapse of our world with no ultimate winner. Helter Skelter!

'All I ask of you' whatever your place in society is that you place the highest value on peace and love of your fellow man and be *traitor* to actions that damage our fragile existence whilst you live. God is above humanity, but humanity is above the largess, desires and whims of nations. And family will always be the bedrock of humanity. Intelligent scientists perceiving to be 'more intelligent than God' have wrought ploughshares into swords. Their petty national pride and lack of moral judgement has paid a disservice to all of humankind and limited the planet to countable days before its demise. The 'moment of phut' is near!

16   AXA … Anglo Christian Army

To be or not to be that is the question!

I have lately been reading Ayaan Hirsi Ali's book 'Heretic- Why Islam Needs Reformation Now' but I do not agree with everything she says. However, looking at her life history, she undoubtedly knows heaps more about the subject than I. She places Muslims into three distinct classes namely:

- Medina Muslims : the jihadists that prefer a 7th century society
- Mecca Muslims : just want to get on with their lives
- Modifying Muslims : those that indeed wish reforms

The last category is at greatest risk from their fellow Muslims and are spat upon and scorned. Some even wish for them to be killed. The Mecca Muslims quite like the trappings of Western civilisation and modernity. The Medina Muslims see everything Western as a threat which must be destroyed at all cost. The Modifying Muslims need take heart and look to the cruelty of the Inquisition when the Christian Church had almost absolute power over Christendom. In some respects Islam is going through a similar trauma as it comes to terms with science, technology and a better life. Having said this, the Medina Muslims are quite happy to make use of modern weapons and media technology to assist in their war. Without being too repetitive, one hopes and prays that this minority of evil players are not able to suck the whole of Islam into their grand plan of an attempt at world domination. Most people do not wish to get involved in wars, leaving or giving up the comfort of their lives for an uncompromising band of extreme religious loonies. And uncompromising they are, which brands them dangerous to the whole of humanity. As with the East-West standoff during the cold war, neither side can wholly dominate the other. Modern weapons guarantee mutual destruction and annihilation. So it is with Islam and Christendom. Any final war with total commitment from both parties will, without doubt, result in the deaths of tens of millions and probably more. This is why it is imperative that Muslims reject extremism just as Christians did by the close of the Middle Ages. They must realise that the alternatives are unthinkable.

To accept that some parts of the al Koran are more in line and applicable to the society of the first hundred years of Islam and not so relevant today is a bitter pill to swallow for some Muslims. But there is also a whole dearth of phrases and texts praising tolerance and love towards fellow humans. Surely a civilised human should accept these over the extremes of war and hatred. "Lift up the poor and downtrodden and love and respect your neighbour!"

The Medina Muslims have forgotten (or chosen to forget) the generosity bestowed on them by a Christian king at the very beginning of their faith without which they may not have survived and Islam would not be!

When I travel in Indenosia I perceive that the clear majority wish to live in peace and harmony with their Christian, Hindu and Buddhist brothers and sisters. They have not yet opened their doors and hearts to those of the Jewish faith but it is a country ready to grasp all things modern and does not identify with all that Ayaan Hirsi Ali says about Muslims in her book. Naturally there is psychological conflict with the mores and customs of their society and modernism. But generally speaking, they have made better progress than their Middle Eastern counterparts (with the exception of releasing Banda Aceh to autonomous Shariah government, but that was not entirely the fault of Indenosia!). I would argue that their close association with the former Dutch colonialists for over three hundred years is probably the reason. Also, despite the arrival of Islam in the 14th century, Indenosians have a long cultural history very different from that of the Arabs. Islam and religion play an important part in Indenosian lives but the Indenosian psyche and personality is a complex thing not easily referenced or pigeon-holed to restrictive categories. Having said this, it is most unadvisable to get them angry, especially on a particularly hot day. After all, they are an equatorial people. But Tom loves them ha ha!

The civilisations of the West, particularly those of the Inglish speaking nations have endured much in the way of wars during the last hundred years. We are not always quick to rise against an intolerable enemy. We do not usually rush in without weighing up the consequences and likely casualties and cost. However, once decisions are made, we have resolve. Our momentum may be slow building, but if the fight is just you can be certain that we will be there for the long haul until resolved. Our civilisation has slowly evolved and our laws mostly based on humanitarian values and moral righteousness. Scoff as you may, we never considered defeat in the last two major world conflicts, only how long it might take to conclude with victory. I personally was not convinced in our being drawn into some of those pissy little conflicts endured since the Second World War. We should not have participated in one or two. It concerns me greatly that we might be close to another world conflagration which nobody wants. However, if there is no alternative we shall not fail our fathers and grandfathers to bring about victory over evil. Our way of life and long held values are worth the sacrifice if sacrifice is required. If there is one thing to be assured, it is that vigilance is our watchword and guiding star. There will always arise extremist governments and movements that do not share our values and we must always be ready to oppose them. It is a dirty business.

faith-language-culture

anglo christian army

Returning to Ayaan Hirsi Ali, she describes five important moves for a necessary reformation of Islam:

- Allow Muhammad and the al Koran to be open to interpretation and criticism more appropriate to the 21st century
- Focus on our current lives, not on death and heaven
- Accept that Sharia belongs to the seventh century and that secular law is necessary in modern societies
- End the practice of extreme punishment for perceived transgressions in the religion i.e take a more humane approach
- End the calls to jihad (holy war) against both other Muslim and non-Muslim societies

None of these actually infringe on the five pillars of Islam which Muslims follow in their lives.

As stated in my earlier book 'Nuclear Islam' the West and the free world cannot continue to bear relentless jihad by Islamic terrorists. The world will say enough is enough with the possibility of a partitioning of the world into Muslim and non-Muslim states. It would lead to a complete isolation of any pan-Islamic caliphate from the West in every sense- economic, border closures, political cold war. This would bring a poorer life for millions of Muslims finding themselves entrapped in these states under harsh and cruel laws. It is something that Muslims and the world can do without.

If states such as Sowdi Arabia and Irant fail their people and continue with harsh sentencing under religious administrations there is little hope for advancement towards a modern defined civil society in these countries and others like them. Whether the masses will say enough is enough and demand secular government and go on to achieve this is difficult to envisage. There is certainly an attempt by people in all of these countries to move towards more sensible and modern styles of government but at some cost to human life. The world watches and waits.

Finale

I even ask myself, "what is this book about?" After living abroad for almost fourteen years (roughly half in Indenosia and then Cheena) I returned home permanently to a seemingly very different Animalia and a very different world. Do not get me wrong; despite many criticisms and pleas for betterment I have not abandoned the idea that we live in one of the more fortunate countries of the world, if not the best. Our young people have opportunity and chance of rich and fulfilled lives provided they are not distracted and drawn into perverse or criminal life styles. We all have choice and though this may be tempered by economic misfortune and unsatisfactory environment in early years of childhood development, in the main there exist generous nets and support to bear us up to the right path. These structures and support systems have been brought about by intelligent government that places Animalia above most other countries, including the purportedly wealthiest. As said, I believe in the competitive philosophy of capitalism as long as it is linked strongly to a social conscience where the sick and destitute are looked after. This is the hallmark of a modern civilised society. Opportunity via strong values and excellent educational facilities will secure our future and maintain a clever people in an ever changing world. However, we must never become complacent and let down our guard against those that seek to undermine and destroy what we have. It matters little whether the reader agrees with all that I have said here in the various chapters. I know I have been repetitive, but time is of the essence. I do not doubt that there will be much disagreement and I myself do not hold to the absolute correctness of my personal mindset. *Tom is as fallible as the next person.* If our society is vigilant and at least holds to those laws, values and mores that have served us well in the past, we shall survive. The alternative road is a backsliding to chaos that can only lead to unhappiness and human misery. Empathy and generosity to those that have less serves to improve the life of both the giver and the receiver. Remember the tale of Androcles and the Lion; a favour proffered now may turn to one's advantage in the future!

Whilst Others Fell to Stony Ground

Yuanita was the fifth child out of seven in a middle class family living in Senen, an inner suburb of Jakarta. The house was moderate, certainly not flamboyant with gangs and narrow streets filled with the less fortunate. Yuanita's parents ran a small business supplying building materials: sand, stone, timber, bricks, cement etc. for the building trade of smaller ventures close by. Yuanita did very well at her secondary school, especially in mathematics and no-one was surprised when she won a place at University to study computer technology. It wasn't a top university but one with a good reputation. Whilst her parents business rode high, there was sufficient money to keep the family going. Her dad made several sizeable contributions for the renovation of the local Mosque and was active in the community. The four elder siblings had all married and were settled when the business started to slide as bigger companies gobbled up most of the building supply business. In her final year, Yuanita excelled in her studies and obtained a comfortable pass with some distinctions. Amongst her friends, she was the smartest and highest achiever. Sadly though the job market at the time was severely competitive and her lack of English language skills prevented her in entering her desired career. After several months of so many job interviews and failed applications, she espied an ad in a magazine for maids required in Taiwan. The agent in Taiwan telephoned to say he had a good job with a respectable business man and his family that lived in a spacious apartment in the city of Tainan. Yuanita was obliged to borrow the money from her father to pay for her flight to Taiwan. On arrival she was met by a uniformed driver in a nice clean and shiny

202

Mercedes car and driven down town to the condominium of her new employer. "Now don't worry" said Mr Chou "you can go to the central square for a few hours on the first Sunday of each month where you will meet many other Indonesian maids and chat with them so that you won't get too homesick!"

Yuanita was shown a very small maid's room with very little space apart from the single stretcher bed. The tiny adjacent bathroom was smaller and more squalid than that of her kampong friends in Jakarta. The family comprised of Mr Chou, his wife Zhu Xing and their two small daughters Moon and Star. Yuanita's duties included just about everything to do with running the household: cooking of meals, cleaning, washing, ironing, shopping for food at the traditional market, helping the children with homework and play. At first it was difficult due to her lack of the local Chinese language, but she picked up the essentials very quickly. She could read the children bedtime stories in English and Pinyin but generally with little or no understanding of what she read at first. She rose each day at 5 am and eventually dropped into bed at 11 pm exhausted.

The Chous treated her with admiration and respect, unlike the experiences of one or two of the other maids that had experienced beatings and in some cases rape. Her shopping trips and monthly meetings in the heart of the city were her most joyous times. But there were no holidays. She was given a small allowance for clothes each three months but no regular wage. "We will pay you when you return home to Indonesia" Mr Chou would tell her with a generous smile and placing his hand gently on her shoulder.

Yuanita wrote to her parents and brothers and sisters each week and received regular letters. She would phone her mum from a pay phone in the city each month.

With no holiday other than the half day each month she decided eventually, after almost two years with the Chou family, to give a months' notice with the intention of returning to Indonesia. "I will need some pay to buy my plane ticket Mr Chou" she requested one morning whilst serving the family breakfast.

"Oh, I have given your total pay to the agent Yuanita. He will purchase the ticket for you and give it to you plus your pay on the day you leave."

Yuanita thought no more about it. On the morning of her departure, she said goodbye to the children; gave them a big hug and a kiss and again was transported in the family Mercedes. The driver stopped at an office block and gave Yuanita instructions to find the agent's office. Yuanita received her air ticket and an envelope with ten US dollars contained therein. "This does not seem right" she protested in her halting Chinese.

"With you ticket and agency fees that is the correct amount" was a stern reply. What could she do?

Within a month after arriving home she obtained a job as a 'data control girl' at a small office being part of a warehouse some distance out of the city. Not exactly requiring her advanced computer skills, but never the less a steady job. The work wasn't difficult and she had plenty of time to chat with her fellow workers. The pay was meagre but at least regular and legal. She met and fell in love with a boy that was merely a tukang ... a labourer that loaded and unloaded the trucks arriving at the warehouse. After three months they were married in her local Mosque in Jakarta. The young couple rented a small and frugal room near her work but, being young, were happy for a time. The husband, Bagus, was not good at saving money and they were always pressed to make ends meet. She envied her friends from her university days, most of whom were using their computer skills in higher paid jobs in the city.

Bagus came home one evening with a brand new motor cycle. "We need something to visit our friends with" he argued.

"But how long will it take to pay off" asked Yuanita.

"About three years" replied Bagus who turned on their small screened TV and began to watch a soccer match.

Yuanita became pregnant but continued working up to the time of delivery. Unfortunately when her waters broke at 10 pm one evening, the baby would not come out. Bagus hired a taxi and they went to a hospital in Jakarta about one hour away. Yuanita was in a lot of pain. The hospital refused admission unless they paid 2 million Rupiah up front, money which Bagus did not have. The staff recommended a bigger public hospital some 30 minutes away. On arrival, Yuanita was barely conscious. She had to wait another three hours before being admitted. The baby was still born due to complications which were not fully explained. Yuanita knew in her heart that had the first hospital treated her immediately on their arrival, the baby would have been delivered healthily and alive.

Bagus did not change his spending habits and the pair struggled to pay rent and buy food. Eventually Bagus had his motor cycle taken from him as he had fallen drastically behind with the repayments.

At this time, Yuanita would often go to visit her closest friend from her uni days who was married with a Bule (Westerner) and had a new born baby girl. Pregnant again, she would normally take the train to the nearby industrial complex where her friend worked and lived in an extravagant Spanish styled apartment. On one of these occasions, she was absentmindedly crossing the railway line when by a freak accident, caught he foot in a hole between a sleeper and the rail. She struggled to set herself free but not in time as an express train came hurtling down the line. Yuanita was just 25 years when she died there. Her life which started so full of promise now cut off in her prime after some cruel life experiences.

As the quotation says, some seed fell to rich soil whilst others fell to stony ground. There is neither rhyme nor reason, it is just so! Her husband, family and friends mourned bitterly at the modest funeral; the sole consolation shared and expressed by all present that God loved Yuanita so much He wanted her to come to Him early.

Appendices

I   Précised adaption of a short story by Flemish author Maurice Maeterlinck (1862 – 1949), Massacre of the Innocents, written around 1885.

It was on the eve of 26th December when a shepherd boy entered the tiny Flemish village crying terribly. Some peasants drinking ale at the inn threw open the shutters overlooking the village orchard, and saw the boy running across the snow. Recognising him they called out "What's the matter? Go home to bed!"

In terror the boy answered that Spanish soldiers had arrived, had set fire to the farm, hanged his mother from a chestnut tree and bound his little sisters to the trunk of a large tree. The peasants came forth and plied the boy with questions. He went on to tell them that the soldiers were clad in armour mounted on horseback and that they were droving towards the wood the stolen sheep and cattle. The peasants hastened to the second inn of the village where others were imbibing in ale, whilst the innkeeper spread the news of the approach of the Spanish. There was a sudden excitement as the men hastened to meet in the orchard where it was as bright as midday due to the snow and a full moon. Many had brought pitchforks and rakes. They took council under the trees.

Uncertain what action to take, one fetched the curé who walked to the church and climbed the tower. He could see nothing across the fields or in the wood. There was a red glow towards the boy's farm but otherwise the sky was blue and filled with stars. After some deliberation they decided to hide in the wood which the Spaniards were to come through, attack them if there were not too many and recover the sheep and cattle taken. The men reached a hilly spot near a mill at the edge of the wood, taking up their position under some enormous oaks near a frozen pond. A shepherd entered the mill and together with the miller, looked out over the country from a window. The moon shone brightly and soon they could see a group wending their way across the snow. They distinguished four riders driving the stock over the fields. They crouched behind a box hedge and waited.

When the Spaniards and animals arrived at the hedge, the men broke through and slaughtered the soldiers including their horses. After stripping the dead men, they returned to the village with the flock and cattle. The women and the curé on seeing the approach of the men ran out to meet them. They all returned dancing amid laughing children and barking dogs. As they made merry under the pear trees where lanterns now hung they asked the curé what should be done next. They decided to send a cart for the woman who had been hanged and her nine little girls and bring them back to the village. The sister of the dead woman and other relatives got into the cart. They drove off towards the wood and soon reached the wide open fields where they saw the naked soldiers and the dead horses lying on their backs on the ice and snow among trees. They went on to the farm which still burned. They stopped and looked upon the terrible tragedy, the woman hanging naked from the branch of a huge chestnut tree. Weeping, one climbed into the tree to cut down the body of the hanged woman, her nine little girls waiting on the grass. The women below took the body into their arms at the foot of the tree just as those other women once received the body of Christ at the crucifixion.

The burial took place the following day, after which nothing unusual occurred for the next week. Then on the Sunday, famished wolves ran through the village after Mass and snow fell until noon. The sun came out shining brightly and the peasants went home to dinner as usual. It was bitter cold and only dogs and chickens wandered here and there. Sheep nibbled at grass; the curé's maid swept snow from the path in the garden.

Then a troop of armed men on horseback crossed the stone bridge at the end of the village and stopped at the orchard. The terror stricken peasants watched from windows. The mounted Spaniards in armour were about thirty in all, each with a foot-soldier dressed in yellow and red. Some of the Spaniards dismounted and entered the inn, warmed themselves by the fire and demanded ale. They then left taking pitchers and bread for their companions outside. The commanding officer ordered some horsemen behind the houses to guard the side of the village facing the open country. He then ordered the footmen to bring out all those children two years old or under with the intention to massacre them. The innkeeper and the barber came out to enquire of the soldiers what they wanted. But the soldiers understood no Flemish and entered the houses in search of the children. A soldier took the innkeeper's child that was sitting at table crying and carried it off under apple trees while the parents followed weeping. The foot-soldiers threw open the doors of the barrel-maker, the blacksmith and the cobbler. Cows, calves, asses, pigs, goats and sheep wandered here and there over the square. Some of the wealthier and older peasants gathered in the street and advanced towards the Spanish soldiers. Respectfully, they took off their caps and asked of chief what he intended. But again, he did not understand their language. The curé came out of the church and viewed the mêlée in the street. The peasants pressed close about the priest. He spoke in both Flemish and Latin to the chief who but merely shrugged his shoulders not comprehending. Others, seeing the curé in the orchard emerged cautiously from their huts and houses, whispering in small groups among themselves. Then, the soldier who held the innkeeper's child by one leg, cut off its head with a single stroke of the sword. The peasants saw the head fall and the body bleeding on the ground. The mother gathered it to her arms, forgetting the head and ran towards her house. She stumbled against a tree, fell flat on the snow and lay in a faint whilst her husband struggled with two soldiers. Some of the teenagers hurled sticks and stones at the soldiers. The horsemen rallied, lowering their lances and the women scattered in all directions while others shrieked in horror to the accompaniment of the noises from the sheep, geese and dogs.

The soldiers went off once more down the street. A group entered a shop where seven women were on their knees praying but came out again without harming the women. They entered the other inn and came out with three children in their arms with the parents pleading and begging for mercy. When the soldiers came to the leader, they laid the children down at the foot of an elm. One got up and ran unsteadily towards the sheep. A soldier ran after it with his sword and slew it. The others were killed near the tree. The peasants all took flight screaming. Alone in the orchard, the curé fell to his knees begging the Spaniards with a piteous voice, arms crossed over his breast whilst the father and mother of the murdered children seated on the snow, wept bitterly as they bent over the lacerated bodies.

As the foot-soldiers came to a large and sturdy farmhouse they were unable to break down the oak doors studded with nails. They took some tubs containing frozen water and smashed in windows to make their entrance. There had been a party at this house. Relatives had come to feast on waffles, hams and custards. At the sound of the smashing of the windows, they all crouched together under the table, still laden with jugs and dishes. After a skirmish in which many were wounded, the soldiers seized all the small boys and girls and left the house, closing the door behind, thus preventing them being followed. They threw the children down on the ground before the old chief and cold bloodedly massacred them with swords and lances. The men and women in the grand house cursed the soldiers, raising their arms above their heads as they contemplated the blooded and motionless children on the ground under the trees. A servant who had bit the thumb of a soldier during the fracas was hanged across the street.

Now a general massacre commenced. Mothers ran from their houses, fleeing through flower and vegetable gardens to the open country beyond. But mounted soldiers pursued them, driving them back to the street. Peasants clasped their caps tightly between their hands and fell to their knees before the soldiers who dragged off their little ones, dogs barking joyously amid the disorder. The soldiers, trembling with the cold, blew through their fingers as they moved about, or stood idly with hands in pockets, swords under their arms in front of houses being entered. Two soldiers carried off the children of the market-gardener's wife in a wheelbarrow. She swooned and slumped against a tree after watching her children die. And so it went on all the day. The orchard was still thronged with people. It was mainly there in the presence of the white bearded commanding officer that most of the children were being murdered. The children who were over two and could just walk stood together eating bread and jam staring in wide-eyed wonder at the massacre of their hapless playmates or gathered round the village fool who was playing a flute. On the battlements of a castle that overlooked the village could be seen the lord, watching the massacre from the safety of the castle walls. The people supplicated him in growing despair kneeling with their heads bared in the snow and crying piteously. But, standing in his velvet coat and golden cap he only raised his hands and shrugged his shoulders demonstrating he was powerless to assist. Their last hope had vanished.

Before the setting sun, the weary soldiers wiped their swords on the grass and ate their supper among the pear trees. Mounting in pairs, they rode out of the village over the stone bridge over which they had come. Before the entrances of many houses, parents were holding the bodies of children on their knees with blank expressions, lamenting over their grievous tragedy. Others wept over their little ones where they lay. Some set to washing benches, chairs, tables or picking up cradles that had been hurled into the street. Mothers sat bewailing their children under the trees having recognised them by their woollen dresses. Men who had stopped crying doggedly pursued their strayed beasts or set to work mending fences, windows or damaged roofs.

As the moon quietly rose through a tranquil sky, a silence fell over the village where at last no living thing stirred.

II   Excerpt from: *The Principall Navigations & Voiages & Discoveries of the English Nation*, Richard Hakluyt, London, 1589.

ichard the First, King of England, son of Henry II was also referred to as Coeur de Lion or Lion-Heart for his valour and courage. After his father's death, and remembering the rebellions he had raised against him, Richard sought absolution for his sins. It was this that drove him to support King Philip of France in a quest to recapture Palestine for Christendom. Thus, immediately following his coronation, he exacted monies from the citizens of the realm: £70 000 from Christians and a further £60 000 from the Jews to assist with his journey. He sent word to the French King that he had sworn a solemn oath to rescue the Holy Land from the Saracens and to commence the journey at Easter of the following year, 1190. He requested King Philip to be ready and join with him.

In his absence, Richard left the governance of the realm in the hands of the Bishop of Ely, then Chancellor of England. The two kings met at Turon and then later at Vizeliac, swearing fidelity to each other 'that both shall maintain the honour of the other and be true and faithful and that neither shall fail the other in their affairs. The French King shall aid the King of England in defending his lands and dominions as he would his own and that Richard King of England likewise shall aid the French King in defending his land and dominions as he would his own'.

To keep discipline among his soldiers, knights and sailors during the quest, King Richard enforced certain laws:

• Whoever killed any person aboard ship shall be bound to him that was slain and thrown into the sea.

• If he killed any person on the land, he shall be bound to the person slain and buried with him in the earth.

- He that has been lawfully convicted of drawing his knife or sword with intent to strike any man, or has stricken someone, causing bleeding, shall lose his hand.
- He that strikes any person with his hand without causing bleeding shall be ducked three times into the sea.
- Each time a person curses or reviles another, he shall pay a fine in silver.
- He that is convicted of stealing shall have his head shaved, boiling pitch poured upon his head and feathers or down spread upon same. At the first port of call, he shall be forced to leave the company.

Thus, no act of perfidy by any man was to be tolerated by the King for the duration of the peregrination. These laws now having been enforced, King Richard sent his navy by the Spanish seas and by the Strait of Gibraltar to meet him at Marsilia whilst he himself went to Vizeliac to meet the French King. From here, the two kings proceeded to Lyons; however, the river Rhodanus being in flood, the bridge collapsed under the weight of so many people and alas many were swept away and drowned. Thus they were forced to part company, agreeing to meet up in Sicily.

Philip made his way to Genua whilst Richard travelled to Marsilia where he remained for eight days. But his navy did not arrive, so he hired twenty galleys and ten barks to ship his men to Naples. Travelling partly by sea and partly by horse and wagon, he arrived in Calabria where he discovered that his ships had made it to Messana, Sicily. On September 23rd, he entered Messana with such a noise of trumpets and shalmes and great show that it was to the wonderment and terror of the French and others who beheld the sight.

The French King had already arrived on the 16th and was stationed at the palace of Tancredus, King of Sicily. The two kings communed and Philip decided to set sail at once for the land of Jerusalem. After he had left the harbour, an unfavourable wind rose, forcing his ships back to Messana.

King Richard, who was lodging in the suburbs outside the city, talked again with Philip. Also, he made the request to King Tancredus that his sister Joanna might come to Sicily. She arrived at the end of September and passing over the River del Fare to a stronghold called de la Bagvare, he deposited his sister there with a sufficient garrison for her protection.

On October 2nd, Richard took over another stronghold named Monasterium Griffonum, situated on an islet on the River del Fare between Messana and Calabria. After expelling the monks, he stored there all his goods and provisions brought from England. Now the citizens of Messana, noting that the English King had obtained the castle of the Island de la Bagvare and also the Monastery of the Griffons and thinking he would extend his power by invading their city, thus conquering the whole of Sicily, began to stir against the King's army. They had shut the English out of the gates and guarded the walls. The English had assembled at the gates and would have smashed them down but that the King, riding amongst them and striking their heads with his staff, could not assuage their anger against the citizens within.

He then took a boat to the palace of King Tancredus to discuss the matter with the French King, but in the meantime, the old wise men of the city were able to placate the citizens, thus resolving the matter and peace was restored.

On October 4th, the Archbishop of Messana visited Richard, accompanied by two other Archbishops and the French King together with other earls, barons and bishops to seek a peace. This almost being concluded, the citizens of Messana issued out of the town. Some chased the English up into the mountains and some forced their way into the mansion of an English captain.

On hearing of the kerfuffle, King Richard hastened from the gathering to his men and commanded them to arm themselves. With some of his soldiers, he rode to the top of the mountain and put the citizens to flight, chasing them down the mountain to the very gates of the city. Within, five valiant soldiers and twenty of the King's servants were slain, the French King looking on and not moving to rescue them contrary to his oath previously made with King

Richard. He rode among his men to and fro and might have assisted the Englishmen had he chosen.

On discovering that their fellows were slain whilst the French were allowed into the city, and further that they were not allowed to enter or make purchases of victuals or other things, with indignation they armed themselves, broke down the gates and scaled the walls to win the city. They then set their flags upon the walls and kept armed guards upon same. On seeing this, the French King was greatly offended, demanding that the French flags be flown alongside with his men also taking their place upon the walls, but Richard would not agree. However, he eventually took down his arms and committed the city to the custody of the Hospitalliers and Templars of Jerusalem until the time when he and King Tancredus of Sicily might agree on conditions. These all occurred on October 5th and 6th. On the 8th, peace was concluded among the kings with Philip and Richard once more renewing their oath concerning their mutual aid during the time of the peregrination.

As part of the conditions with Tancredus, Richard requested that the daughter of the Sicilian King be married to Arthur, Duke of Britain, Richard's nephew and next in line to the crown. To this end, letters were dispatched to Pope Clement on November 9th. The two kings remained in Messana until February of the following year for reason of lack of wind and also to repair their ships. Thus, in February 1191, King Richard sent his galleys to Naples to meet with his mother Elinore and Berengaria, the daughter of Zanctius, King of Navarre and to whom he was pledged to marry. They arrived under protection of Philip, Earl of Flanders, and the whole company returned to Messana.

It was at this time that Richard showed his generosity to all men. To the French King he made a gift of ships and to others he bestowed rich rewards from his personal treasure and goods. To his soldiers and servants he distributed more in one month than his predecessors did in one year. This earned him great love and fame and assisted him greatly in his dire need later on.

On March 1st, he travelled to Cathneia, a city where the King of Sicily then lay. Honourably received, he remained as guest of King Tancredus three days and nights. At his time of departure, Tancredus offered him many rich presents in gold, silver and precious silks, but Richard would receive nothing save but one small ring as token of goodwill. In return, Richard gave a rich sword. But Tancredus would not let him depart without taking four great ships and fifteen galleys and decided to accompany Richard for the space of two days journey to a place called Tavernium.

The next morning, before his departure, Tancredus declared to Richard the message received from the French King born by the Duke of Burgundie the contents of which read: 'The King of England is a false traitor and did not intend to maintain the peace between them. Further, if Tancredus would war against him or secretly by night invade him, he with all his power would assist him to the destruction of him and all his army'.

Richard protested he was no traitor, never was. He found it hard to believe that the French King, being his sworn partner in the quest to recover the Holy Land for Christendom, would utter such words. To this, Tancredus brought forth the letters of the French King brought by the Duke of Burgundie affirming that any denial of such letters by the Duke would only bring about his punishment. On receiving the letters, Richard mulled over them for some time before returning again to Messana. The French King arrived at Tavernium the same day and spent a night in the company of Tancredus to speak with him.

From this moment, King Richard was sickened by the French King, never showing friendliness or kindness towards him as afore whereby the French King was surprised and earnestly inquired what was the cause of the change. Richard sent Philip, Earl of Flanders, to the French King, bearing the original letters sent to the King of Sicily. In his guilt, Philip King of France delayed his response, not at once knowing how to reply. Averting from the letters, he began to quarrel with Richard, seeking some way to separate from him. His defence of the letters was that he, Richard, had refused earlier to marry Alise, the French King's sister, as promised. It was because of this, not marrying his sister Alise that he was bound to be his enemy while he lived. For Richard's part, he replied that he could by no means marry such a woman in so much as his father had carnal copulation with her and also had by her a bastard son. For proof, he was able to call upon many witnesses to testify before the French King.

In conclusion, by means of counsel and persuasion by those close with the French King, agreement was made so that King Philip did acquit Richard from his bond to marry his sister. Richard was in turn bound to pay King Philip two thousand marks each year for the term of five years. Again, peace between them was concluded on March 28th. Philip left the haven of Messana at the beginning of Easter and brought his army to the siege of Achon.

After their departure, Queen Alinor, the King's mother, accompanied by Berengaria, arrived in Messana for the marriage with Richard. Richard left the haven on April 20th and sailed for Achon with 150 great ships and fifty-three great galleys containing his army. On Good Friday about 9 am rose a tempest from the south, scattering his navy. The King was driven to the Isle of Creta, making anchor at Rhodes Harbour. The ships carrying the King's sister, the Queen of Sicily and Berengaria – the King of Navars' daughter – together with two other ships were driven to the Isle of Cyprus.

After this storm, Richard sent forth his galleys to recover his sister and fiancée as well as his dispersed navy. His sister and future wife were safe in the Port of Lymszem on the Isle of Cyprus, but the two accompanying ships were lost and with their crews and passengers drowned, including the King's Vice Chancellor, later found with the King's seal still about his neck. Isakius, the then King of Cyprus (also named Emperor of the Gryffons) took and imprisoned all the Englishmen cast up on his coasts as well as taking possession of all items of worth found upon those drowned. He also took possession of the two ships that had entered his haven containing those ladies aforementioned.

On hearing these tidings; Richard, in great wrath, gathered his galleys and set sail for Cyprus. At first he politely told King Isakius how his men on their quest to the Holy Land were unfortunate to be borne by bad weather to his shores. He requested three times for the release of the ladies, his men and all their goods, but Isakius at each request, conveyed that he had no intention of releasing the prisoners or returning any goods.

When Richard heard how light this King Isakius made of his humble and honest petition and how nothing might be retrieved without violent force, he commanded his men to arm themselves and follow him ashore, willing them to place their trust in God and not doubt that the Lord would stand with them and give them the victory. The King in the meantime stood by the coasts where the Englishmen would arrive and prepared with swords, billes and lances and other weapons. Boards, chests and other objects were piled up before them to make a wall of defence. Few were harnessed and most were without skill or experience in feats of war.

With his soldiers, Richard first set his bowmen in front; who, with their shot, quickly made way for others to follow. Soon winning the land, they pressed so fiercely upon the Gryffons that at long last, after clash and blows, the King of Cyprus was put to flight with Richard valiantly pursuing. Many were slain and many more made captive, but the King of Cyprus avoided capture due to nightfall. Richard achieved a great victory and returned to the port town of Lymszen which had been deserted, finding there great abundance of corn, wine, oil and victuals.

The next day Joanna, the King's sister, and Berengaria the maiden entered the port and town of Lymszem with fifty great ships and fourteen galleons so that the whole navy converged there, totalling 254 tall ships and about sixty galleons. The King Isakius, seeing no escape by the sea, pitched his tents just five miles from the English army, swearing that he would again give battle. But in the early hours of the morning of the day set for battle, Richard's army set upon the tents of the Gryffons. Being asleep and unprepared, a great slaughter was inflicted with the King of Cyprus running away naked, leaving his tents and pavilions to the Englishmen. These were full of horses and treasure and included the King's personal standard, the lower part of which entailed a streamer wrought with gold.

Returning with victory to his sister and fiancée, on May 12th Richard married Berengaria, daughter of Zanctius – King of Navarre – on the Isle of Cyprus at Lymszem. The King of Cyprus at length submitted to Richard with condition of payment of 20 000 marks in gold and return of the captives and further, he in person to attend upon King Richard to the land of Jerusalem in God's service with four hundred horsemen and five hundred foot soldiers. In return, Richard promised that he retain his castles, his only daughter and keep his kingdom.

The King of Cyprus swore fidelity and allegiance to King Richard before Guido, King of Jerusalem; and the Prince of Antioch, but this King Isakius was again in defiance of Richard who again encircled the land of Cyprus with ships and men-at-arms that the people of Cyprus soon yielded. On recapture, Isakius was bound in fetters of gold and expatriated to the city of Tripolis.

All this being done with regard to the possession of Cyprus, on June 1st Richard bestowed the governorship to Radulphe, son of Godfrey, Lord Chamberlaine. Richard departed Cyprus with his ships and galleys on June 5th and sailed towards the siege at Achon. Arriving the next day at Tyrus, its citizens would not permit him to enter the city. Whilst crossing the sea on the following day, he met with a great bark filled with soldiers and armed men totalling about fifteen hundred. This bark sailed with the French colours set, but indeed were Saracens sent with barrels of gunpowder (not yet known to the English) to assist in the defence of the city of Achon. But Richard, being of good perception, did not fall for this ruse and immediately set upon them, thus spoiling their plan. Most were drowned with but a few taken prisoner. The news of this was a discomfort to the citizens of Achon and an advantage to the Christians. Richard arrived at Achon on June 7th, the siege having already proceeded for many months. Rather than see the walls undermined, towers thrown down and the city destroyed, the citizens at length surrendered to the two kings.

Further assistance to the Christians was due to a spy within the city who, from time to time, would drop letters over the wall written in Hebrew, Greek and Latin disclosing the various feelings and goings on within and further, giving tactical advice to the Christians without. After the taking of the city, the identity of the spy was never discovered. Thus on July 12th, the princes and captains of the Saracens met at the tent of the Templars to seek terms of peace and give up the city:

- that the Kings should have the city of Achon delivered into their hands with all contained therein
- that five hundred captives of the Christians be surrendered and returned into Achon
- that the Holy Cross be returned together with one thousand Christian captives and together with two hundred horsemen selected from those of the Saladin
- that two hundred thousand Byzantine citizens be held as surety by the kings for forty days under threat of death to ensure all the aforementioned terms be realised.

Thus agreed, the kings sent their soldiers and servants into the city to take one hundredth of the richest and best and lock them up in well guarded towers. For the most part, citizens must remain in their houses. Those that would be baptised and receive the faith of Christ should be free to go whither they would. So, many for fear of death pretended to be baptised, but afterwards reverted to their faith under Saladin as soon as they were able. Noting this, the kings commanded that none should be baptised against their will.

On July 13th, after having obtained the city, the two kings divided between them all things contained therein: people, gold and silver, furniture etc. to the extent that little remained as booty for the knights and barons who quickly displayed their displeasure. Hearing of this, the kings quickly saw to it that their wishes be satisfied. On July 20th, Richard requested of the French King that they renew their oath, combine their armies and agree to stay in the land of Jerusalem a further three years to recover the whole country, but Philip would undertake no such oath. Richard entered the city with his wife and sister and took up residence in the palace whereas the French King remained at the houses of the Templars until the end of the month. At the beginning of August, the French King decided to travel to Tyrus then depart the Holy Land, leaving his half of the city in the hands of Conradus the Marques. Richard and all the princes of the Christian army begged him to stay, remarking that it was a pity he had come so far just to leave undone that for which he came. But he could not be dissuaded and on August 3rd, the French King sailed for his homeland.

After his departure, the Saracens broke all the peace agreements. Neither did they return the Holy Cross or the captives and sent no money. Word was sent to King Richard that if he executed any of the Byzantines, those Christians still imprisoned would be beheaded. The Saladin sent great gifts to Richard and requested that the time limit be extended beyond the forty days, but Richard refused both gifts and the request. At this, the Saladin decreed that the Christian captives be beheaded on the August 28th approaching. Richard, however, seeing that the time limit was exhausted on August 20th, caused the beheading of some 2500 of the Saracen captives openly in the sight of the Saladin's army. Only a few of the higher ranking were preserved for further bargaining. Richard then ventured towards the city of Joppe which he found completely deserted of Saracens and so moved on to Ascalon; however, Ascalon had been stripped of all valuables on order of the Saladin with most of the people gone, as similar it was now throughout the whole land of Siria, giving Richard free passage with no resistance. No Saracen prince dared confront King Richard and his army.

Of all these achievements, Richard sent letters to England and also to the Abbot of Claravale in France and was now hoping to return home by the following Easter. The two kings had accomplished much and indeed might have much more had they not fallen out. No sooner had Philip returned home, he invaded the country of Normandy, willing Richard's brother John to take over the Kingdom of England in his brother's absence. John conspired with Philip of France.

Hearing of these events whilst in Siria, Richard made peace with the Turks and decided that the following spring he would commence his journey home to England. Due to stormy weather near Histria and driven to a port in the town of Synaca, Richard was captured by Duke Lympold of Ostria and immediately sold to the Emperor for sixty thousand marks. The Emperor had him imprisoned and Richard was held for the space of a year and three months whilst the ransom was being sought in England.

The barons and bishops of England withstood John's attempt at seizing the throne. It was concluded that a ransom of £104 000, part to the Duke of Ostria and the remainder to the Emperor, be raised for Richard's release. To this end, the valuables of the church such as gold and silver chalices, crosses, candlesticks, plates and the like, together with public contributions from friars, abbots and subjects were accumulated. A part instalment was paid and for the balance, hostages and pledges were taken. Permission was gained from the Pope that priests might celebrate with chalices of latten and tin. It was later rumoured that the treacherous Duke of Ostria was shortly afterwards punished by God in the shape of plagues and misfortunes rendering him to die just a year later in 1196. Thus, Richard was finally delivered to his native England after his honourable deeds for Christianity in the Holy Land.

Guiliemus Neobrigensis, *Actes and Monuments of the Church of England*
Translated from the Latin by M John Foxe.
Reproduced here by the kind permission of *The Hakluyt Society*, London, UK.

CONFLICT	COMBATANTS		OUTCOME
Italian War 1494–1498	**League of Venice** Papal States Republic of Venice Kingdom of Naples Kingdoms of Spain Duchy of Milan Holy Roman Empire Republic of Florence Duchy of Mantua Kingdom of England (from 1496)	Kingdom of France Swiss mercenaries	**Victory** Forced FRENCH retreat
Second Ottoman-Venetian War (1499–1503)	Republic of Venice Castile and Aragon	Ottoman Empire	**Defeat** Venetian strongholds of Modon and Coron fall to the Ottomans Cephalonia and Ithaca to Venice

Italian War 1499–1504	Duchy of Milan Kingdom of Naples Castile and Aragon (from 1501)	Kingdom of France Papal States Republic of Venice Castile and Aragon (to 1501)	**Victory** Louis XII of France ceded Naples to Ferdinand II of Aragon French control of the Duchy of Milan
War of the League of Cambrai 1508–1516	**1508–10**: Venice **1510–11**: Papal States Venice **1511–13**: *Holy League*: Papal States Venice Spain Holy Roman Empire England Swiss mercenaries **1513–16**: Papal States Spain Holy Roman Empire England Duchy of Milan Swiss mercenaries	**1508–10**: *League of Cambrai*: Papal States France Holy Roman Empire Spain Duchy of Ferrara **1510–11**: France Duchy of Ferrara **1511–13**: France Duchy of Ferrara **1513–16**: Venice France Scotland Duchy of Ferrara	**Defeat**

Spanish conquest of Iberian Navarre 1512	Crown of Castile Crown of Aragon	Kingdom of Navarre	**Victory** Navarre south of the Pyrenees annexed to Castile
Spanish conquest of the Aztec Empire 1519–1521	SPANISH conquistadores Tlaxcala	Aztec Empire	**Victory** Aztec empire is annexed to Spanish Empire
Italian War of 1521–1526	Spain Holy Roman Empire England Papal States	France Swiss mercenaries Republic of Venice	**Victory**
War of the League of Cognac 1526–1530	Spain Holy Roman Empire Republic of Genoa	France Swiss mercenaries Papal States Republic of Venice Republic of Florence Kingdom of England Duchy of Milan	**Victory**
Little War in Hungary 1530–	Holy Roman Empire	Ottoman Empire	**Indecisive** John Szapolyai

224

c.1552	Archduchy of Austria Kingdom of Bohemia Royal Hungary Kingdom of Croatia Spain Papal States	Moldavia John Szapolyai's Hungarian kingdom Wallachia Serbian Despotate France	recognized as King of Hungary Ferdinand I's lands in Hungary guaranteed
Spanish conquest of the Inca Empire 1531–1572	Spanish conquistadores Indian auxiliaries	Inca Empire	**Victory** Former Inca lands incorporated into Viceroyalty of Peru
Yaqui Wars 1533–1821	Crown of Castile (1533–1716) Spain (1716–1821)	Yaqui **Yaqui Allies:** Mayo Opata Pima	**Defeat** Eventual Mexican victory in 1929
Italian War of 1536–1538	Holy Roman Empire Spain Swiss mercenaries	Kingdom of France Ottoman Empire	**Indecisive** Truce of Nice Savoy and Piedmont acquired

			by France
Arauco War 1536–1825	✖ Spanish Empire Kingdom of Chile	Mapuche, Huilliche Pehuenche and Picunche warriors	**Defeat** Establishment of the Bío-Bío River as frontier Mapuches are independent until the occupation of the Araucania in 1883
Third Ottoman–Venetian War 1537–1540	**Holy League**: ▨ Republic of Venice ✖ Spain ✚ Republic of Genoa ▮ Papal States ✖ Kingdom of Naples ▨ Kingdom of Sicily ▦ Knights of Malta	Ottoman Empire ⚜ France (until 1538)	**Defeat**
Mixtón War 1540–1542	✖ Spain	Caxcanes	**Victory**
Tiguex War 1540–1541	✖ Spain	Tiwa Indians	**Victory**
Italian War of 1542–1546	✖ Spain ▦ Holy Roman Empire	⚜ France ✚ Swiss mercenaries	**Inconclusive**

	Saxony Brandenburg Kingdom of England	Ottoman Empire Jülich-Cleves-Berg	
Schmalkaldic War 1546–1547	Empire of Charles V: Spain Holy Roman Empire Duchy of Saxony Kingdom of Hungary Kingdom of Bohemia and other Lands of the Bohemian Crown	Schmalkaldic League: Electorate of Saxony Hesse Electorate of the Palatinate Bremen Lübeck Brunswick-Lüneburg Other German territories	**Victory** Capitulation of Wittenberg: Schmalkaldic League dissolved, Saxon electoral dignity passed to the Albertine House of Wettin
Chichimeca War 1550–1590	Spain Indian allies	Chichimeca (Zacateco, Guachichil, Guamare, Pame)	**Defeat**
Italian War of 1551–1559	Spanish Empire Holy Roman Empire Kingdom of	Kingdom of France Swiss mercenaries Republic of	**Victory** Peace of Cateau-Cambrésis Spain is confirmed as the dominant

	England 🏛 Republic of Florence 🇩🇰 Duchy of Savoy	Siena Ottoman Empire	power in Italy France renounces its claim in Italy but wins the Three Bishoprics (Metz, Toul and Verdun) in Lorraine and the Pale of Calais from England.
French Wars of Religion 1562–1598	**Catholics**: ⛪ Catholic League ✖ Spain 🇩🇰 Duchy of Savoy	**Protestants**: ❄ Huguenots ➕ England	**Defeat** Uneasy truce The Edict of Nantes granted the Huguenots substantial rights in certain areas Paris and other defined territories were declared to be permanently Catholic Failure of France's enemies to weaken France and to gain territories
Philippine revolts against	✖ Spain Filipino loyalists	🇫🇷 Dagohoy rebel group other Philippino	**Victory** Most revolts failed

Spain 1567–1872		rebel groups ——————— 🇬🇧 British supporters	
Eighty Years' War 1568–1648	❌ Spanish Empire 🦅 Holy Roman Empire	🟧 United Provinces ➕ England 🛡️ Nassau 🔱 France	**Defeat** Peace of Münster Independence of the Dutch Republic SPANISH retention of the Southern Netherlands
Fourth Ottoman-Venetian War 1570–1573	**Holy League**: 🏴 Republic of Venice ❌ Spain 🟨 Papal States ❌ Kingdom of Naples ➕ Republic of Genoa 🏴 Kingdom of Sicily 🐝 Grand Duchy of Tuscany 🏴 Duchy of Urbino 🟥 Duchy of Savoy 🟥 Knights of Malta	Ottoman Empire	**Defeat** Cyprus under Ottoman rule
Second	❌ FitzGeralds	➕ Kingdom of	**Defeat**

Desmond Rebellion 1579–1583	of Desmond ✕ Spain ▌ Papal States allied Irish clans	England 🏳 Kingdom of Ireland allied Irish clans	Famine throughout Munster Plantation of Munster
War of the Portuguese Succession 1580–1583	✕ Spain 🛡 Portugal loyal to Philip of Spain	🛡 Portugal loyal to Prior of Crato ✚ France ✚ England ▬ United Provinces	**Victory** The Iberian Union: Acquisition of the Kingdom of Portugal and its colonial possessions by Philip II of Spain
Cologne War 1583–1588	✚ Ernst of BavariaPrince-Elector, Cologne, 1583–1612 🛡 House of Wittelsbach 🛡 Free Imperial City of Cologne 🛡 Philip of Spain, and for him: 🛡 House of Farnese 🛡 House of Isenburg-Grenzau 🛡 House of Mansfeld	✚ Gebhard, Truchsess von Waldburg, Prince-Elector, Cologne 1578–1588 🛡 House of Neuenahr-Alpen 🛡 House of Waldburg 🛡 House of Palatinate-Zweibrücken 🛡 House of Nassau 🛡 House of Solms-	**Victory**

	(main line) House of Berlaymont-Flyon *and others*	Braunfels *and others*	
Anglo-Spanish War 1585–1604	Spanish Empire Portugal under Philip of Spain French Catholic League Irish alliance	Kingdom of England United Provinces Kingdom of France Portuguese loyal to Prior of Crato FRENCH Huguenot forces	**Indecisive** Status quo ante Treaty of London
Irish Nine Years' War 1594–1603	Alliance of Irish clans Spain Scottish Gaelic mercenaries	Kingdom of England Kingdom of Ireland	**Defeat** Treaty of Mellifont (1603) Flight of the Earls (1607)
Acoma War 1598–1599	Crown of Castile	Acoma	**Victory**
Dutch-Portuguese War 1602–1663	**Kingdom of Portugal** *Supported by:* Crown of Castile (until 1640) Kingdom of Cochin Potiguara Tupis	**Dutch Republic** *Supported by:* Kingdom of England (until 1640) Johor Sultanate Kingdom of Kandy Kingdom of	**Inconclusive** Treaty of Hague Formation of the Dutch Empire Portuguese Restoration War Portuguese victory

		Congo Kingdom of Ndongo Rio Grande Tupis Nhandui Tarairiu Tribe	in South America and Africa, Dutch victory in the East
War of the Jülich Succession 1609–1614	**1610: Supporting Emperor Rudolph:** Holy Roman Empire Principality of Strasbourg Prince-Bishopric of Liège **1613–1614: Supporting Wolfgang William:** Spain Palatinate-Neuburg Catholic League	**1610: Opposed to Emperor Rudolph:** Margraviate of Brandenburg Palatinate-Neuburg United Provinces Kingdom of France England Protestant Union **1613–1614: Supporting John Sigismund:** Margraviate of Brandenburg United Provinces England Protestant Union	**Victory** Treaty of Xanten: Jülich-Berg and Ravenstein to Wolfgang William. Cleves-Mark and Ravensberg to John Sigismund. Wesel under SPANISH control
Thirty Years' War	**Roman Catholic States and Allies**	**Protestant States and Allies**	**Defeat**

| 1618–1648 | Holy Roman Empire Catholic League Austria Bohemia (after 1620) Spanish Empire Hungary Kingdom of Croatia Denmark-Norway (1643–1645) | Sweden (from 1630) France (from 1635) Denmark-Norway (1625–1629) Bohemia (1618–1620) United Provinces Saxony Electoral Palatinate (until 1623) Brandenburg-Prussia Brunswick-Lüneburg England (1625–1630) Transylvania Hungarian Anti-Habsburg Rebels | Peace of Westphalia

Protestant princes allowed to continue religious practices

Habsburg supremacy curtailed

Rise of France and the Bourbon dynasty

Rise of the Swedish Empire

Decline of feudalism

Decentralization of the Holy Roman Empire

Franco-Spanish War until 1659

Substantial decline in the power and influence of the Catholic Church |
| First Genoese-Savoyard | Spain Republic of Genoa | Kingdom of France | **Victory** |

War 1625		🚩 Duchy of Savoy	France surrenders its claims on Savoy and Valtellina and withdraws its troops from the Piedmont and the Republic of Genoa, stipulated by the Treaty of Monzón Reconquest of some territories in the French Riviera by the combined forces of Spain and the Republic of Genoa
Anglo-Spanish War 1625–1630	✖ Spain	✚ England ▬ United Provinces	**Victory** Treaty of Madrid
Spanish expedition to Formosa 1626	✖ Spanish East Indies	Kingdom of Middag	**Indecisive** SPANISH establishment in Formosa
War of the Mantuan Succession 1628–1631	**Supporting the Duke of Guastalla:** 🦅 Holy Roman Empire ✖ Spain	**Supporting the Duke of Nevers:** ⚜ France	**Indecisive** Peace of Regensburg (1630) Treaty of Cherasco

234

	🟥 Duchy of Savoy		(1631)
Franco-Spanish War 1635–1659	✖ Spain 🟦 Royalists of the British Isles (from 1657)	France ✚ Commonwealth of England (from 1657)	**Defeat** Treaty of the Pyrenees
Catalan Revolt 1640–1659	✖ Spain	🟥 Principality of Catalonia France	**Victory** Revolt crushed Treaty of the Pyrenees County of Roussillon and the northern half of Cerdanya ceded to France
Portuguese Restoration War 1640–1668	✖ Castile and Aragon	Kingdom of Portugal **Supported by**: France (1641-59) ✚ Kingdom of England (after 1662)	**Defeat** Treaty of Lisbon Charles of Spain recognizes the sovereignty of the House of Braganza over Portugal and its colonial possessions Portugal cedes Ceuta to Castile
Neapolitan Revolt	✖ Spain	Neapolitan Republic	**Victory**

		France	Revolt crushed

1647–1648		France	Revolt crushed
Anglo-Spanish War 1654–1660	Spain Royalists of the British Isles	Commonwealth of England France (1657–59)	**Indecisive** Treaties of Madrid (1667 and 1670) Acquisition of Jamaica, the Cayman Islands, Dunkirk and Mardyck by the Commonwealth of England
War of Devolution 1667–1668	Spanish Empire **Triple Alliance:** Dutch Republic Kingdom of England Swedish Empire	France	**Indecisive** Treaty of Aix-la-Chapelle (1668)
Franco-Dutch War 1672–1678	Dutch Republic Holy Roman Empire Spain Denmark-Norway Electorate of	France England Sweden Bishopric of Münster Archbishopric of Cologne	**Defeat** Treaty of Nijmegen Treaty of Westminster

	Brandenburg		
Second Genoese–Savoyard War 1672–1673	✚ Republic of Genoa *Supported by:* ✖ Spain	▰▰ Duchy of Savoy	**Victory** Status quo ante bellum
War of the Reunions 1683–1684	✖ Spanish Empire 🦅 Holy Roman Empire ✚ Republic of Genoa	🔱 France	**Defeat** Truce of Ratisbon
Nine Years' War 1688–1697	**Grand Alliance**: ▬ Dutch Republic ✚ England 🦅 Holy Roman Empire ✖ Spain ▰▰ Piedmont-Savoy ▰▰ Sweden (until 1691) ✖ Scotland	🔱 France ▭ Irish and Scottish Jacobites	**Indecisive** Treaty of Ryswick Louis XIV recognizes William III of Orange as King of England, Scotland and Ireland France retains Alsace (including Strasbourg) and surrenders Freiburg, Breisach and Philippsburg to the Holy Roman Empire, regains Pondicherry (after paying the

			Dutch a sum of 16,000 pagodas) and Nova Scotia
			Spain recovered Cataloni a from France, and the barrier fortresses of Mons, Luxembour g and Kortrijk
			The Duchy of Lorraine was restored to Leopold Joseph from France
War of the Spanish Succession 1701–1714	Kingdom of France Spain loyal to Philip Bavaria (until 1704) Duchy of Mantua (until 1708)	Holy Roman Empire: Austria Prussia Hanover England (until 1707) Scotland (until 1707) Great Britain (from 1707)	**Defeat** Treaty of Utrecht (1713) Treaty of Rastatt (1714) Treaty of Baden (1714) Philip is recognised as King of Spain, but once more renounces any claim to the throne of France. Spain and Britain sign the *Asiento*

		Dutch Republic Duchy of Savoy Kingdom of Portugal Spain loyal to Charles	Spain cedes the Spanish Netherlands, Kingdom of Naples, Duchy of Milan and Sardinia to the Habsburg Monarchy, Sicily t o the Duchy of Savoy and Gibraltar and Minorca to Britain France is guaranteed all its former conquests but recognizes British sovereignty over Rupert's Land and Newfoundland and cedes Acadia and its half of Saint Kitts to Great Britain The Dutch Republic retains various forts in the Southern Netherlands and

			annexes a part of Spanish Guelders. Spain cedes the Colony of Sacramento to the Portuguese Empire
Huilliche rebellion 1712	✕ Spanish Empire	Huilliches of Chiloé	**Indecisive** Key encomenderos killed Suppression of the rebellion Encomienda mildened
Seventh Ottoman-Venetian War 1714–1718	Republic of Venice Austria (from 1716) Portugal Order of Malta Papal States Spain Himariotes	Ottoman Empire	**Defeat** Treaty of Passarowitz Morea ceded back to Ottoman Empire
War of the Quadruple Alliance 1718–1720	Spain Jacobites	Great Britain France Holy Roman Empire Dutch Republic Savoy	**Defeat** Treaty of The Hague

Anglo-Spanish War 1727–1729	Spain	Great Britain	**Indecisive** Treaty of Seville (1729)
War of the Polish Succession 1733–1738	Poland loyal to Stanisław I France Spain Kingdom of Sardinia Duchy of Parma	Poland loyal to Augustus III Russian Empire Habsburg Empire of Austria Saxony Kingdom of Prussia	**Victory** Treaty of Vienna Augustus III ascends the throne Bourbon territorial gains
Spanish–Portuguese War 1735–1737	Spanish Empire	Portuguese Empire Brazilian colonial forces	**Defeat**
War of Jenkins' Ear 1739–1748	Spanish Empire	Great Britain	**Indecisive** Status quo ante bellum Treaty of Aix-la-Chapelle (1748)
War of the Austrian Succession 1740–1748	France Prussia Spain Bavaria (1741–45) Saxony (1741–42) Sicily and Naples	Habsburg Monarchy Great Britain Hanover Dutch Republic Saxony (1743–45) Kingdom of	**Victory** Treaty of Aix-la-Chapelle Maria Theresa retains the Austrian throne

	✚ Republic of Genoa(1745–48) ⬜ Sweden (1741–1743) ⬜ Kingdom of Sardinia (1741–1742)	Sardinia (1742–1748) ⬜ Russia (1741–1743, 1748)	Prussian control of Silesia confirmed Duchies of Pama, Piacenza and Guastalla restored to the Spanish Bourbons
Seven Years' War 1756–1763	France Austria Russia (until 1762) Spanish Empire (from 1762) Sweden (1757–1762) Saxony Mughal Empire (from 1757)	Great Britain Prussia Hanover Brunswick-Wolfenbüttel Iroquois Confederacy Portugal (from 1762) Hesse-Kassel Schaumburg-Lippe	**Defeat** Treaty of Saint Petersburg (1762) Treaty of Hamburg (1762) Treaty of Paris (1763) Treaty of Hubertusburg (1763) *Status quo ante bellum* in Europe TRANSFER of colonial possessions between Great Britain, France, and Spain
Spanish–	Spanish	Portuguese	**Victory**

War	Victor	Defeated	Outcome
Portuguese War 1776–1777	Empire	Empire	First Treaty of San Ildefonso Portugal remains neutral during the American Revolutionary War
American Revolutionary War 1775–1783	American Union France (1778–83) Spain (1779–83) Co-belligerents: Netherlands (1780–83) Mysore (1779–84) Vermont (1777–83) Oneida Tuscarora Watauga Association Catawba Lenape	Great Britain Loyalists German mercenaries Co-belligerents: Onondaga Mohawk Cayuga Seneca Cherokee	**Victory** Peace of Paris American independence Britain loses area east of Mississippi River and south of Great Lakes & St. Lawrence River to independent American States & to Spain Spain gains East Florida, West Florida and Minorca Britain cedes Tobago and Senegal to France. Dutch Republic cedes Negapatnam to Britain.

War of the Pyrenees 1793–1795	Spain Portugal FRENCH Émigrés	France	**Defeat** Peace of Basel Second Treaty of San Ildefonso
Anglo-Spanish War 1796–1808	Spain	Great Britain	**Inconclusive** Treaty of Amiens (1802) Belligerence resumed in May 1804 Cessation of hostilities and de facto Anglo SPANISH alliance upon outbreak of the Peninsular War (1808) Trinidad ceded to Britain (1802) Minorca returned to Spain (1802)
Quasi-War 1798–1800	United States Batavian Republic Great Britain	France Spain	**Indecisive** Convention of 1800 Peaceful cessation of Franco-American alliance

			End of FRENCH privateer attacks on American shipping American neutrality and renunciation of claims against France
War of the Oranges 1801	France Spain	Portugal	**Victory** Treaty of Badajoz Question of Olivença Portuguese territory returned, except Olivenza, and border territories, which remained in Spanish possession France territorial guarantees in Trinidad, Port Mahon (Minorca) and Malta, as well as lands north of Brazil
War of the	French	**Third Coalition:**	**Victory**

Third Coalition 1803–1806	Empire ▬ Etruria ▬ Batavian Republic ▬ Italy ▬ Spain ▬ Electorate of Bavaria ▬ Württemberg	▬ Holy Roman Empire ▬ Russian Empire ▬ United Kingdom ▬ Kingdom of Naples ▬ Kingdom of Sicily ▬ Sweden ▬ French counter-revolutionaries ▬ French royalists	Treaty of Pressburg Dissolution of the Holy Roman Empire Creation of the Confederation of the Rhine Hostilities RESUME few months later with the formation of a Fourth Coalition against France
Invasion of Portugal 1807	▬ French Empire ▬ Spain	▬ Portugal	**Victory**
Peninsular War 1808–1814	▬ Spain ▬ United Kingdom ▬ Portugal	▬ French Empire ▬ Napoleonic Spain	**Victory** Treaty of Paris
Bolivian War of Independenc e 1809–1825	▬ Spain Royalists	▬ United Provinces of the Río de la Plata ▬ Republiquetas	**Defeat** Independence of Bolivia
Mexican War of Independenc e 1810–1821	▬ Spain ✗ Mexican royalists	▬ Insurgents ▬ Army of the Three Guarantees (1821)	**Defeat** First Mexican Empire gains independence from Spain

246

	Royalists	Patriots	Defeat
Argentine War of Independence 1810–1818	*Royalists* Viceroyalty of the Río de la Plata Viceroyalty of Peru	*Patriots* United Provinces of the Río de la Plata Chilean exiles	**Defeat** Argentine victory and emancipation from Spanish colonial rule Slavery partially abolished
Chilean War of Independence 1810–1826	Spanish Empire Viceroyalty of Peru Mapuche allies	Chile United Provinces Mapuche allies	**Defeat** Chilean emancipation from Spanish colonial rule
Venezuelan War of Independence 1811–1823	Kingdom of Spain	Venezuela Gran Colombia New Granada	**Defeat** Venezuelan independence
Peruvian War of Independence 1811–1824	**United Liberating Army** United Army (Argentine-Chilean) Gran Colombia Republic of Peru Peruvian patriots	Kingdom of Spain Viceroyalty of Peru Peruvian Royalists	**Defeat** Peru becomes independent of the SPANISH monarchy

War of the Seventh Coalition 1815	**Seventh Coalition:** 🏴 United Kingdom 🏴 Prussia 🏴 Austrian 🏴 Russian Empire 🏴 Hanover 🏴 Nassau 🏴 Brunswick 🏴 Sweden 🏴 Netherlands 🏴 Spain 🏴 Portugal 🏴 Sardinia 🏴 Sicily 🏴 Tuscany 🏴 Switzerland 🏴 French Kingdom	🏴 French Empire 🏴 Kingdom of Naples	**Victory** Second Treaty of Paris End of Napoleonic Wars Second exile of Napoleon and second Bourbon Restoration Beginning of the Concert of Europe
Spanish reconquest of New Granada 1815–1816	🏴 Kingdom of Spain	🏴 United Provinces of New Granada	**Victory** Reconquest of New Granada by the SPANISH monarchy
Ecuadorian War of Independence 1820–1822	🏴 Spain	Independence Armies	**Defeat** Independence of Ecuador from Spain

Spanish reconquest attempts in Mexico 1821–1829	Spanish Empire	Mexico	**Defeat** Spain recognizes the independence of the United Mexican States in 1836

MODERN

	Kingdom of France *Armée de la Foi*	Partisans of the Cortes	**Royalist victory**
Portuguese Civil War 1828–1834	Liberal Forces of Queen Maria II Spain (Since 1834) United Kingdom France (Since 1830)	Absolutist Forces of King Miguel Spain (Until 1833)	**Liberal victory** Concession of Evoramonte: Constitutional monarchy is restored Dom Miguel renounces all his claims to the throne and goes into exile.
First Carlist War 1833–1839	Forces of Queen Isabella II United Kingdom French	Carlists: Forces of Infante Carlos Forces	**Liberal victory** British mediated Convention of Vergara.

	Kingdom [flag] Forces of Queen Maria II	of King Miguel	
Second Carlist War 1846–1849	[flag] Spain	[X] Carlist insurgents	**Liberal victory**
Cochinchina Campaign 1858–1862	[flag] Spain [flag] Second French Empire	[flag] Dai Nam (Nguyễn Dynasty)	**Victory** Treaty of Saigon: Cochinchina becomes a FRENCH colony.
Hispano-Moroccan War 1859–1860	[flag] Spain	[flag] Morocco	**Victory** Treaty of Wad-Ras: Morocco recognises Spanish sovereignty over Sidi Ifni and Western Sahara.
Dominican Restoration War 1863–1865	[flag] Spain	[flag] Dominican Republic	**Defeat** Restoration of Dominican sovereignty
Chincha Islands War 1864–1866	[flag] Spain	[flag] Peru [flag] Chile **Joined in 1866:** [flag] Ecuador [flag] Bolivia	**Defeat** Peace treaties between Spain and Perú (1879), Bolivia (1879), Chile (1883) and

			Ecuador (1885).
Ten Years' War 1868–1878	Spain	Cuban rebels	**Victory** Pact of Zanjón
Third Carlist War 1872–1876	Kingdom of Spain (1872–73) I Republic (1873–1874) Kingdom of Spain (1875–1876)	Carlist insurgents	**Royal Victory**
Little War 1879–1880	Spain	Cuban rebels	**Victory**
First Melillan campaign 1893–1894	Spain	Rif tribes Morocco	**Victory** Treaty of Fez: Morocco pays war reparations of 20 million pesetas and pledges to pacify northern provinces. Melilla hinterlands ceded to Spain.
Philippine Revolution 1896–1898	Spain Captaincy General of the Philippines	Filipino Insurgents	**Defeat** Expulsion of the SPANISH colonial government during Spanish–

251

War	Spain/allies	Opponents	Outcome
			American War (1898)
Spanish–American War 1898	Spain	United States	**Defeat** Treaty of Paris: Spain loses sovereignty over Cuba and cedes the Philippine Islands, Puerto Rico, and Guam to the United States for the sum of $20 million.
Second Melillan campaign 1909–1910	Spain	Rif tribes	**Victory** Melilla territory extended to Cape Three Forks and the Bḥar Ameẓẓyan lagoon
Rif War 1920–1926	Spain France	Republic of the Rif	**Victory** Debellation of the Republic of the Rif
Spanish Civil War 1936–1939	Republican Foreign volunteers Soviet Union (1936–1938) Mexico	Nationalist Italy Nazi Germany Portugal Foreign	**Nationalist victory** Defeat of the Second Spanish Republic Beginning

		volunteers	of Franco's dictatorship
Ifni War 1957–1958	Spain	Morocco	**Victory** Treaty of Angra de Cintra: Morocco recognizes SPANISH sovereignty over Ceuta and Melilla and pays war reparations.
Basque conflict 1959–2011	Francoist Spain (1959–1975) Spain (1975–2011) France	Basque National Liberation Movement	**Inconclusive** ETA declares definitive cessation of its armed activity.
Sahara secret War 1973–1975	Spain	Polisario	**Inconclusive** Madrid Accords Polisario continues the struggle against Morocco.
1st Iraq Gulf War 1991	Kuwait	Iraq	**Victory** Kuwait regains its

	🇺🇸 United States 🇸🇦 Saudi Arabia 🇫🇷 France 🇪🇬 Egypt 🇸🇾 Syria 🇬🇧 United Kingdom Other Allies		independence
Bosnian intervention 1992–1996	⬛ NATO	🟦 Yugoslavia	**Victory** Dayton Accords: Siege of Sarajevo lifted. Bosnian Serbs return to negotiations.
War in Afghanistan (2001-)	🏴 Afghanistan 🟢 ISAF	Islamic Emirate of Afghanistan	Fall of Taliban régime Osama bin Laden killed Ongoing Taliban insurgency
2nd Iraq War 2003–2004	⬜ Multi-National Force – Iraq Iraq after the fall of Saddam Hussein	Iraq under Saddam Hussein Various insurgents	**Victory** Fall of Ba'athist rule in Iraq Deployment

	Iraqi Kurdistan		in Najaf Spanish withdrawal in 2004
Libyan intervention 2011	Many NATO members acting under UN mandate and Anti-Gaddafi forces several Arab League states Sweden	Pro-Gaddafi forces	Fall of Gaddafi regime Muammar Gaddafi killed National Transitional Council take control

IV   Australian Casualties in Wars

Australian Casualties of Wars

ADF Casualties	Died	Wounded	Civilian Deaths
Colonial 1788- 1901			
Frontier War 1788-1934			Settlers 2500 Natives 20000
Sudan 1885	9	3	
South Africa- Boer War 1899-1902	559	735	
China- Boxer Rebellion	6	0	
WWI 1914-1918	61508	155000	
WWII 1939-1945	39767	66553	
Occupation of Japan 1946-1951			
Korean War 1950- 1953	341	1216	
Malayan emergancy 1950-1960	51	27	
Indonesian Confrontation 1963-1966	16	8	
Vietnam War 1962-1975	519	2398	
Iraq-1 Gulf War 1990-1991			
Afghanistan 2001-present	43	256	
Iraq-2 2003-2009	3	27	
Peace Keeping 1947-present	9	22	
Iraq-3 against ISIL 2014- present*	-	-	Volunteers Joined IS 3* 129*

* to June 2015

V   Crime

Extreme Crime Rates 2013

Total Homicide Victims

male	female	Total	per 100000	most common weapon	
				knife	firearm
273	157	430	1.9		

Murder Victims

male	female	Total			
157	92	249	1.1	87	

Attempted Murder

male	female	Total			
99	58	157	0.7	54	51

Manslaughter

male	female	Total			
17	7	24	0.1		

Total Deaths

male	female	Total			
174	99	273	1.2		

VI   Road Deaths 2014

2014 Fatality Data on Australian Roads

By State:

TOTAL ACT	10	0.9%
TOTAL NSW	309	26.8%
TOTAL NT	39	3.4%
TOTAL QLD	223	19.3%
TOTAL SA	107	9.3%
TOTAL TAS	35	3.0%
TOTAL VIC	249	21.6%
TOTAL WA	181	15.7%
TOTAL AUS	1153	100.00%

By Type:

Bicyclist (includes pillion passengers)	45	3.9%
Driver	532	46.1%
Motorcycle pillion passenger	5	0.4%
Motorcycle rider	187	16.2%
Passenger	230	19.9%
Pedestrian	151	13.1%
Unclassified	3	0.3%
Total Fatalities	1153	100.0%

VII Drug Related Deaths

Death by Drug Overdose and Drug Related

	2005	2010	* predicted 2015
TOTAL:	1468	1507	1898
Heroin	131	125	138
Methadone	106	112	118
Cocaine	17	23	26
Antidepressants	200	216	262
Amphetamines	79	88	255
Alcohol	178	170	204
Benzodiazopines	249	230	258 includes ice
Cannabis	20	17	12
Paracetemol	52	49	57
Tobacco	80	92	112
Other	356	385	456

VIII Police Shootings 2014

Police Shootings 2014

	2014		Compare 2008-2011
	Fatal	Non-fatal	Fatal
Queensland	4	2	0
NSW	3		7
Victoria	1		2
Tas	0		1
SA	1		0
WA	1		0
NT	0		0
ACT	0		1
Totals:	10		14

IX   Mental Illness

Mental Illness

anxiety
bipola disorder
depression
schizohrenia
substance abuse disorder
personality disorder
psychotic disorder
psychososial disorder
temporary breakdown
combination disorder

15% of people seriously affected by mental illness eventually die by suicide and a small percentage will be shot by the police

up to 85% of homeless people have a mental illness

a mental health issue is normal and may be stress due to some temporary life factors

45% of Australians aged 16 to 85 years will experience a common mental health-related condition such as depression, anxiety or a substance use disorder in their lifetime... that's bullshit! 100% of people experience one of these!

men are four times more prone to suicide than women

X   Causes of Death

Causes of Death

	2005		2013	
Heart Desease/Failure	24576	22.5%	19766	16.9%
Brain/Dementia	16500	15.1%	21410	18.3%
Lung Cancer	7264	6.7%	8217	7.0%
Colon Cancer	2688	2.5%	4234	3.6%
Breast Cancer	2656	2.4%	2892	2.5%
Other Cancer	8678	8.0%	9045	7.7%
Drugs/Alcohol	40365	37.0%	43560	37.2%
HIV/Hepatitis	103	0.1%	111	0.1%
Suicide	4410	4.0%	4830	4.1%
Falls	956	0.9%	1920	1.6%
Road Accidents	897	0.8%	1123	1.0%
Totals:	109093	100.0%	117108	100.0%

AGE - SPECIFIC SUICIDE RATES   2010

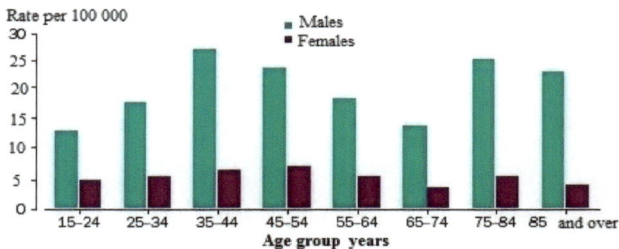

Total Male: 165
Total Female: 46

Total: 211   per 100 000   (i.e 4326 for 2010)

258

XI   Murders of Animalian Civilians by Islamic Terrorists   2000 -2014

Deaths/Murders of Australians Attributed to Islamic Terrorists

	2000	2001	2002	2003	2004	2005	2006	2007	2008	2009	2010	2011	2012	2013	2014
In Australia	0	0	0	0	0	0	0	0	0	0	0	0	0	0	2
Abroad	0	11	88	0	0	0	0	0	0	3	0	0	0	0	*20+

NOTES:

*1 volunteer fighting in Iraq against IS
19 murdered by IS in Syria after joining
(> 6 killed in Syria alongside rebel forces)

Other possible deaths in Islamic countries
not ever identified as terrorist approx. 12

Terrorist attacks on Australians by other
religious groups in India and elswhere approx. 8

(Column annotations: 9/11 attack on World Trade Center NY, USA; Kuta Bali bombings; Marriott & Ritz-Carlton bombings Jakarta; Islamic State Iraq and Levant)

XII   Autism Spectrum Disorder & Learning Disabilities

Autism Rates (Autism Spectrum Disorder) and Learning Disabilities for Selected Countries

		population milions	ASD rate per 10 000	total with ASD	proportion male (IQ < 70)	proportion male	proportion female	autistic males with learning disability	autistic females with learning disability	total males with a learning disability	total females with a learning disability	total persons with a learning disability	percentage persons with a learning disability
Australia	2012	22.34	52	115400	47%	80%	20%	43390	10848	130171	32543	162714	0.7%
	2009	21.25	30	64400	46%	82%	18%	24292	5332	72875	15997	88872	0.4%
UK	2011	62.2	142	700000	48%	85%	15%	285600	50400	856800	151200	1008000	1.6%
	1966		5										
	1978		20										
	2005		90										
	2006		116										
USA	2011/2012		200										
Sweden	2001/2007		115										
Sth Korea	2011		265										
World Median	2013		62										

Most of these statistics must be viewed with caution due to
definitions and sampling techniques. In some cases data is
for narrow age ranges and do not reflect the picture for the
overall population.

Researchers comparing findings of prevalence studies from different parts of the world over the past few years have come up with a more conservative median estimate of prevalence.
They conclude that the both the increase in estimates over time and the variability between countries and regions are likely to be because of broadening diagnostic criteria

There was considerable variation in the prevalence of autism across age groups, with a marked drop off
in prevalence after peaking in the 5 to 9 years age group. A similar pattern can be seen in the data from
2009. There are several possible reasons for this variation in prevalence across age groups such as
diagnostic issues, survey scope and methodology.

ALL PERSONS WITH AUTISM AGED 0-39 YEARS, by Age—2009, 2012

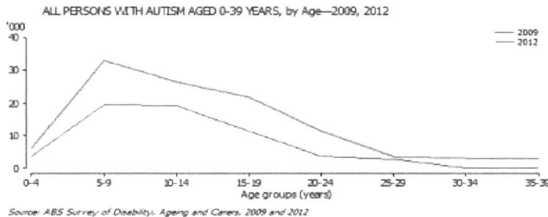

Source: ABS Survey of Disability, Ageing and Carers, 2009 and 2012

The criteria used to diagnose autism have been subject to some variation over time.

XIII Migrants that Should Not Have Been Allowed In 1946-1966

Migrant Arrivals 1946-1966*

		Number should have been REJECTED! **	#
Argentina	4750	24	0.50%
Albania	3850	10	0.25%
Austria	26000	294	1.13%
Belgium (and Congo)	525	3	0.50%
Brazil	1200	9	0.75%
Bulgaria	850	9	1.00%
Canada	13500	3	0.02%
China+Hong Kong+Macao+Formosa	26000	8	0.03%
Colombia	350	2	0.50%
Croatia	21000	263	1.25%
Czechoslavakia	4100	31	0.75%
Denmark	6500	16	0.25%
Egypt	22300	56	0.25%
Estonia	2500	25	1.00%
France (and Algeria)	3900	23	0.60%
Germany	225500	3834	1.70%
Greece	126800	190	0.15%
Hungary	15600	94	0.60%
India	17300	2	0.01%
Italy+	296800	2523	0.85%
Latvia	3900	49	1.25%
Lithuania	2850	36	1.25%
Malta	59800	6	0.01%
New Zealand	47900	19	0.04%
Netherlands (and Indonesia)	136000	748	0.55%
Norway	1200	6	0.50%
Poland	21700	141	0.65%
Portugal	3200	4	0.13%
Romania	8450	68	0.80%
Russia (USSR)	4200	17	0.40%
Slovenia	3250	33	1.00%
South Africa	9700	3	0.03%
Spain	7900	43	0.55%
Sweden	2500	8	0.30%
Switzerland	2200	22	1.00%
UK and Republic of Ireland##	791800	79	0.01%
Ukraine	8800	110	1.25%
Uruguay	850	11	1.25%
Yugoslavia	42500	425	1.00%
Other Europe	24300	134	0.55%
USA	30100	21	0.07%
Other South America	4400	77	1.75%
Other North Africa	3000	23	0.75%
Other Asia	60000	78	0.13%
Middle East	13500	41	0.30%
Illegal	7750	233	3.00%
TOTAL	**2121075**	**9496**	**0.45%**

Official Number: 2113098

NOTES

* Based on Department of Immigration NOTE: stated country not necessarily that of original citizenship!

\# Estimates per 100 immigrants entering Australia

** Persons known to have been either:
1. members of the Nazi Party
2. members of the Ustashi, Arrow Cross and other national fascist movements
3. associated with the murder of Jews, Gypsies, Muslims and innocent civilians
4. High ranking officers of the German Armed Forces
5. High ranking officers in the Italian Armed Forces
6. High ranking officers in quisling armed forces or police that assisted the Nazis
7. Known to have commited a war crime
8. members of the SS, Gestapo or othe secret services under the control of the Nazis

+ rejected figure does not include all that served under Mussolini in the police or armed forces
Also this figure undoubtedly includes many that were not Italian citizens

estimated 35000 from Republic of Ireland over this period

IN SUMMARY WE SEE THAT THE AUSTRALIAN AUTHORITIES BETWEEN 1946 AND 1966 FAILED IN THEIR DUTY BY ALLOWING IN EXCESS OF 9000 IMMIGRANTS THAT WERE OF A DANGEROUS CHARACTER AND LIKELY TO DO HARM IN AUSTRALIA TO THEIR FORMER ENEMIES... I.E. THOSE AUSTRALIANS THAT WERE IDENTIFIED AS BRITISH OR FROM ALLIED COUNTRIES DURING THE WAR.
THE GREATER FEAR OF COMMUNISM OUTWEIGHED COMMON SENSE IGNORING THE DANGER AT THE TIME DOWN TO THE PRESENT.

XIV   Recognition of Sources of Materials:

Levenda, Peter. Ratline : Soviet Spies, Nazi Priests, and the Disappearance of Adolf Hitler   ISBN   9780892541706

Levenda, Peter (2012-04-17). Ratline: Soviet Spies, Nazi Priests, and the Disappearance of Adolf Hitler (Kindle Locations 4201-4202). Nicolas-Hays, Inc. Kindle Edition.

Thomas, Gordon. The Pope's Jews: The Vatican's Secret Plan to Save Jews from the Nazis   ISBN 9780312604219

Aarons, Mark. Sanctuary! Nazi Fugitives in Australia   ISBN   085561 332 7

Aarons, Mark and Loftus, John. Ratlines: How the Vatican's Nazi Networks Betrayed western Intelligence to the Soviets   ISBN   074931002 2

Goeritno, Ir. KGPH, Soeryo, Hitler Mati di Indonesia: Rahasia Yang Terkuak, Indonesia: Titik Media, 2010

Geller, Pamella. Stop the Islamization of America

Ayaan Hirsi Ali. Heretic- Why Islam Needs a Reformation Now
ISBN   9780732299057

Robertson, Geoffrey. Mullas Without Mercy   ISBN   9780732299057
The Iraq Report A Special Investigation By Andy McSmith

McSmith, Andy (2015-01-23). The Iraq Report: A special investigation by Andy McSmith. Independent Print Limited. Kindle Edition.

Scotland's Future. Published by the Scottish Government, November 2013. Kindle Edition.

Law, Tom. Nuclear Islam and Other Stories. Sid Harta 2006.
ISBN   977509702

A. N. Leont'ev, A. R. Luria, & A. Smirnol (Eds.), Psychological research in the U.S.S.R (Vol. 1, pp. 11–54) Moscow 1931

Australian Bureau of Statistics… various

Also:

AFP
Al Jazeera
Associated Press
ATV (Hong Kong)
Australian War Memorial
BBC
Blogs- China.com
Blogs- sina.com.cn
Bloomberg News
Bulloger.com
Caijing
CCTV9 Beijing
Channel 4 with Lindsey Hilsum
China Daily
China News Service (ifeng.com)
China Review News
Christian Science Monitor
CNN
Der Spiegel
DPA Taiwan
euronews
Facebook.com
Forbes.com
Fox News
Global Times
Islamicjewhatred.com
jewwatch.com
Los Angeles Times
Malcolm Moore's Telegraph blog
Microsoft News
MITBBS.com
National Press Club
New York Times

PC World
petergardner.info
People's Daily, China
Radio Free Asia
Reclaim-Australia.com
Reclaim-Australia.net
Reuters
roomfordebate.blogs.nytimes.com
RTÉ News
San Francisco Sentinel
Sky News
South China Morning Post
Southern Metropolis Weekly
Telegraph
The Australian
The Guardian
The Melbourne Age
The Sydney Morning Herald
The Wall Street Journal
The Wall Street Journal: China Journal
tianshannet.com
TIME Magazine
Times Online
TVB News (Beijing)
Twitter.com
Washington Post
Wikipedia
Xinhua
Xinjiang TV
Yahoo News Photos, yahoo.com

About the Author:

Tom Law has worked and lived in the alpine district of eastern Victoria for most of his adult life as a science and mathematics teacher. He built a solid rock house and threw down deep roots, raising a family and enjoying all that the mountains had to offer. At a later stage in his life he worked firstly in Indonesia and then in China for several years. Having returned to his favourite haunt, nook and singing gullies he is again raising a young family with an Indonesian wife. His view of the outside world away from his immediate paradise takes on somewhat cynical perspectives as he sees the faltering of great civilisations in danger of collision. In particular he worries about the country he lives in and the directions in which it is heading.

WANT A BMMCC T-SHIRT?

THEN GET IT AT:

http://longership.deco-shirts.com

Other Works by Tom Law:

Nuclear Islam and Other Stories.   Sid Harta   2006.
ISBN 977509702

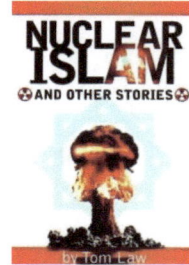

A look at the threat of Nuclear War in the political landscape of today. Some comments on the environment and other contemporary issues.

Boy in Blue Raincoat.   Longership
ISBN 9780980725841

A boy growing up in the remote hills of eastern Victoria finds unexpected adventure and love. Explores his close relationship with his dad and the small timber mill community in which he finds himself.

Scotlands Choice. Longership
ISBN 9781500463205

Predominantly a book of cartoons leading up to the referendum on Scottish independence. Humorous but not to be taken too seriously!

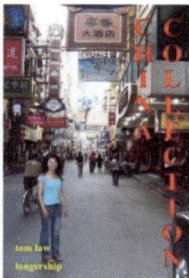

China Collection. Longership   ISBN 9780980725889

Poetry on political and environmental observations written over a period of six years whilst working in Jiangsu province, China.

More can be viewed at: http://longership.com